noise

Universal Language
Pattern Recognition
Data Synaesthetics

a series of exhibitions about information and transformation
curated by Adam Lowe and Simon Schaffer

Cambridge 22 Jan - 26 March 2000

Kettle's Yard
The Whipple Museum of the History of Science
The Cambridge University Museum of
Archaeology and Anthropology
and in association with the
Fitzwilliam Museum's exhibition, Digital Images

London 28 Jan - 1 May 2000

The Wellcome Trust Two10 Gallery

KETTLE'S YARD

Acknowledgements

n01se has been conceived and devised by Adam Lowe and Simon Schaffer and our first and warmest thanks are to them.

We are very grateful to all the artists, writers and lenders who have participated with such enthusiasm and generosity.

The exhibition has been made possible by grant-aid from Cambridge City Council, The Calouste Gulbenkian Foundation, The Henry Moore Foundation, The Elephant Trust, and the collaboration of The Wellcome Trust who have also supported this publication.

We also wish to thank our colleagues in participating museums and galleries: Liba Taub and Catriona West of The Whipple Museum of the History of Science, Anita Herle and Robin Boast of The University of Cambridge Museum of Archaeology and Anthropology, Craig Hartley of the Fitzwilliam Museum, Ken Arnold and Denna Jones of The Wellcome Trust, Professor Malcolm Longair, Head of the Department of Physics and the Cavendish Laboratory, Michael Dorling of the Sedgwick Museum, David McKitterick of Trinity College Library, Professor John Parker and Alex Goodall of the Botanic Gardens, all of the University of Cambridge, Pete James of Birmingham Central Library, Simon Chaplin of The Royal College of Surgeons, David Tovee of University College, London, the Hypermedia Research Centre, University of Westminster, Caroline Fuchs of Galerie Berndt and the following who have helped in a variety of ways: John Purcell Paper, Ilford, Sony Computer Science Lab Paris, The Royal College of Surgeons, Tragacanto Madrid, The GeoSphere Project Santa Monica, The Ashmolean Museum, Big Bills, London Electronic Arts, ZKM, Lisson Gallery, The Churches Conservation Trust,
and Sian Ede, Julie Lawson, Peter Weibel, Hans Ulrich Obrist, William Owen, Colin Franklin, James Jegede, Julian Rothenstein, Nando Guereta, Peter Fleissig, Griff Williams, John Wright, Rufus Moore and Yuka Lowe,

Designed by Adam Lowe
Cover design by Piers Wardle
Edited by Alfred Birnbaum
Printed by Aldgate Press
Web design by Jeremy Quinn
Published by Kettle's Yard

ISBN 0 90 7074 78 2

Kettle's Yard
Castle Street, Cambridge, CB3 0AQ
www kettlesyard.co.uk/noise

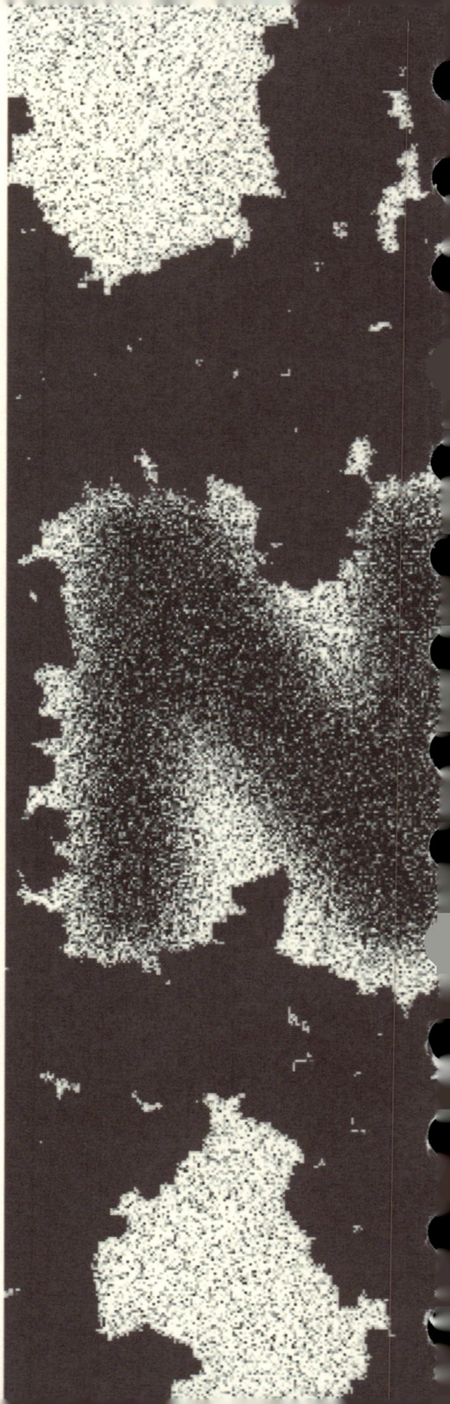

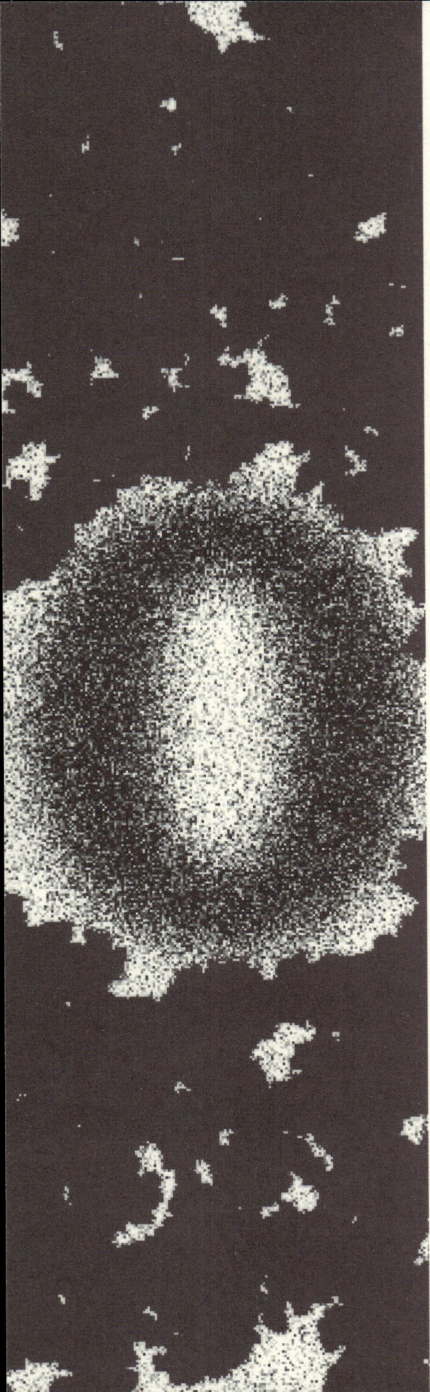

Tabatha Andrews
William Armstrong
Art and Language
Charles Babbage
Stephen Baker
Joe Banks (Disinformation)
Richard Barbrook
William Bateson
Evgen Bavcar
Robin Boast
Patrick Blackett
Jerry Brotton
Soraya de Chadarevian
Adrian Cussins
John Dee
Umberto Eco
Richard Feynman
Manuel Franquelo
Peter Galison
Joy Garnett
Merrill Garnett
Joseph Grigely
Roger Guillemin
Sebastian Guillié
Mercurius Van Helmont
Anita Herle/Su Dalgleish
Lynn Hershman
Jeff Hughes
Margaret Watts Hughes
Lisa Jardine
Bill Jones
Athanasius Kircher
Bruno Latour
Malcom Longair
Mike Lynch
Paul D Miller (DJ Spooky)
Iwan Morus
Gracie Ngale Morton
Sven Nebel
Joseph Nechvatal
Ben Neill
Pictic Balls
Roy Porter
Marc Quinn
Jonathan Ree
Michael Rees
Giles Revell
Kathleen Rogers
Romandson
Brian Rotman
Stan Vanderbeek
Tom Van Sant
Ludwig Von Siegen
Julian Simmons
Nicola Schwartz
Lillian Schwartz
Robert Shannon
Bessie Nakamarra Sims
Paddy Japaljarri Sims
Brian Cantwell Smith
Luc Steels
Bruce Sterling
Jozue Tanaka
John Tchalenko
Dave Tovee
John Tresch
Burhan Tufail
Catherine Wagner
Piers Wardle
Peter Weibel
CTR Wilson
John Wilkins
Peter Wollen
John Woodward
Charles Wynn-Williams

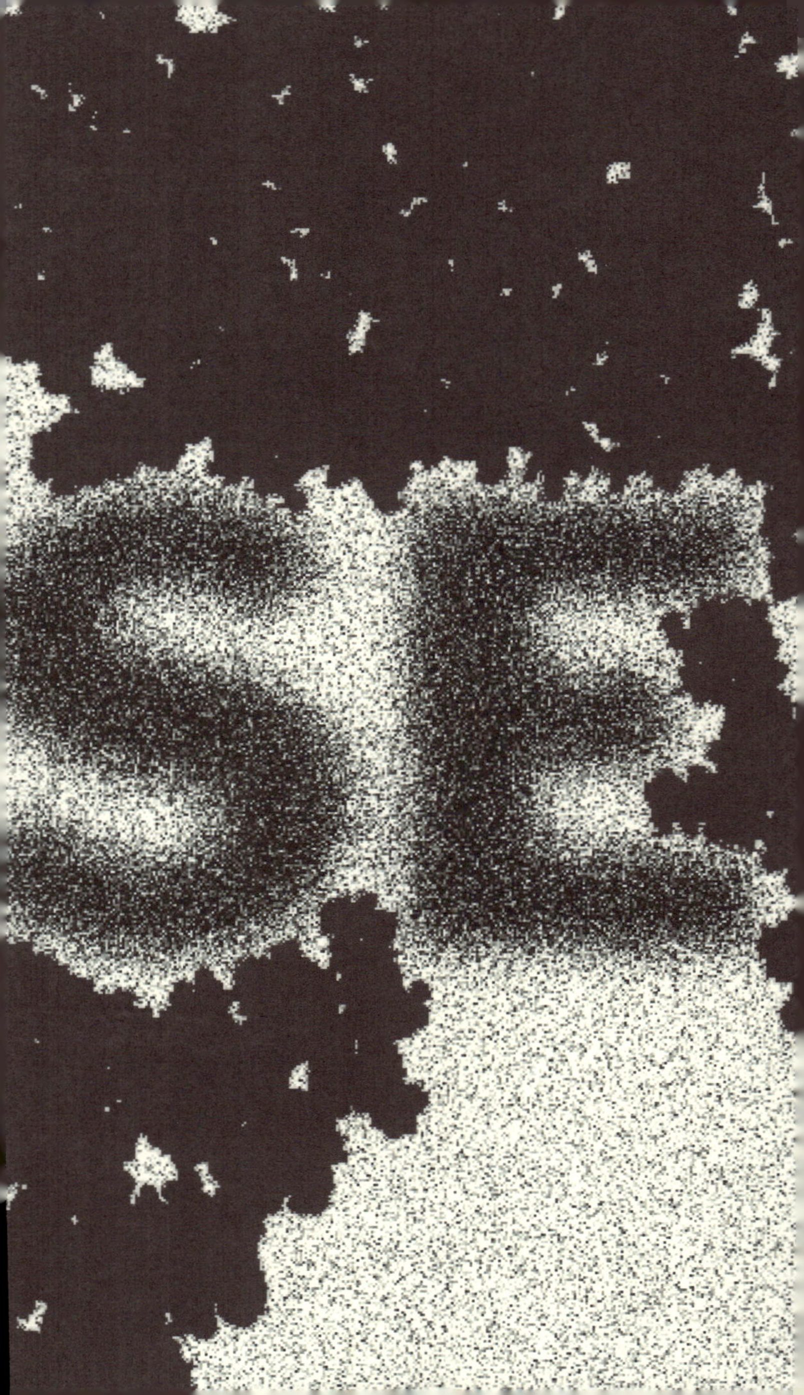

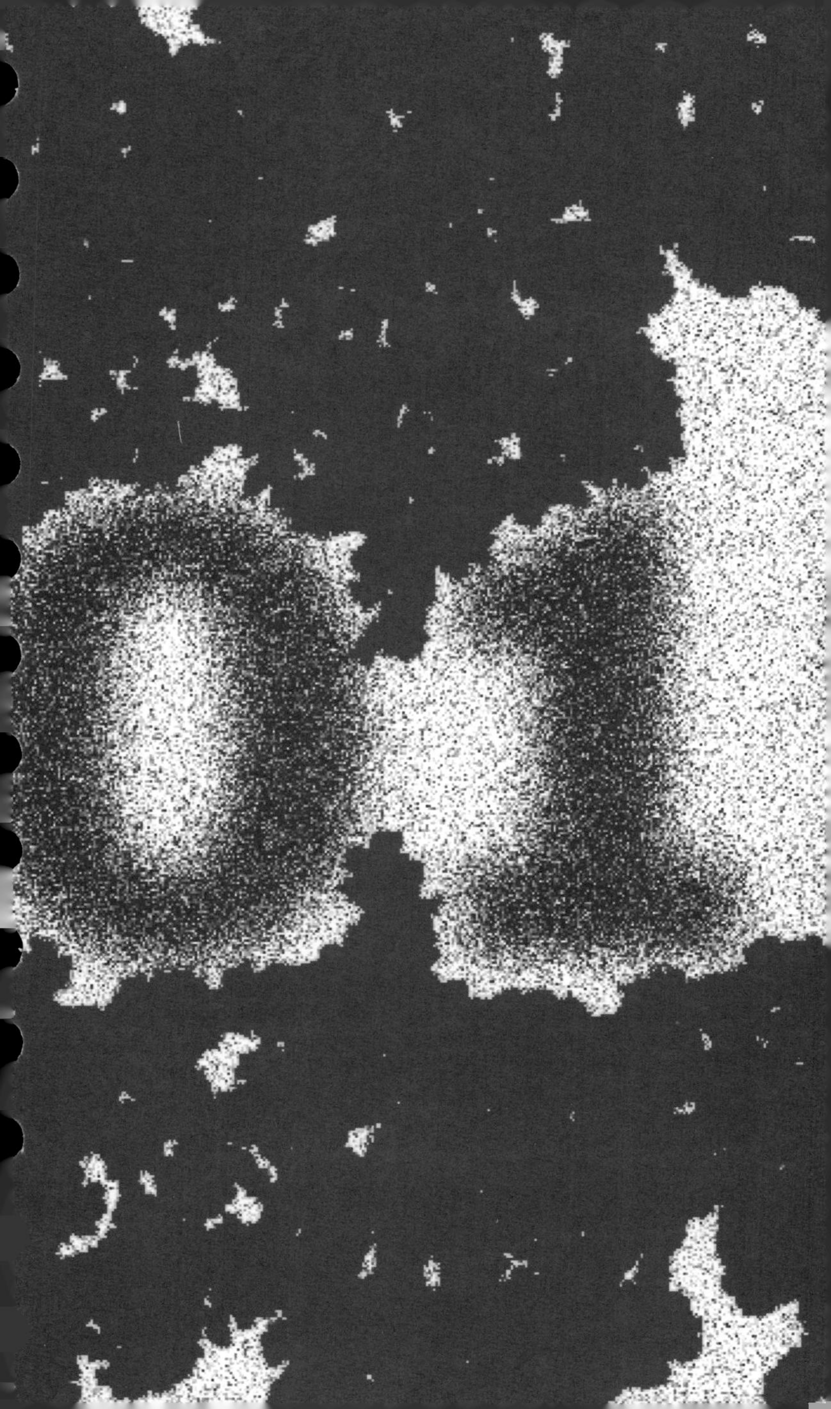

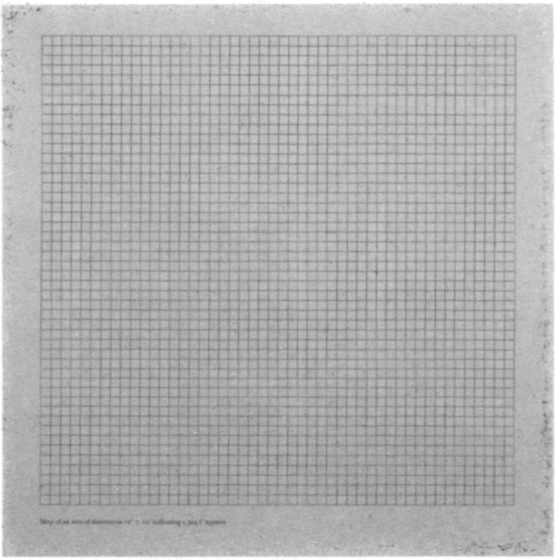

Photograph: Dave Morgan

Art and Language *Map of Itself* 1967
Book print 37 x 46 cms
Courtesy the Artists and Lisson Gallery London

"Look at the television," she said. "Please look, Jim."

He looked again. "Nothing," he said. "Turn off my goddam VCR. No, wait! Let *me* do it."

"Look very hard," Irene said. Her voice trembled. "Can't you understand?"

He looked again, seriously this time.

And he saw something. He would never have noticed it, if she hadn't pointed it out to him first. Static was static, meaningless, just noise, confusion, chaos.

But with a quiet shock of comprehension he found he could actually see something there. Some kind of definite order, inside that boiling sea of hissing multicoloured flecks. A movement, a form, something that almost made sense to him, just past the edge of his understanding. A nibbling, brain-itching thing, just like an oiled key that would open a new world up, with the proper focus, with the proper twist . . .

"Holy smoke,"he said staring. "Have they got satellite TV in this dump? That's some kind of interference pattern, or something. What the hell is it?"

Irene stared raptly at the set. The fear had faded from her face. "It has beauty," she said.

Jim stared again. "What the heck kind of....did you mess with my hookup? Turn off the VCR."

"Not yet," she said. "It's too interesting."

He leaned over angrily, snapped the recorder off.

The TV jumped immediately into a network morning show, cheerful grainy-faced network idiots.

"How did you do that, huh? What buttons did you push?"

"Nothing," she said. "I look, that's all. I look very hard. Only confusing at first. But then, I can see it !"

Bruce Sterling Jim and Irene *Globalhead* (Bantam Books 1992)

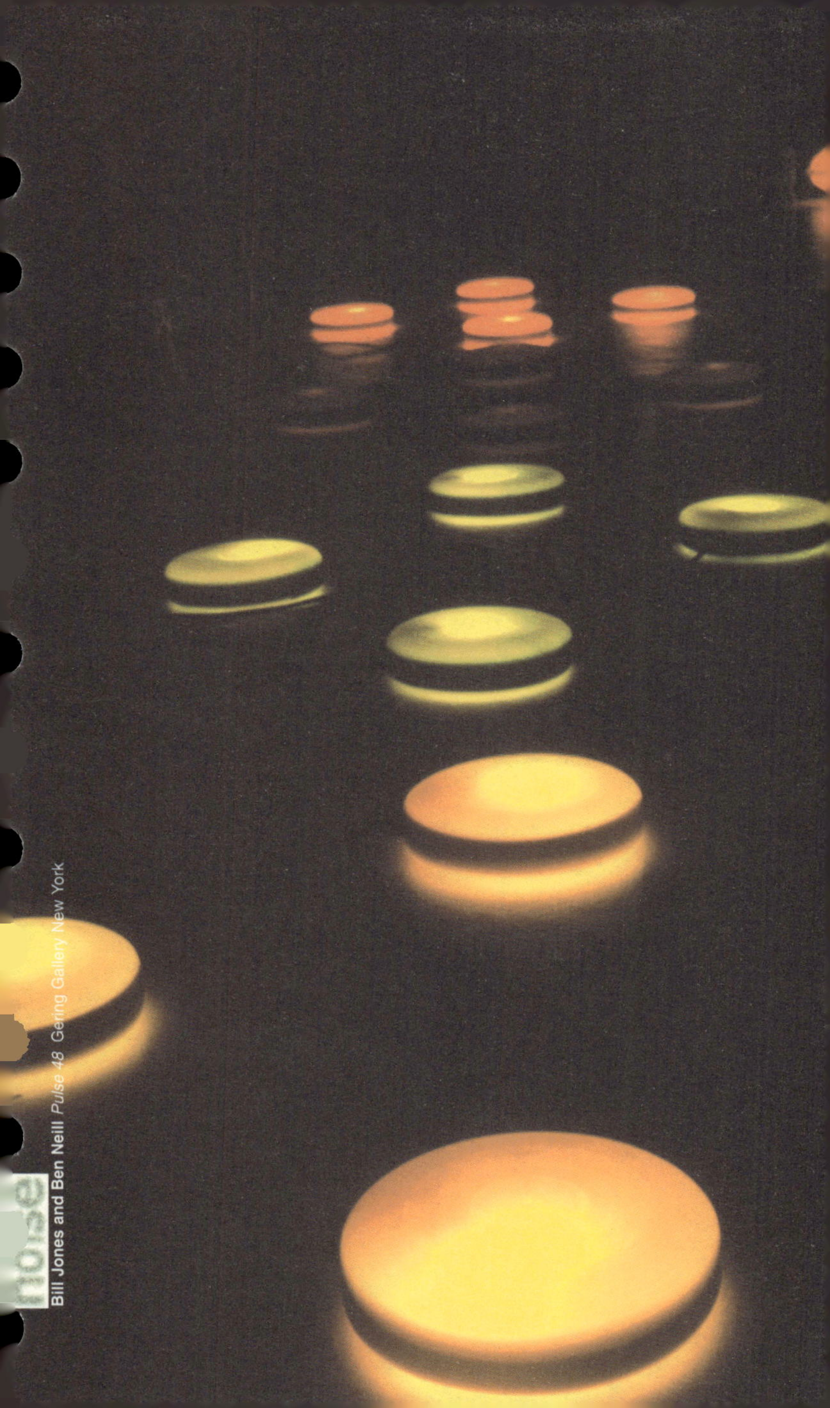

noise

Bill Jones and Ben Neill *Pulse 48* Gering Gallery New York

noise

Preface

n01se is an exhibition and a book about how we perceive and how we communicate our perceptions.

We normally take noise to be a nuisance that other people make, a cacophony that prevents us from being heard, or even from thinking. But the noise of a crowded room is of conversations, of thoughts and information being exchanged. And, what's more our conversation is part of it.

Noise is the stuff which we want to suppress. We try to extract what we need and strip away what seems irrelevant: the scientist, perhaps, by pursuing a line of deductive research; the artist, traditionally, by a process of abstraction. (The ethnic cleanser has his own methods.)

But who is to say that what you or I select is more true or real, valid or exciting than what we discard? And might that stripping away be an act of impoverishment? One person's noise might well be another person's information, and one researcher's wastebasket could lead to a hundred new lines of enquiry.

For thousands of years people have sought the means to make things more visible, to clarify and order and, hence, understand what they see, and to communicate and share their discoveries. But, while selection involves omission, communication requires the transformation of raw data into language and medium. The cave painters of Altamira used charcoal, mud and iron oxide in an art of supreme abstraction to capture their perception of animals in flight. Now we are able to present a 'precise', 'one-to-one', 'digital' 'replica' of the 'reality' of those cave walls.

n01se takes its cue from that capacity of modern digital technology to separate and order information and apparently reveal our world 'as it is' - by collaging photographic images to construct a view of the earth from space with not a cloud in the sky - or a compilation picture of the underside of a ladybird with every detail in precise focus. But is a cloudless - noiseless - world the truth?

Putting this preface together is a similar exercise but **n01se** is, appropriately, an anthology of many voices. They seek out some of the precursors of the new technology and suggest how notions of universal language, synaesthesia and pattern recognition are not unique to digital computing but have always been with us and are intrinsic to all human communication. They also propose that noise, far from being an unnecessary hindrance, is the essential excess from which information can be drawn, in which it can rediscover its context and through which it can be transformed and communicated.

n01se is a celebration of that excess, the disorder which allows order to emerge.

Michael Harrison
Director, Kettle's Yard

Contents

Synaesthesia, the process of mixing messages across media, turning sounds into pictures and words into things.

n01se, of course, has many stories to tell, not just one carefully selected pathway. Instead of presenting one safe set of signs from the messy complexity of arts, sciences and everyday life, all homogenised and nicely packaged for cook/chill consumption, **n01se** probes many different ways of seeing and being in the world. Chances are your own sense of order is already someone else's **n01se.**

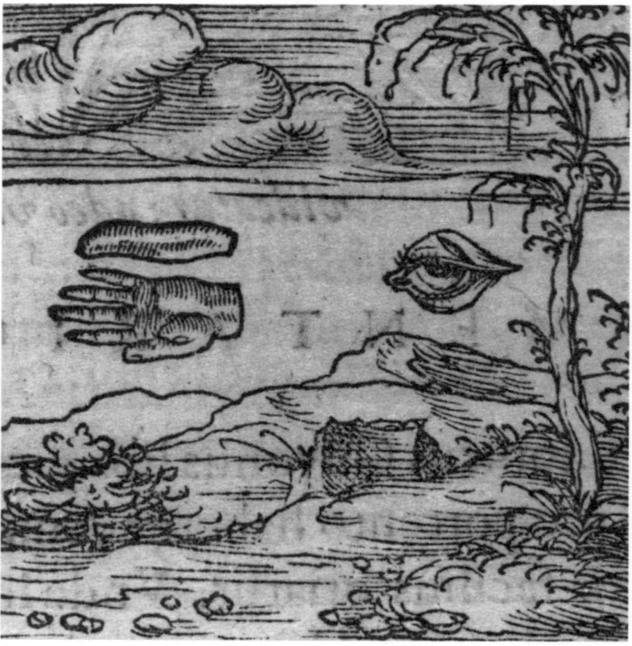

Horapollo, *Hieroglyphica* Lyons 1626
Reproduced by permission of the Master and Fellows of Trinity College Cambridge

Book 1; Number 26; 'Speech'
To symbolise speech, they draw a tongue and a bloodshot eye. For the primary element of speech is the voice, and the secondary is the eyes. And when they wish to symbolise speech differently, they draw a tongue placed above a hand: thus giving the primacy of speaking to the tongue, and the second place to the hand, which carries out the desires of the tongue.

All Babble and Baggage?

Simon Schaffer

n01se is news. At least, that's what the word meant five centuries ago. Now the big noise is digital, posing as "anti-noise". Digital technologies seem to offer an escape from the incoherence and decay of our contemporary world by offering means of ordering, preserving and transmitting information for open access and use — everything hard-edged and crisp, with no scratches, crackles or pops. Here's the recipe: break down messy complexities into strings of discrete units, package them compactly for easy transport, recompose convincing or even improved versions by clever recombination of individual units. It sounds very new, utilising the latest electronic technology. And most unworldly, a counter to things falling apart. It hardly seems to require much maintenance either. Digital mastery gives us exact versions of the original — only better. The promise of perfect permanence, enhanced no end.

n01se is a set of connected shows that showcase and question the digital, with the aim of reclaiming its antecedents. Re-read the recipe, and it's a paraphrase of Noah: building the Ark, selecting ordered pairs of living beings, preserving them from flood and chaos, then reconstructing a better, brighter world. The Ark soon became a model for the first museums, whose rooms were stocked with carefully selected objects recovered from the wreck of the past, all arranged and classified, admired and understood. The puzzle for all Ark builders was selection. Digitizers have always had this problem: what principles by which to set down patterns? Are such patterns already out there in the world? Or do they merely result from the way we choose to select and arrange?

If digitisation has a longer history than credited, it's also much more earthy. It requires hard work and great care. Could Noah know, thanks to conversations with his God, just how many kinds of real things there were on Earth? For error would have been fatal for those left behind (drowned, forgotten) or those wrongly included (parasites, viruses, the worm in the bud). Language is always a key to digital selection. Do Hebrew script or hieroglyphs or ideograms or Morse code or megabytes or //html really hold the secrets of eternity (or maybe the way to a quieter life)? If we had a sign system that was an amazingly accurate version of what's out there in the world, it should be easy to see how to make our selection and later optimise our success rate. But digitasl visionaries always find someone to blame for their pains. Early Christians blamed the Serpent; Occidentals blamed Orientals; Charles Babbage, designer of the Difference Engine, blamed the Luddites; Alan Turing, theoretician of the Universal Computing Machine, blamed the intellectual aristocracy . . boffins and geeks blame hackers and literati. All these undercover agents are accused of
bringing down the pure world of signs to the mundane mess of mere **n01se**.

But villains are often also heroes. Chaotic images of spark discharges, the buzz of interference, random mutations churning away inside every chromosome can all become the sources of innovation, development and aesthetic pleasure. n01se offers choice — alternate cases among these signals. It shadows the dream of a ***Universal Language***, the haunting possibility of recapturing what was lost, of building a yet newer kind of sign system to make the labours of digitisation easy and appealing. n01se also plays with ***Pattern Recognition***, the way in which we know things to be real, or make them real using the very tools of selection and recomposition. Are such digital patterns facts or artefacts? **n01se** even feels its way around

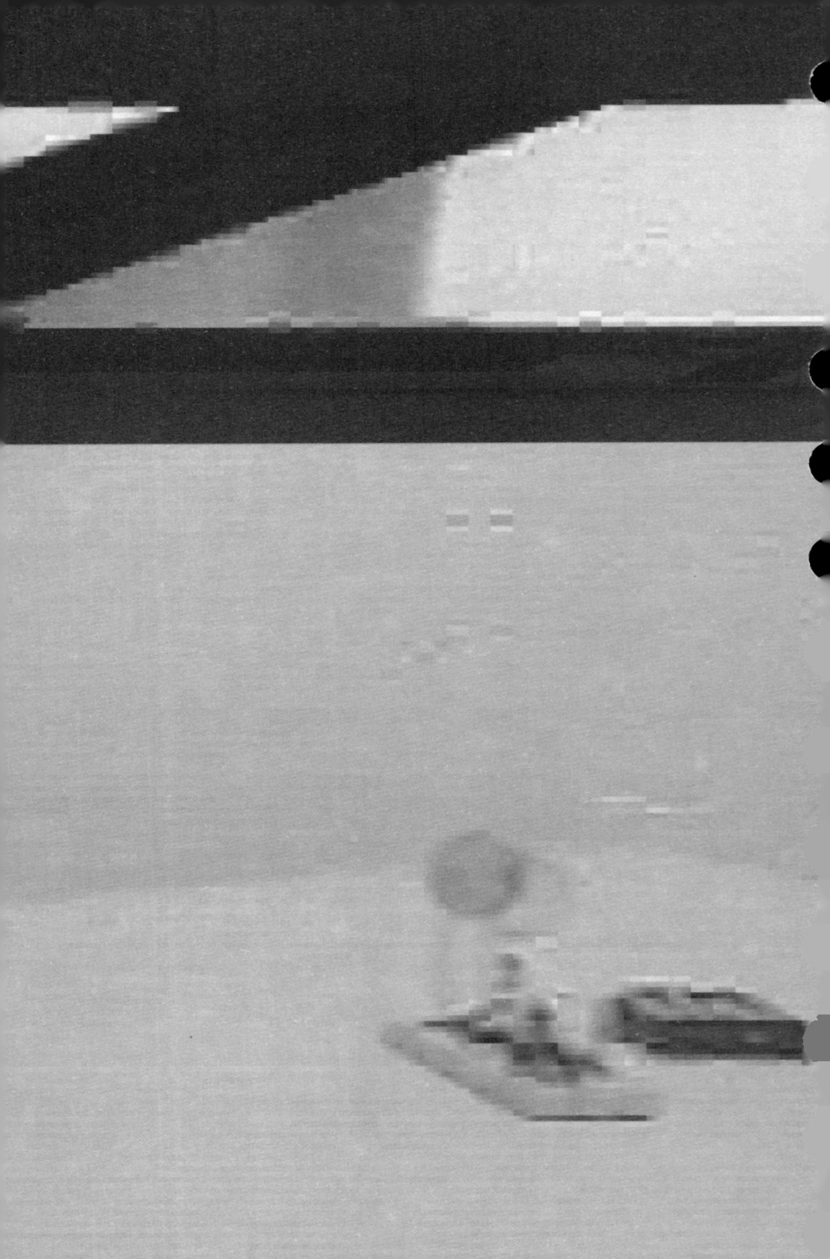

A corrupted video image of **Manuel Franquelo's** installation *The Preacher and Chorus*
Central Fine Arts, New York

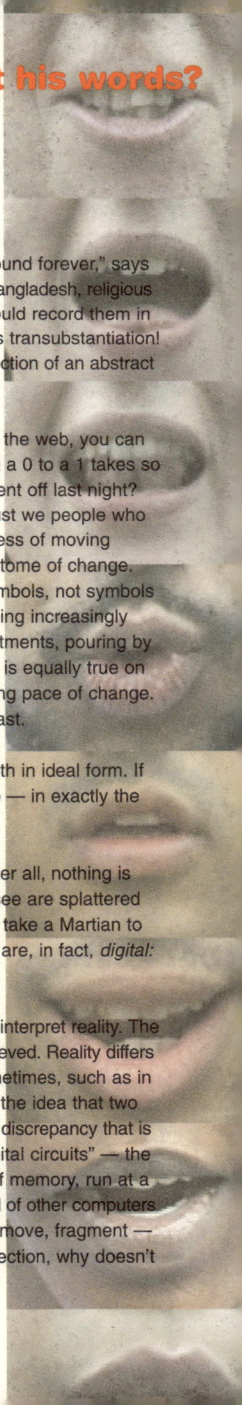

Where is the man who has lost his words?

Digitality and Noise

BRIAN CANTWELL SMITH

Purity, stability, perfection — the promises of digitality. "Perfect sound forever," says Sony. No scratches, no noise, no irritating static. And no decay. In Bangladesh, religious manuscripts disintegrate, victims of insects and humidity. If we could record them in digital form, we're told, they would be immune to rot. Scanning as transubstantiation! It seems as if Plato's heaven is being replaced by the eternal perfection of an abstract realm of 0s and 1s.

If epochal stability is the mark of the digital, so too is change. On the web, you can create, duplicate, modify with unprecedented abandon. Switching a 0 to a 1 takes so little energy it is essentially free. Want to adjust that memo you sent off last night? No problem! Click, click, click; just one more email. And it's not just we people who change things; convergent networks and routers are in the business of moving things around, not keeping them fixed. Computing itself is the epitome of change. *Mathematics plus time*, it's been called. It is the *processing* of symbols, not symbols themselves. Plus, the symbols and media are themselves becoming increasingly dynamic: streaming video, QuickTime movies, virtual reality enactments, pouring by at megabytes per millisecond. And what is true of the technology is equally true on the human side: eruptive start-ups, multi-mega-mergers, a dizzying pace of change. For a revolution based on stability, the digital world sure moves fast.

Fixity and fluidity — digitality stands testament to both. And to both in ideal form. If you want stability, it will stay. If you choose change, it will change — in exactly the ways you specify.

It's odd that such perfection is attainable, in this messy world. After all, nothing is *really* digital. Attach an oscilloscope to a digital line, and all you see are splattered variations of bewildering complexity. Seriously: how long would it take a Martian to figure out that these intricate whiplashes of electronic alternation are, in fact, *digital: naught but strings of 0s and 1s?*

Pure digitality is a myth — an abstraction in terms of which we (re)interpret reality. The digital ideal (indicated in the figure with a dashed line) is never achieved. Reality differs by an unavoidable *discrepancy* (indicated with hash marks). Sometimes, such as in audio, the discrepancy cannot avoid making an impact (mocking the idea that two pressings of the same CD must sound identical). But it is not the discrepancy that is mysterious. What is magic is that sometimes — in so-called "digital circuits" — the discrepancy *doesn't seem to matter*. Computers have gigabytes of memory, run at a gazillion instructions per second, and are linked to an untold myriad of other computers on the network. If every one of these systems — every bit, step, move, fragment — is "fallen," failing to meet the inaccessible standard of digital perfection, why doesn't the discrepancy bring the whole thing down?

Or to put it positively: how do we build perfection, on top of such messy foundations? How on earth does the digital idealisation work so well, if in reality it is so unerringly defiled?

The answer has to do with *containment*. Rather than eliminate discrepancy (a hopeless task), digital circuits *control* it. The genius of digitality involves figuring out ways to ensure that *discrepancy doesn't propagate*. Whenever a signal gets (dare we say it?) *noisy*, we reshape it, clean it up, put it back on the straight and narrow — with Orwellian (even Stalinesque) efficiency. Memory on your laptop computer is *refreshed* 60 times a second. If it were not, then — like those Bengali manuscripts — it too would rot away, decay, collapse in frangible chaos. It takes work (and battery power) to prop up a digital myth — even to maintain a digital illusion of doing nothing at all!

What is stunning is that we have figured out how to build devices to maintain the illusion — for a while. In the end, they too will fail. Not even digitality can go where moths and rust do not corrupt. But this side of heaven, digitality has come as close to perfection as we can get.

What about noise? Is discrepancy noise? Often; but not always. A small company in California listens to random cell phone calls, throwing away all the signal. It turns out, for every handset, that its discrepancy serves as a kind of analogue signature. Given the inevitable contingencies of manufacture and materials, each device is slightly different. Those differences are reflected in the particular shape of the error or discrepancy (Tolstoy should be happy; we diverge in our own peculiar ways). The companys job is to monitor the character of the disctepancy, and sound an

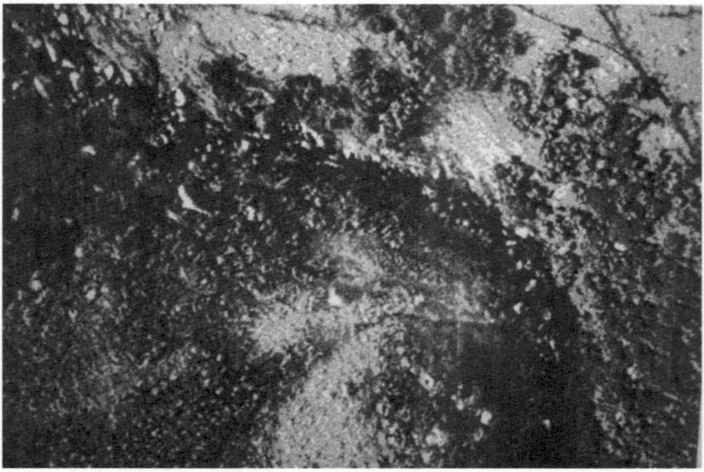

Julian Simmons *Aerial Series* 1997 Ink plotter on paper
This image is from a series of 12 ink drawings produced by Julian Simmons on his drawing machine from a black and white photograph taken with a remote controlled camera attached to a kite.

alarm when it inexplicably changes. That's how phone companies detect when a phone number has been stolen and implanted on a different unit. There is money in being a discrepancy sleuth. Admittedly, discrepancy is sometimes painful. It degrades the music, crashes the machine. But it can be valuable. Cell-phone discrepancy is useful, because it *correlates* — with particular, concrete handsets. The same is true of pirate software: discrepancies on CD-ROMs contain tell-tale traces of illegal duplicating factories. Does that mean noise = uncorrelation? No, that can't be right, either. Sometimes lacking correlates is a priceless advantage: the Kohinoor Diamond; a favourite childhood path; the touch of her lips, that last night in Kathmandu.

Moreover, even when digitality is achieved, it is no proof against noise. We go to heroic lengths, controlling discrepancy, to build digital computers, networks, communication channels. The result has been substrates for new levels of cacophony. Network routers and web servers usher up email, memos, the odd poem, downloads from Antarctic webcams. But they have also unleashed a deluge of advertising, spam, bureaucratic trivia. Chaos contained, a kind of modernist perfection, has given us a new platform on which to raise the clamorous din to unprecedented heights.

Noise isn't challenged by the digital era. Noise isn't analogue or digital; it comes in 57 varieties. Noise isn't static or dynamic; it embraces both formats. Noise isn't correlation or uncorrelation; dreary repetition and exquisite particularity put paid to categorical containment. Noise is wily and durable – crafty enough to work its way into, under, through, around, and on top of any perfected ideal.

Is noise the absence of meaning? That might cut deeper — if only we knew what meaning was. Problem is, meaning itself can be noisy. So many things mean so little. Empty promises. Protestations of political pundits. A disenchanted world, robbed of sacred significance.

"Where is the man who has lost his words?" asks Zhuangzi, "I want to have a word with him."

Is noise all we have to protect us from the silence of perfection?

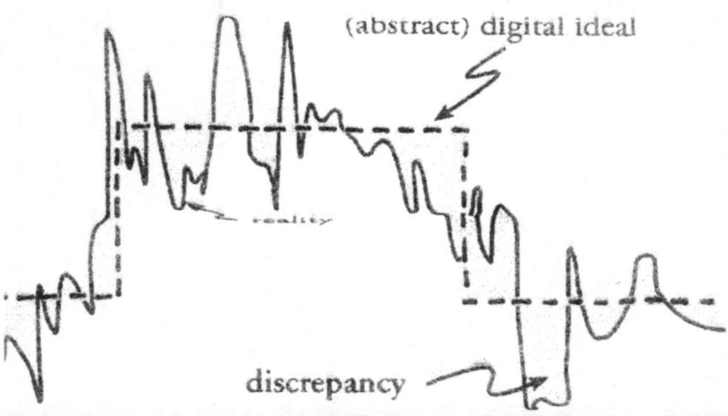

… of human gender do not fit such abso-
… as a potential contrast with com-
… are different from organisms exactly
… neatened-up categories, bi-
… this is to say, this sense of neatness is rather
… at the level of the substrate, computers are
… in the sense discussed above. The claim is much
… computers have, they have in a perfectly
… down automata or not, universal or
… will not run Microsoft Word, are
… won't reboot after a crash. In no
… will the answer to a constitutive
… or "somewhat" or "more or less." It is ex-
… absoluteness, moreover, that
… and inhuman, i.e., it is ex-
… categories of the
… inevitably metaphorical,
… as lived that drives the wedge be-
… and the (strictly) humane.

… is that there need not be a continuous
… voltage or volume or frequency, in terms of

… ultimately require strong arguments.
… it is … develop an intuitive
feeling for what is going on.
… three distinctions
… and its referent, (ii) between …
… system and the "external world" in which
… implicated in the analysis of any interpreted or
… not only computers, but also people, as well
… language, books, and e-mail. The first dis-
… gets at the ineliminable fact that …
… represents, encodes information
… towards a task domain or subject
… or conceptual split between syntax and
… how a system works (i.e., issues about
… effectiveness) from more distal …
… the symbols mean or represent …
… in some sense even more basic: it is …
… is a system or entity at all. What is
… constitutes the system itself, …
… or external world.
… as applicable to people …
… What makes computers special, how-
… mathematical traditions from which
… theory frameworks, is that …

[illegible] and [illegible] in place to preserve [illegible] and prop up [illegible] the digital ab-
[illegible] employ phenomenally complex error recovery
[illegible] and even recover the idealised digital "signal" in the
[illegible] tracks of destruction. Internet packets are
[illegible] when they have eroded en route beyond the point
[illegible] are stored redundantly; fragile memories
[illegible] critical applications are run on three identical
[illegible] one fails. The full gamut of such coding strategies
[illegible] is extraordinarily impressive. Certainly the popu-
[illegible] could examine a CD and simply "read off" the
[illegible] an outright error.[2]
[illegible] the "digital" level of abstraction [illegible] the level at which two
[illegible] identical, for example [illegible] is higher (more abstract)
[illegible] physical tokens. This is one reason why differ-
[illegible] CD can sound different, different digital pressings of
[illegible] We see and hear at the lower, continuous,
[illegible] able to what is digitally ignored: the inelim-
[illegible] of approximation, contingent particulars of the
[illegible]

[illegible] of modern systems, however, is not at
[illegible] with a more inclusive kind of discreteness:
[illegible] digitality [illegible] digitality at the level of concepts.
[illegible] enough, and similar to the basic case. A concept is
[illegible] discrete, just in case, at an abstract level:

Indiscrete Affairs

Brian Cantwell Smith[a]

1 [illegible]ECTION AND PROTECTION

[illegible] knows that computers are digital. Or at least that *most* computers are [illegible]. Sure enough, there are exceptions: analogue computers for solving dif[illegible] equations, resembling old telephone exchanges; ultra-modern ana[illegible] VLSI chips that mimic the human cochlea and retina; continuous Turing [illegible]; dreams of organic and quantum computers not based on zeros and [illegible]. Still, the invention of the digital computer is widely taken to have been [illegible] of the major developments in the history of computing. Think of what [illegible] along with it: abstract symbols, universal machines, programming lan[illegible] and the Internet. To say nothing of CDs, personal computers, e-mail, [illegible] reality. Somehow or other, digitality [illegible] or discreteness, to use an equiva[illegible] [illegible] is at the core of the computer revolution.

[illegible] does 'digital' mean? That's difficult to say [illegible] but perhaps less difficult [illegible]. As suggested in Figure 1, two things are required. First, the flat top [illegible] implies that to be digital, or to exemplify a digital property, re[illegible]

Brian Cantwell Smith Teaches Computer Science, Cognitive Science and Philosophy at Bloomington Indiana. Previously he worked for fifteen years at Xerox Palo Alto Reseach Centre.

Julian Simmons Artist currently completing a PHD at the Royal College of Art. His work with computer drawing machines involves a variety of ways on making traces and introducing tactile qualities into mechanically made marks.

An 'SDMI-compliant' Internet music player will search for any mark revealing that a recording is an unauthorised copy from the Internet, and refuse to play it. The mark must survive conversion between analogue and digital formats and resist hackers who may try to remove it, while not degrading the sound.
Some spread a thin layer of coded noise under the audio, while others subtract tiny frequency bands from the music and add code-containing noise to the gaps.
Barry Fox, *Silent Safeguard,* in New Scientist, No. 2200, 21/08/99

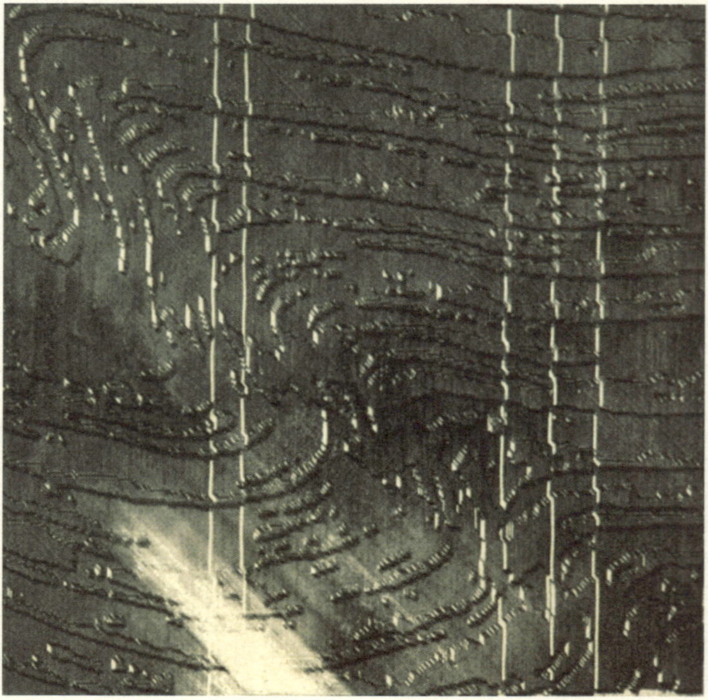

Julian Simmons *Geological Fold* 1997 Etching
Tonal information from a black and white photograph of a geological fold was sent to the computer driven drawing machine which used a sharp point to score lines into the surface of an etching plate coated with a hard ground.The plate was then biten in acid and printed The printing machine, recording tone rather than movement, mimics the plotting action of a seizmograph, a tool used to record earth movement during earthquakes.

What language do angels speak?

The Search for the Perfect Language

UMBERTO ECO

John Dee *The Book of Enoch*
by permission of the Syndics of Cambridge University Library

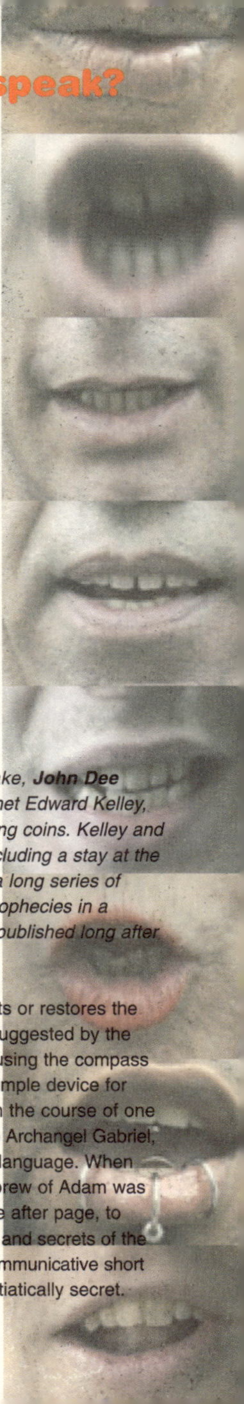

In a large house furnished with library and laboratory at Mortlake, ***John Dee*** *composed a scheme for a new geometrical alphabet. Later he met Edward Kelley, an occult investigator who'd already had his ears cut off for forging coins. Kelley and Dee travelled together in central Europe between 1583-1589, including a stay at the Habsburg capital of Prague. With Kelley's help, Dee conducted a long series of angelic conversations in which spirits dictated revelations and prophecies in a secret code, the language of Enoch. These conversations were published long after Dee's death in 1659 and reviewed by* ***Robert Hooke****.*

Thanks to its universality, Dee can claim that his language invents or restores the language of Adam. Dee's graphic analysis of the alphabet was suggested by the practice of Renaissance artists of designing alphabetical letters using the compass and set-square. Thus Dee could have thought of a unique and simple device for generating both concepts and all the alphabets of the world... In the course of one of the angelic colloquies, Dee found himself in the presence of the Archangel Gabriel, who wished to reveal to him something about the nature of holy language. When questioned, Gabriel simply repeated the information that the Hebrew of Adam was also the primal language... After this, the text continues, for page after page, to expatiate on the relations between the names of angels, numbers and secrets of the universe. This perfect language would be based upon a sort of communicative short circuit, capable of revealing everything, but only if it remained initiatically secret.

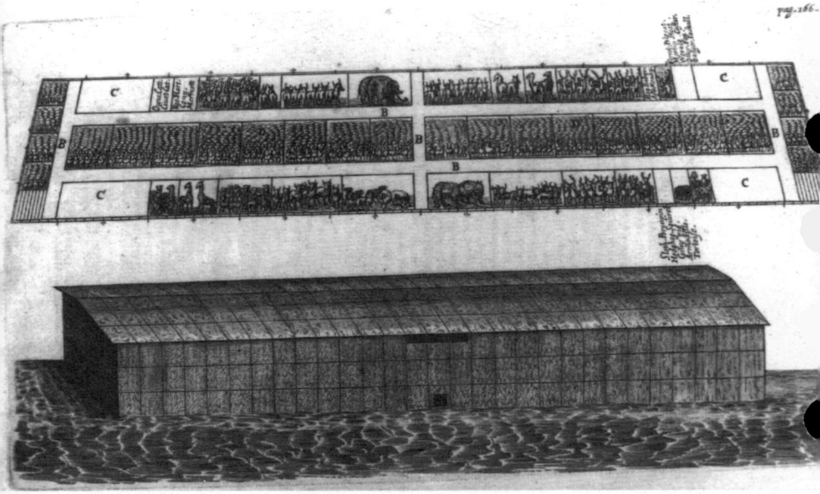

John Wilkins' design for the Ark *Essay Towards a Real Character and a Philosophical Language.*
by permission of the Syndics of Cambridge University Library
The enclosure in the centre contains meat to sustain the carnivores during their time afloat. Wilkins calculated that 1,825 sheep would be required.

Athanasius Kircher *(1602-1680). A German Jesuit who first wanted to travel as missionary to China, then briefly hired as the successor of Johann Kepler in the job of Imperial astronomer in Vienna; but after shipwreck in the Mediterranean became in 1635 resident expert at the Jesuit College in Rome. There he taught mathematics, studied hieroglyphics and constructed a vast museum of antiquities, marvels and exotica. He published huge works on heavens and earth, on music and magic, on Noah's Ark (1675) and the Tower of Babel (1679)*

After an examination of the history of the world from the Creation to the Flood, and, from there, to the confusion of Babel, Kircher traced its subsequent historical and anthropological development through an analysis of various languages. Kircher never questioned Hebrew's priority as the holy language; this had been explicitly revealed in the Bible. He held it as self-evident that Adam, knowing the nature of each and every beast, had named them accordingly. Kircher was thinking of Adam defining the properties of the various animals by permutating the letters of their names. To be precise, first the names themselves mimic some property of the animals to which they refer: 'lion' for example is written ARYH in Hebrew, and Kircher takes the letters AHY as miming the heavy sound of a lion panting…
...At this point, Kircher took the story up to the present. Linguistic change is seen as caused by the separation and mixture of peoples. He is also able to identify the process of creolization which can occur when two languages are put into contact with one another.

John Wilkins *(1614-1672). Natural philosopher and priest, and Oliver Cromwell's brother-in-law, who was in turn head of Wadham College Oxford and Trinity College Cambridge before moving to London in the 1660s where he became the first secretary of the Royal Society. He published works on the inhabitants of the Moon and on*

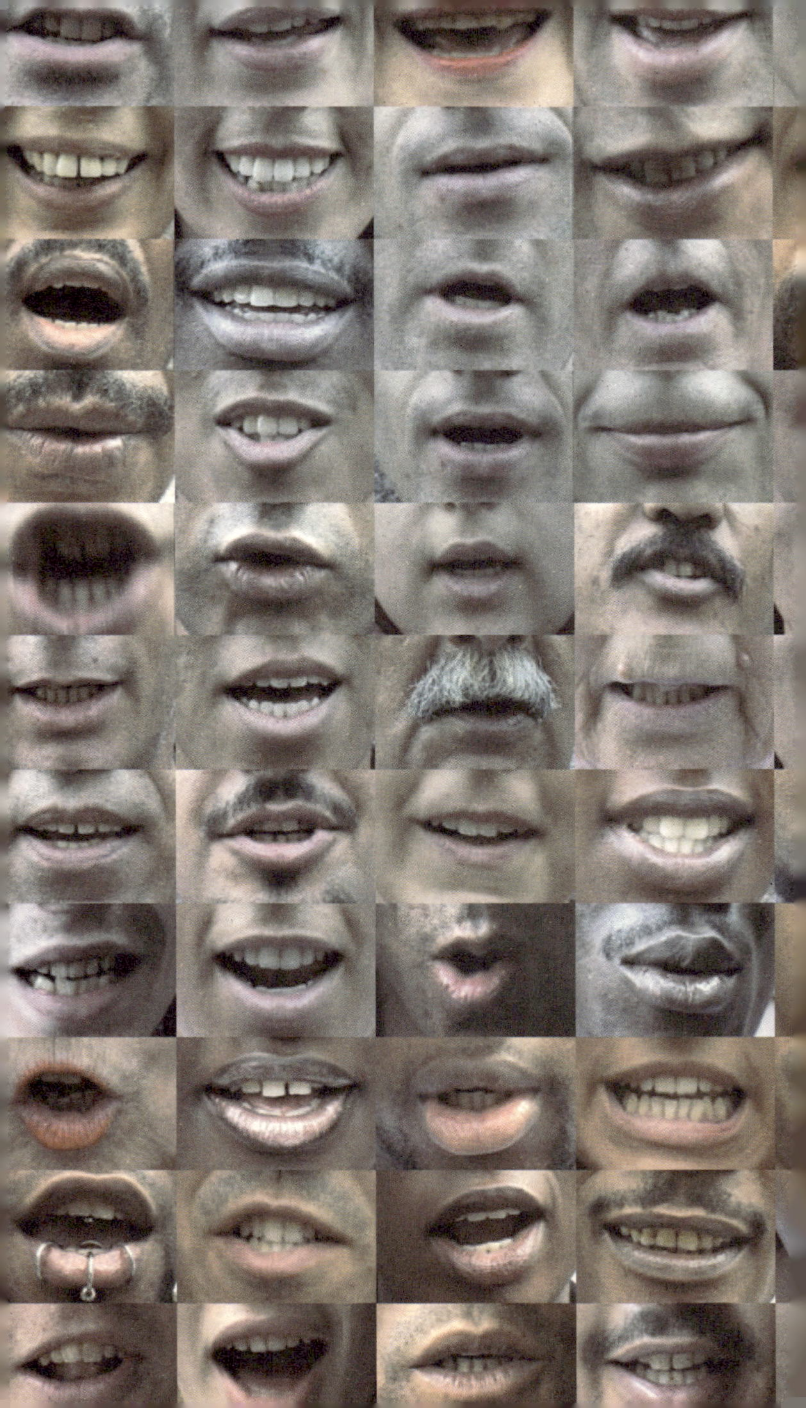

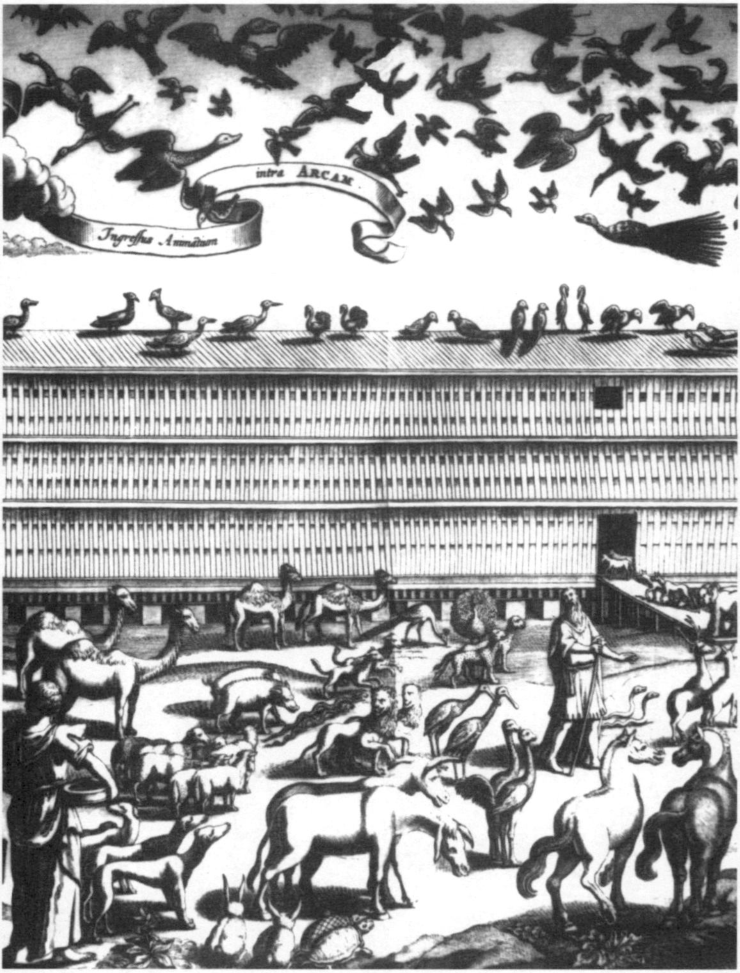

Top; Noah leading the animals into the Ark in pairs.
Left Building the Ark
Athanasius Kircher.*Arca Noë* 1675 detail
With kind permission of the department of Zoology, Balfour and Newton Libraries, University of Cambridge

Building the Ark required great human effort, as witnessed in the prints illustrating Kircher's *Arca Noë* , a book dedicated to the 12 year old king of Spain, Charles II. Not only did Noah have to design and supervise the construction of the boat but also to source, identify, name and capture all the creatures.

cryptography and worked on blood transfusion and hearing aids. Much concerned with the number of animals aboard Noah's Ark, Wilkins designed a universal language which he wanted to publish in 1666, but his book was then destroyed in the Great Fire of London. The scheme finally appeared in 1668, in which year Wilkins was made Bishop of Chester.

Wilkins' *Essay towards a Real Character and a Philosophical Language* was the most complete project for a universal and artificial philosophical language that the seventeenth century was ever to produce. Wilkins' approach required as a preliminary step a vast review of all knowledge to establish what the notions held in common by all rational beings really were. Wilkins never seriously wondered whether other cultures might have organised the world after a different fashion, even though his universal language was designed for the whole of humanity…Wilkins must classify fundamental and Platonic conceptions, like God, world or tree, together with drinks, like beer, political offices, military and ecclesiastical ranks - in short, the whole notional world of a seventeenth-century Englishman...

...What if we regarded the defect in Wilkins' system as its prophetic virtue ? What if we treated Wilkins as if he were obscurely groping towards a notion for which we have only recently invented a name - hypertext? A hypertext is a program for computers in which every element of the repertory is tied, through a series of internal references, to numerous other nodes. It is possible to conceive of a hypertext on animals where, starting from the unit 'dog', one can get information (1) on the place of dogs on a tree of biological 'taxa' which comprises also cats, horses or wolves; (2) on the properties and habits of dogs; (3) on dogs in history (the dog in the Neolithic, dog in medieval castles, etc.); (4) on the image of the dog in great works of art; and so on…If this were the case, many of the systems' contradictions would disappear, and Wilkins could be considered as a pioneer in the idea of a flexible and multiple organisation of complex data. Yet if such was his project, then we can no longer speak of him in the context of a search for a perfect language; his was instead the search for ways to articulate all that natural languages permit us to say.

Extracted with permission from Umberto Eco
The Search for the Perfect Language
Blackwell, 1995

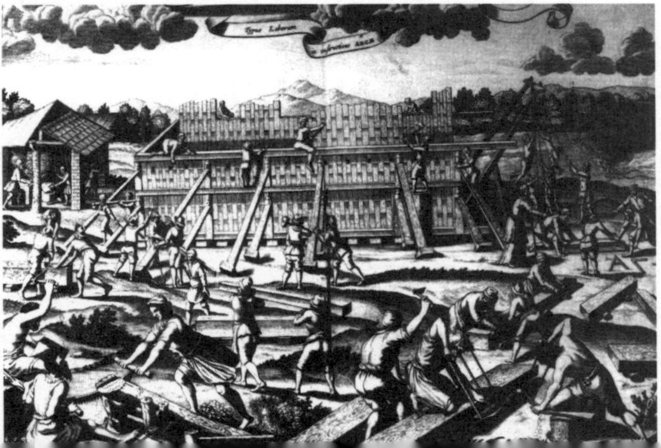

Umberto Eco Semiotician and novelist. He has been professor at the University of Bologna and President of the International Centre for Semiotics and Cognitive Studies at the University of San Marino.

John Tchalenko A film maker involved in perception and eye tracking. He is currently running a research unit at Camberwell College of Arts. Previously Tchalenko was Lecturer in Seismotectonics at Imperial College.

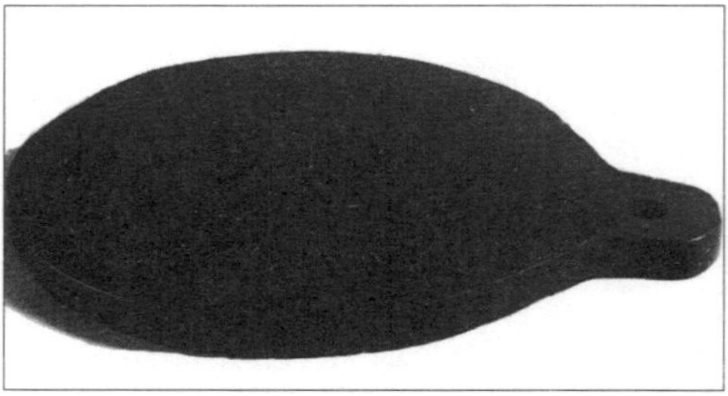

John Dee's obsidian mirror, in which he discoursed with angels in their native language Enochian. It was one of the first treasures to be brought back from South America and is now in the British Museum.

"There were angels in the glass, two four six many of them, each one shuffling into his place in the line like an alderman at the Lord Mayor's Show. None was dressed in white; some wore fillets or wreaths of flowers and green leaves in their loose hair; all their eyes were strangely gay. They kept pressing in by one and two, always room for more, they linked arms or clasped their hands behind them, they looked out smiling at the two mortals who looked in at them. All their names began with A.
John Crowley, *Aegypt* Gollancz 1987

Back cover: stills from *'Dud'* by John Tchalenko
camerawork by Lukas Tchalenko 1999
A 15 minute loop of the close up of lips saying the word Milk in their mother tongue. The word was said three times; spoken normally, posed as a question and then shouted. If you stand at the right street corner in London it is easy to gather together people of many different tongues.

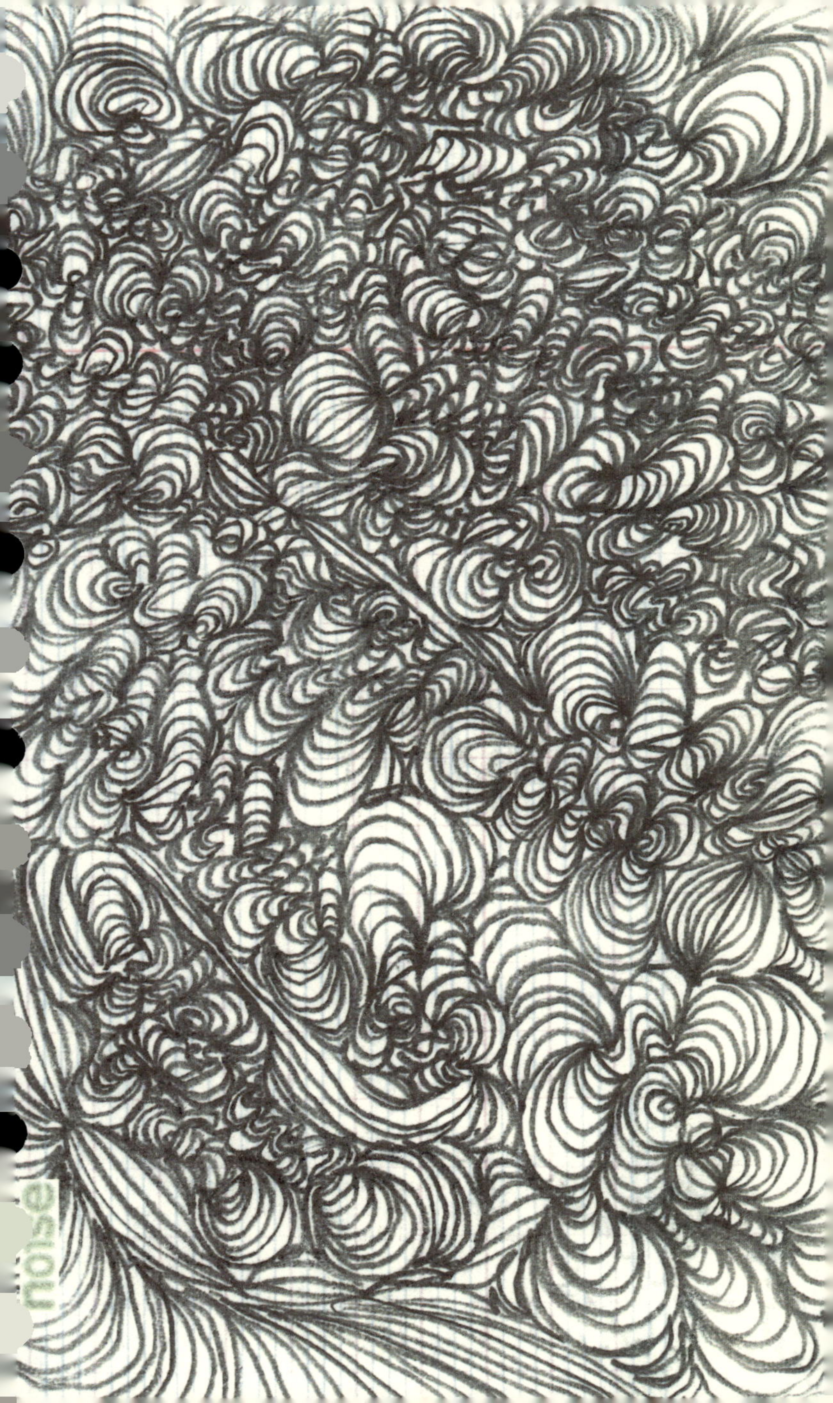
noise

Slow, quietish ~~acoust~~
guitar song
no real rhythum.

Love the naked dude

She said "time to rock n roll"

added drums

its like they keep
warming up to rock
out + then they never
do.

You would miss that if you
could ~~here~~ hear.

LOUD WIND NOW.

Wim Wenders, too.

But I
don't get to
talk much
when we're
walking.

impressions, chance juxtapositions, rapidly assimilated into visual and literary culture. Francesco Balilla Pratella's *Manifesto of the Technics of Futurist Music* (1911) calls for a new music to 'represent the spirit of crowds, of great industrial complexes, of trains, of ocean liners, of battle fleets, of automobiles, and airplanes'. The rhythmic shifts of Stravinsky's *The Rite of Spring* anticipate the collage of sampling technologies. But sampling brings music into the domain of law, of copyright, of authorship ('Musical language has an extensive repertoire of punctuation devices but nothing equivalent to literature's " " quotation marks' - John Oswald). Will inventors, companies, ever patent the sounds of their machines, claim copyright on the hum of industrial cooling units, the clicks of a Geiger counter?

We live in a world of sound, an environment of noise, a universe that can be transformed into, or simply read as, music. The Aeolian Harp: a machine for transforming the environment into sound. Charles Dodge's *Earth's Magnetic Field* maps geophysical statistics into musical data. John Cage's *4' 33"* make ambient sounds into the musical event. Cheap, portable audio equipment allows everyone to make field recordings, if they so choose. The 'Sound-houses' of Francis Bacon's *New Atlantis* (1627) have 'means to convey sounds in trunks and pipes, in strange lines and distances', are places where 'we practise and demonstrate all sounds, and their generation'. Erik Satie's concept of 'Furniture music' as ambient environment - music as background noise, mood-altering sonic input. New spaces for the experience of music, new conditions too, from concert-hall to outdoor rave, from Sony Walkman to elevator. Everything is made possible.

COLOUR-MUSIC

Visual Sensations	Auditory Sensations
2. Hue, saturation, and intensity are dependent in the main upon wave-length, wave-complexity, and wave-amplitude respectively.	2. Pitch, timbre, and loudness are dependent in the main upon wave-length, wave-complexity, and wave-amplitude respectively.
3. A series of greys extending from white to black are due to a mixture of rays of all wave-lengths. Non-neutral greys are due to predominance of some rays of particular wave-lengths.	3. Noise, as distinguished from musical tones, probably due to a mixture of all tones. Noises may differ in pitch. This is due to predominance of certain tones.
4. From a physiological point of view well-marked turning-points in the spectrum are at yellow, green, blue, and red.	4. Salient points in the musical scale—in order ot closeness of physiological relation to the fundamental tone—are octave, fifth, fourth, major third, minor third and sixth.
5. Colour mixtures or fusion of colours.	5. Combination tones, interruption tones, beats, etc.
6. Simultaneous colour contrast. This occurs usually when two or more colours occupy visibly separate spaces in proximity to each other.	6. Tonal fusion, or the sensation produced by a number of notes in a united chord or noise. Ebbingham follows Stumpf in considering that it is a characteristic

A.Wallace Rimmington *Colour Music: The Art of Mobile Colour*
London Hutchinson 1912.

The noise of art?

BURHAN TUFAIL

'Noise has the power to bring us back to life.'
Luigi Russolo, *The Art of Noises,* 1913

The ear and the eye: a ratio and confusion of the senses. White noise, so-called by analogy with white light, is that which comprises all frequencies of sound within range of hearing, just as white light is a summation of colour. The equal energies per Hertz of white noise, when filtered to reduce the volume at each successive octave, gives Pink Noise (equal energy per octave). Natural sounds, rain, a waterfall, or the sound of certain machines, such as a fan, transform white noise into environment. Pink noise approximates the frequency distributions of Western music.
Colour becomes a metaphor for the classification of sound (let's not mention the blues). Metasynth is a computer program that reads digital images as sound - the primacy of the visual redirected towards the auditory. Would digitized images of paintings have distinct sonic signatures? Could we tell a Breughel from a Braque by listening to them? Or a fake Picasso from a real one?
Synaesthetics perceive music associated with shapes and colours: could the deaf one day 'see' visual transformations of symphonies, of folk songs? Des Esseintes, in Huysmans' *A Rebours*, constructs a 'mouth organ' to correlate tastes with sound, in order to recreate symphonies on the tongue.
Daniël Baranoff-Rossiné (1888-1942), Dada sculptor and painter, developed a synaesthetic piano, *piano optophonique,* which projected colours onto a screen for each note.

A doctor listens to a patient's chest. The stethoscope (literally, a device for 'looking at' the chest - more ear-eye confusion) relays heartbeat, breathing, bloodflow - the flows and turbulences of the body, the music of the internal organs. Use a program to read ECGs, X-rays, CAT scans, as music - we already have sonic imaging techniques, let's reverse the direction of the senses. Auditory patterns as diagnostic tool. In a totally 'silent' environment, we are left alone with the sounds of our bodies - true silence is impossible (John Cage's experiences in the Harvard anechoic chamber). Silent films were always accompanied by the whirr of the projector.

New environments, new technologies, recalibrate our definitions of noise, alter perceptions of the ratios of order and disorder. Each new technology brings into the world its own sonic signature, a fresh component in the auditory environment. Technologies of sound redraw the boundaries between natural (codified, assimilated, naturalized) and un-natural (uncategorized, defamiliarized), between the organization of sound as technique, as craft, as 'musicianship', and the opportunistic bricolage of the machinic substitute. Amplification, studio techniques (e.g. dub), tape editing, sampling, turntablism, redefine the space and materiality of music. New instruments (Luigi Russolo's intonarumori, Harry Partch's instruments, the theremin, trautonium, modern electronic instruments) shift music away from established sound, melody and harmony into the realm of sonic texture, of rhythm, timbre, mixology, space. Collage and montage are established principles: the Modernist city is one of fleeting

Joseph Grigely Artist and Associate Professer of Art at the University of Michigan, Ann Arbor. He lost his hearing at the age of 10 and his work takes as its subject the ineluctable differences between speech and writing, reading and listening.

Burhan Tufail Writer. Teaches contemporary American and European literature at the University of London. Freelance music and literary reviewer, currently co-editing two books of essays on Thomas Pynchon. Co-editor of the journal *Interstice*.

Luigi Russolo Italian Futurist. In 1913 He published a manifesto - *The Art of Noises* in which he claimed ancient life was silent and noise was invented in the nineteenth century. He defined six noise families to be played by a futurist mechanical orchestra: 1; Rumbles, Roars, Explosions, Crashes, Splashes, Booms. 2; Whistles, Hisses, Snorts. 3; Whispers, Murmurs, Grumbles, Gurgles. 4; Creaks, Screeches, Rumbles, Buzzes, Crackles, Scrapes. 5; Noises obtained by percussion on metal, wood, skin, stone, terracotta etc. 6 Voices of animals and men: Shouts, Screams, Groans, Shrieks, Howls, Laughs, Wheezes, Sobs.

A live Zebra finch's song includes points at which the sounds change abruptly from a pure tone to a noisy buzz and back again – a hallmark of a system on the edge of chaos.

Bob Holmes, 'Virtuoso Performance', *New Scientist* No.2200, 21/08/99

All the images shown here are from Joseph Grigely *Fragment of White Noise* 1999
Thanks to Amy Vogel and Chris Ofili

Nil by mouth?

Divine Etymology

JONATHAN REE

Nothing ever comes to us as easily as our first language. Its grammatical intricacies and idioms and irregular verbs held no terrors for us when we were very young; we got our mouths round its sounds with careless ease. Acquiring our mother tongue (or mother tongues, if we are bilingual) was literally child's play.

Yet when we encounter new languages later in life, how inscrutable they are. We cannot see the patterns in their babbling streams, let alone echo or repeat or intuit what they mean. And when we realise that these strange languages must feel as natural and obvious to their native speakers as our own first language feels to us, we suffer a primal intellectual bewilderment.

Are all human languages equal, or are some "more natural" than others? What exactly is "natural" about those languages that come naturally to us? What happens if we try to recover the original linguistic standard obscured by centuries of convention and arbitrary variation? If we dig deep enough could we not reach the mother of all mother tongues, what the Greeks called the *etymon* of language, its original natural truth?

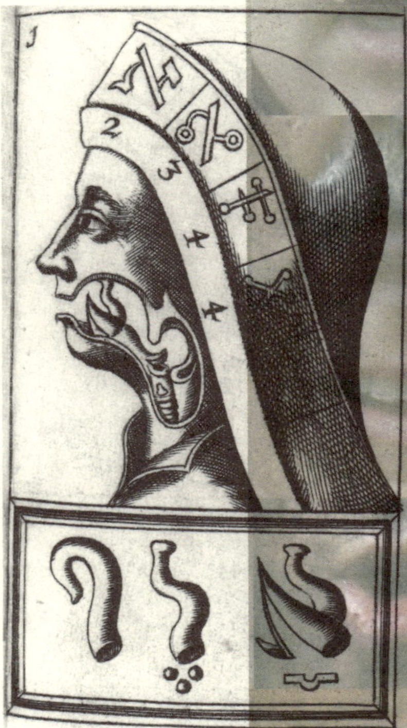

Francis Van Helmont *Een zeer Korte Afbeeling van het Ware Natuurlyke Hebreuwse*
Reproduced by courtesy of the Director and University Librarian John Rylands Library

There has always been a strong element of allegory and myth-making in the search for linguistic origins. Plato's *Cratylus* (ca. 350BC) is perhaps the world's earliest treatise on the would-be science of "etymology", but it is also a satire at its own expense. In it a crazed Socrates sifts through the Greek language for "primary names" — primitive one-syllable words thought to have a "natural fit" with their objects. He suggests, for example, that the sound of a rolled 'r' (the Greek letter *rho*) is natural to the expression of motion, because the tongue is "least at rest". Unfortunately he must admit that many words for movement do not use *rho*.

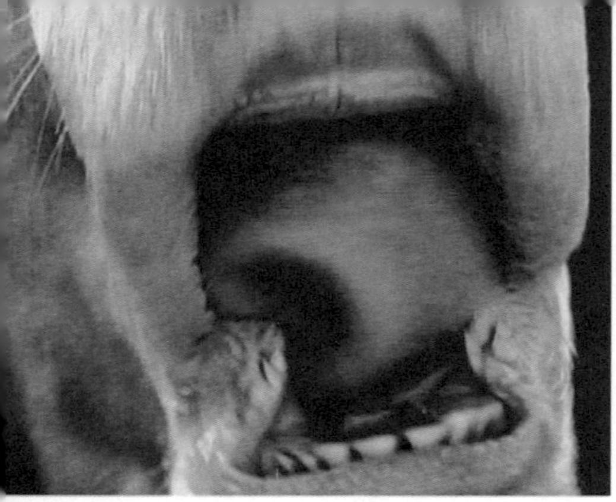

He observes that people could hardly have started inventing words unless some had been agreed on already, so the etymological quest for natural words keeps boomeranging back to the domain of convention and custom from which it sought to escape. “After much study”, Socrates concludes,”I found myself more puzzled than before I began”.

The Biblical account of the origin of language is no less paradoxical. In the first chapter of Genesis, God talks to Himself a lot. “Let there be light”, He says, and decides to call the light Day and the darkness Night. He carries on in the same vein for the rest of the week, steadily elaborating His private language: “Let there be a firmament in the midst of the waters”, and names them Earth and Seas respectively; then “Let the Earth bring forth grass”, and on the sixth day “Let the Earth bring forth the living creature after his kind”, and at last ‘Let us make man in our image’. He now has someone else to talk to, and shows off his week’s work with forgivable pride: “Behold’, He says to His human creatures, ‘I have given you every herb ...and every tree’.

The second chapter of Genesis describes a second invention of language, with God exhibiting beasts and birds to Adam, agreeing magnanimously that “whatsoever Adam called every living creature, that was the name thereof”.

Whether originated in God’s wisdom or Adam’s whimsy, this most ancient account of languages continued unchanged, according to Genesis, for more than a thousand years. When God sent a great flood to wash violence from the face of the Earth, samples of every kind of creature were preserved on Noah’s Ark, and the language of Creation was preserved along with them, so that after the waters subsided the Earth was still ‘of one speech”. But then Noah’s descendants sank into corruption again, and began building a Tower to “reach unto heaven”. God was so affronted by their presumption that He decided to “confound their language that they may not understand one another’s speech”. Nation could no longer speak unto nation, and the only monument to the native language of creation was a decaying half-built tower called Babel.

Both the *Cratylus* and Genesis encourage etymological hopes only to deflate them.

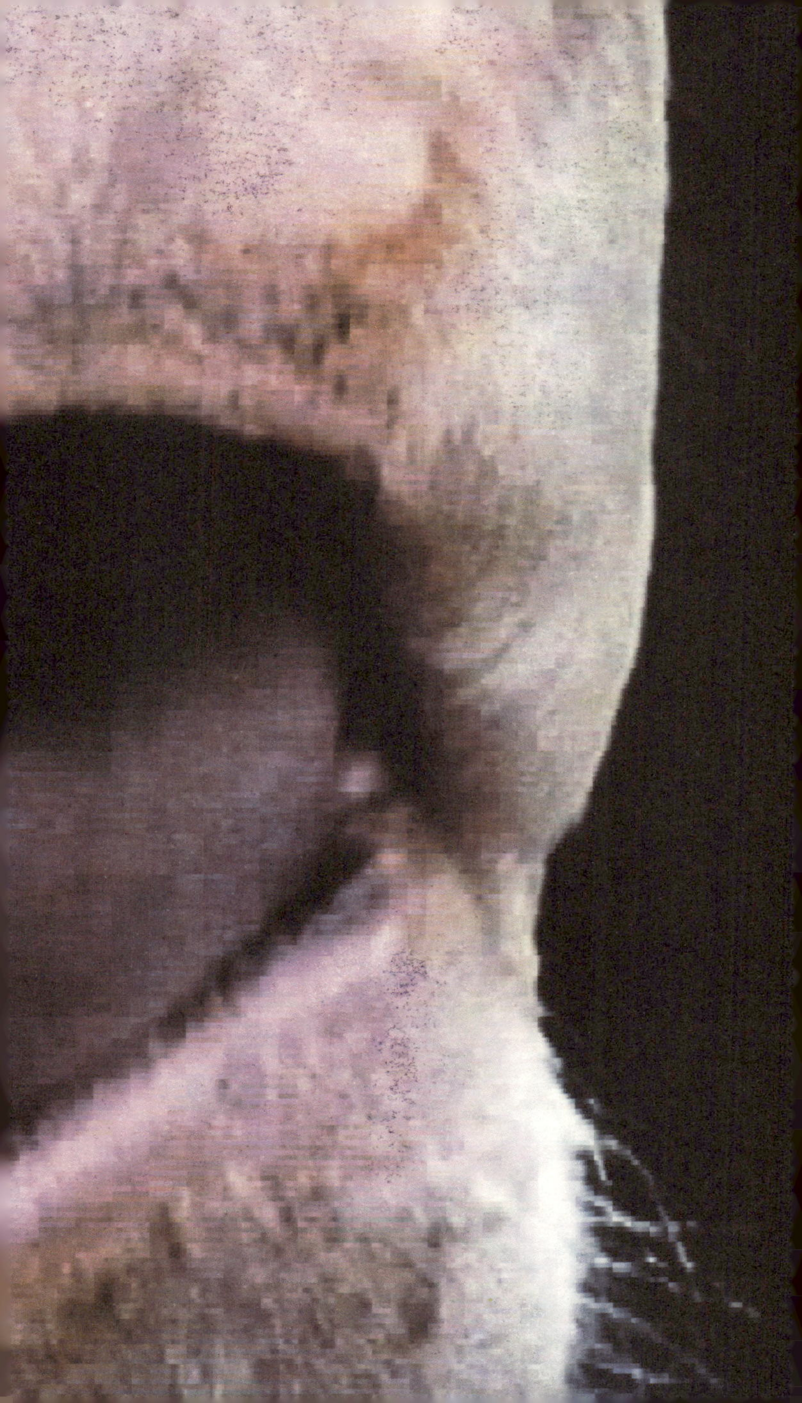

雑音 *zatsu-on* "various sound"

雜音 *zatsu-on* "various sound"

騒音 *so-on* "clamorous sound"

噪音 *so-on* "disruptive sound"

ノイズ *noizu*

五月蝿 *urusai* "mayfly like"

煩い *urusai* "bothersome" "delusive"

賑わい *nigiwai* "tumult"

騒めき *zawameki* "hubub"

乱れ *midare* "tangle" – garble, random

乱 *ran* "tangle" upheaval, disorder, chaos

Korean *hangul* script reputes to have been consciously designed to mimic the physical shape of its vocalisations. The syllabic element ㅇ (unsounded pause) depicts an open trachea, while ㅎ (aspirated *h*) shows air forced through the windpipe. ㅁ (*m*) is a mouth or lips, while ㅂ (*p*) has these lips extending expletively. ㄱ (*k*) is the tongue curved down, while ㄴ (*n*) is the tongue retroflexed up to the soft palate.

Plato's argument suggests that a naturally perfect language existed many generations ago, but implies that we have no hope of retrieving it from the chaos of conflicting conventions that languages have since become. Whereas the Bible teaches that the language of God and Adam was saved from the flood only to be destroyed soon afterwards in the great catastrophe at Babel.

But fresh green shoots of etymological yearning sprang up once more during the Renaissance. Philosophers wondered whether Chinese pictographs or Egyptian hieroglyphs or even the gestural signs of the deaf might not correspond to the original natural language. Christian piety redirected such etymological hopes towards Hebrew; the original text of Genesis placed Hebrew words in the mouths of God and Adam, after all, so it followed that Hebrew itself must be the oldest of all languages, older even than Creation itself.

But how could Hebrew have survived the confusion of tongues? The answer, according to the etymological enthusiast Francis Mercury van Helmont in 1667, was that the sounds of Hebrew were obliterated at Babel but its written form survived unscathed. Helmont also claims to penetrate the alphabetic code and recover the sounds with which it was originally spoken. Hebrew writing, he argues, was essentially pictorial; its characters were portraits of the vocal organs, not representations of objects. Properly interpreted, they depicted the exact positions of lips, tongue and throat required to produce the particular sounds for which they stood.

Helmont dedicates himself to deciphering the vocal instructions encoded in the Hebrew alphabet, and tries to speak accordingly. Despite torture and imprisonment, he perseveres for years, chasing the spectre of scientific triumph: reconstituting the very sounds of the world's first language by which to mimic the exact tones of Adam and Eve or indeed the Serpent in the Garden of Eden — to speak the selfsame words by which God first summoned His creatures into existence. And thus, through etymology, to capture a share of God's original creative power.

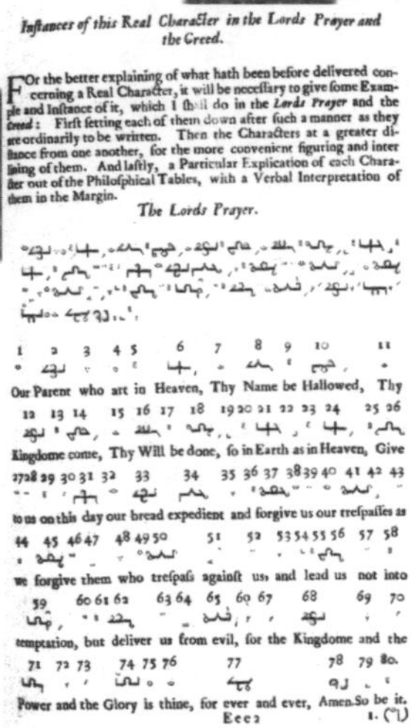
Instances of this Real Character in the Lords Prayer and the Creed.

FOr the better explaining of what hath been before delivered concerning a Real Character, it will be necessary to give some Example and Instance of it, which I shall do in the *Lords Prayer* and the *Creed*: First setting each of them down after such a manner as they are ordinarily to be written. Then the Characters at a greater distance from one another, for the more convenient figuring and interlining of them. And lastly, a Particular Explication of each Character out of the Philosophical Tables, with a Verbal Interpretation of them in the Margin.

The Lords Prayer.

1 2 3 4 5 6 7 8 9 10 11
Our Parent who art in Heaven, Thy Name be Hallowed, Thy
12 13 14 15 16 17 18 19 20 21 22 23 24 25 26
Kingdome come, Thy Will be done, so in Earth as in Heaven, Give
27 28 29 30 31 32 33 34 35 36 37 38 39 40 41 42 43
to us on this day our bread expedient and forgive us our trespasses as
44 45 46 47 48 49 50 51 52 53 54 55 56 57 58
we forgive them who trespass against us, and lead us not into
59 60 61 62 63 64 65 66 67 68 69 70
temptation, but deliver us from evil, for the Kingdome and the
71 72 73 74 75 76 77 78 79 80.
Power and the Glory is thine, for ever and ever, Amen. So be it.
Eee 2

The Lord's Prayer written in John Wilkins' Real Character

Jonathan Ree Professor of Philosophy at Middlesex University

Francis Mercury van Helmont (1614-1698) He travelled Europe as physician and courtly drinking companion. 'He shall always be more prized where he is not than where he is', wrote one acquaintance. When imprisoned by the Inquisition for heresy in 1661-1663, he argued he should be burnt, on the basis of a complex theory of the virtues of pain. He boasted of his ability to teach speech to the congenitally dumb, and explained his account of spiritual speech by analogy with children breaking wind and the bodily retention of semen. The first version of his theory that Hebrew letters are diagrams of the vocal chords was printed in 1667. He then moved to England, met Charles II at Newmarket races, and settled in an aristocratic philosophical community in Warwickshire. He subsequently became a Quaker, returned to Germany in 1679, and resumed his philosophic tourism.

Wolfgang Von Kempelen (1734-1804) Hungarian civil servant. In 1791 Kempelen published a description of a speaking machine which used a clarinet and a bagpipe chanter to imitate the human voice. According to Goethe 'the speaking machine of Kempelen is not very loquacious but it pronounces certain childish words nicely.'

Nicola Schwartz Photographer and video artist.

Tabatha Andrews Artist making installations which exlpore the materiality of sound and light.

An interest in Universal speech often goes hand in hand with the development of mechanical language devices.
In *Rufflette,* a sound installation by Tabatha Andrews, a man and woman say *yes* and *no* alternately. An enigmatically theatrical piece from minimal means.

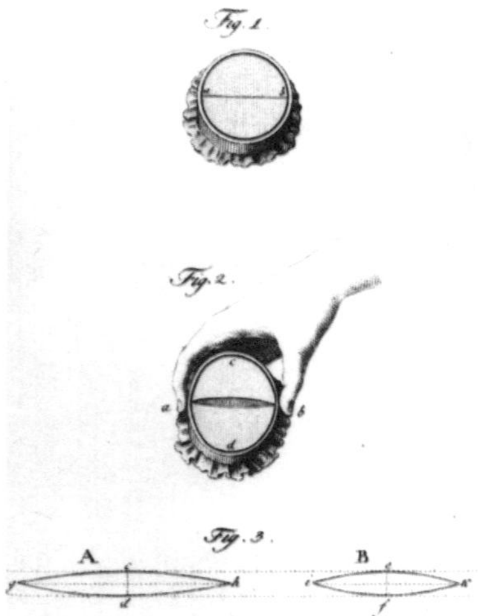

Wolfgang Von Kempelen *Mechanismus der Memschlichen Sprachen Nebst der Beschreibungseiner Sprechenden Maschine* 1791

What do you say we call it?

The Talking Heads Experiment

LUC STEELS

A Wittgensteinian approach. Meanings are not *a priori* Platonic entities independent of language; meanings are the result of embodied interactions with the world, obtained via the role words play in verbal exchanges called "language games". The Talking Heads Experiment explores one kind of language game: a guessing game played by two robotic agents about the scene directly in front of them. One agent acts as Speaker and attempts to draw the attention of the Hearer to some object by transmitting a verbal description of it; the Speaker succeeds if the Hearer correctly guesses which object is "meant".

To play the game, the Speaker segments the scene and performs pattern recognition to extract features — area, shape, colour, position — about the segments selected. The Speaker then conceptualises the focus element "topic" as distinct from those of other segments — be it the largest or the furthest to the left or the green one. Next the Speaker verbalises this conceptualisation using descriptive words selected from its lexicon. The Hearer works the other way round; it queries the words transmitted by the Speaker and applies the resultant meanings back to the scene to find what topic the Speaker intended.

To express conceptualisations, agents need a lexicon relating words to meanings. It must function bi-directionally (words-to-meanings *and* meanings-to-words); it must also store synonyms (more than one word for the same meaning) and ambiguities (more than one meaning for the same word). The agents have not been *given* a lexicon; they must acquire their own common lexicon as a bi-product of the game.

New words accrue in two ways: either an agent creates its own new words from random combinations of syllables; or it stores transmitted words together with possible-meaning guesses inferred from the scene, then uses a hypothesis-test strategy to render lexicons mutually compatible. Agents keep a running score for every word-meaning pair in their lexicon. When word-topic recognition succeeds the score for that pair goes up, and that of other alternates goes down. This dynamic forces the lexicon of each individual agent to progressively conform, and keeps it adapting to any language changes or new meanings that need to be expressed. During the course of the exhibition, a group of robotic agents autonomously constructs a shared language about real world scenes in front of them. Humans can interact with the installation through the Internet; they can teach their agents words and follow the general progress towards the construction of the language.

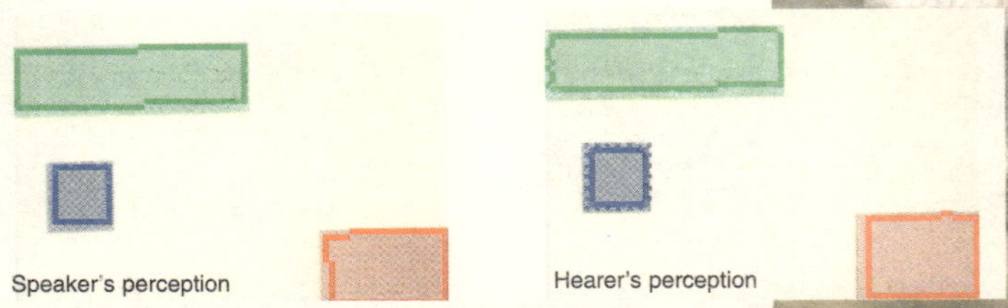

Intriguing questions:
How to bridge the enormous gap between the noisy real world of images and behaviour, and the discrete digital world of symbols and language required for communication and thought? How do language and meaning originate? Why do languages keep changing so as to adapt to the needs of their users? How can a language be transmitted between generations without any central coordination or telepathy?

The installation consists of two computer-controlled robotic camera heads that capture images from 'scenes' in front of them consisting of colored geometric shapes pasted on a magnetic whiteboard. The configurations on the board can be changed at any time, making the robots' world unpredictable and open.

Two robotic structures will be active in this exhibition: one at Kettle's Yard in Cambridge and another one at the Wellcome Institute in London. along with additional installations in Brussels, Paris, Tokyo, Milton Keynes, and elsewhere.

A view of the Talking Heads installation at Laboratorium, a major exhibition at the Museum voor Fotografie in Antwerp.During this exhibition over 1500 agents were created and in excess of 400,000 identification games were played.

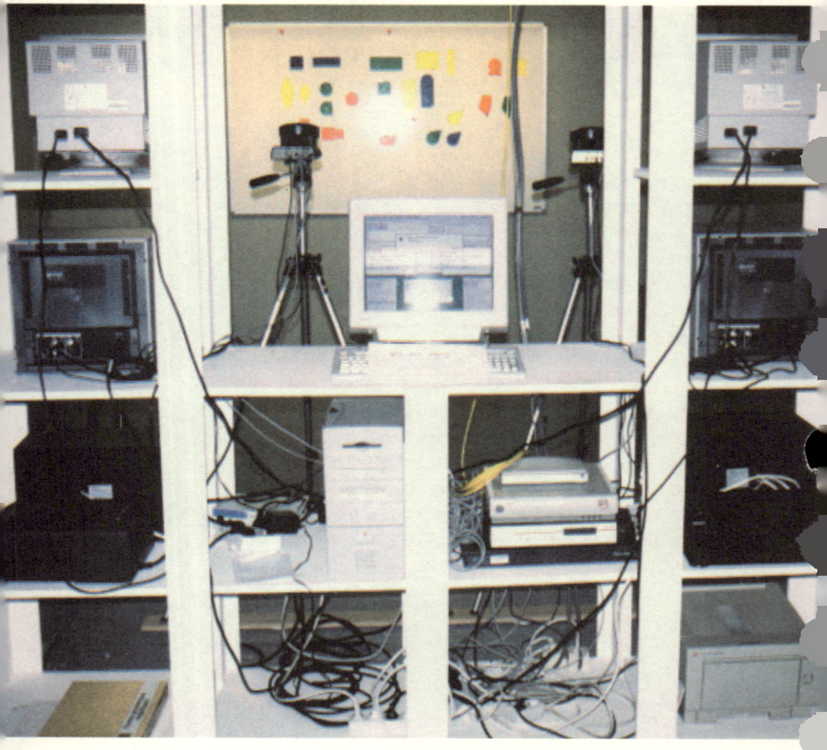

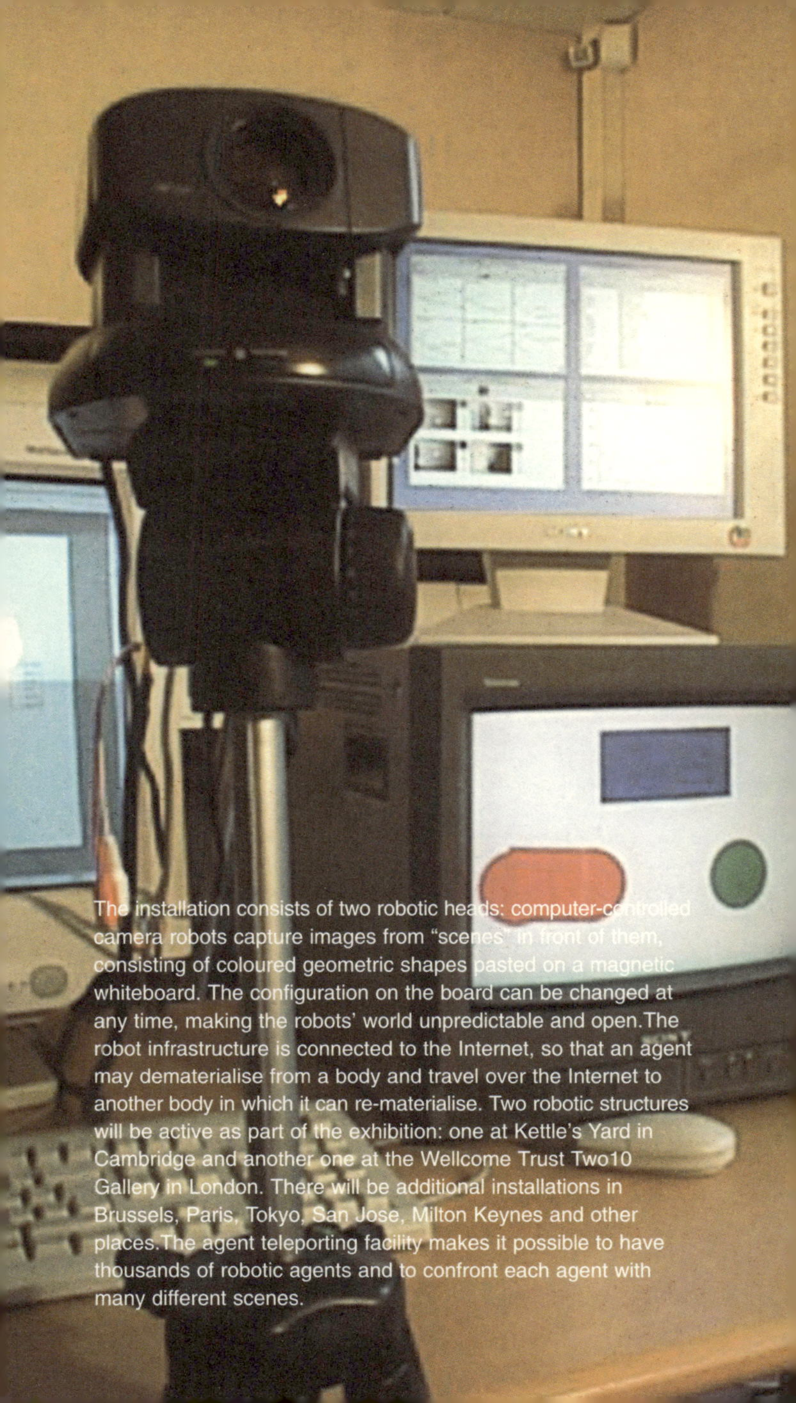

The installation consists of two robotic heads: computer-controlled camera robots capture images from “scenes” in front of them, consisting of coloured geometric shapes pasted on a magnetic whiteboard. The configuration on the board can be changed at any time, making the robots’ world unpredictable and open. The robot infrastructure is connected to the Internet, so that an agent may dematerialise from a body and travel over the Internet to another body in which it can re-materialise. Two robotic structures will be active as part of the exhibition: one at Kettle’s Yard in Cambridge and another one at the Wellcome Trust Two10 Gallery in London. There will be additional installations in Brussels, Paris, Tokyo, San Jose, Milton Keynes and other places. The agent teleporting facility makes it possible to have thousands of robotic agents and to confront each agent with many different scenes.

Each agent has been given a mechanism to `grow' new distinctions by expanding 'discrimination trees'. Each tree identifies one sensory dimension. For example, there is a tree for the area of a segment (scale with respect to the image) which divides the range of possible values into two discrete regions, which would be named in English "small" and "large". Other trees focus on position (left versus right or top versus bottom), shape (rectangular or oval), color, etc. Trees can go as deep as necessary to carve out smaller and smaller sub-regions of a continuous space.

The nodes of the discrimination trees grow in a random fashion but the distinctions that are not successful in the game are pruned. This way the conceptual repertoire of an agent can continue to adapt to the needs of the agent.

Self-organisation.
How do agents manage to reach coherence in their lexicons without a central coordinator and despite all these sources of noise? The answer is self-organisation. Coherence is reached in the same way as an ant society manages to form a coherent path between a food source and the nest, namely by a positive feedback loop. In this case there is a positive feedback loop between use and success: the more a word is successful, the more it is chosen by the agents, and the more success it will have. This causes the agents to settle in an 'attractor' where they all prefer the same word for the same meaning and vice-versa. We see a dampening of synonymy as in the case in natural languages. Noise has the beneficial impact of getting agents out of attractor states (so called local minima) which are not optimal from the viewpoint of the whole although they are a possible solution.

Structural coupling.
How do agents manage to share their conceptualisation of the world without their concepts being innately given (pre-programmed) nor centrally coordinated? The answer is structural coupling, another concept adopted from biology. Two systems have a structural coupling if one creates a context for the other and vice-versa, so that each system develops to be efficiently co-ordinated without any prior design or global control. The conceptual system and the lexicon of each agent is structurally coupled in the sense that agents prune distinctions that are not successful in the language game, and conversely they keep the ones that are useful and successful. This makes the conceptual system progressively better adapted both to the scenes encountered by the agents and the lexicons used in the group. Sources of noise are again beneficial for fostering structural coupling. First of all they help the group to push towards the use of categorisations that are robust against noise. Second, they help agents to explore alternatives and avoid them getting stuck in sub-optimal behavior.

Sources of noise affecting Talking Heads.
The creation of a shared language by a group of autonomous distributed agents is extraordinarily difficult because there are many sources of noise, in the form of disturbances that cause incoherence between the agents:

•Two embodied grounded agents always see the situation from different points of view so that they capture different images. Consequently they may have divergent perceptions and hence great difficulty in arriving at a successful game.

•The word(s) transmitted may not be accurately produced or received. For example, one agent may produce "wabaku" but the other agent may hear "mabaku". This introduces noise in the signal itself and hence possibly confusion among the agents.

•A scene can usually be conceptualised in many different ways, so that there is seldom certainty among the agents whether they share the same meaning. This causes great difficulties in learning the meaning of unknown words.

•The lexicons and conceptual repertoires are never exactly the same as each agent develops them autonomously. This generates in additional sources of confusion. Any theory claiming to explain the origins of word-meaning must confront the handling of noise head on.

Cultural evolution.
Noise plays yet another role, namely as a motor of language evolution. Indeed, natural lexicons evolve - even if there are already perfectly good words in a language. Noise on the word form causes changes in the form which propagate in the remainder of the population. Misunderstandings may destabilise a word and cause its meaning to shift.

Another factor in language evolution is due to changes in the environment. Thus two alternative meanings for a word may be compatible for a while but are then sundered when a series of scenes arises in which the two meanings are no longer both applicable. For example, all objects may be both green and small and therefore there may be a word "sesubipu" which may mean both, until a clear situation arises where a green object is no longer the smallest and a misunderstanding arises.

Semiotic evolution is continually present. Different meanings for a particular word will emerge over over a large number of language games. During specific periods, different words dominate. The word "droite" (originally introduced by a French speaker) gains the dominant meaning "to the right", then shifts to "at the bottom", and then to "very much to the right". Particularly the words introduced by humans have a tendency to undergo this kind of strong evolution because human users do not know which meanings their agents employ.

Constructing perceptually grounded concepts.
What is most remarkable about this experiment is that the robotic agents do not come with pre-programmed ways of conceptualising reality but have to develop their own concepts.

Luc Steels Professor of Artificial Intelligence at the University of Brussels (VUB) and founding director of the Sony Computer Laboratory in Paris.

The **Talking Heads Experiment** is a collective effort by members of the Sony Computer Science Laboratory, Paris and the VUB Artificial Intelligence Laboratory, Brussels. Frederic Kaplan, Angus McIntyre and Joris Van Looveren made major contributions. This research has been sponsored by the Sony Computer Science Laboratory in Paris and a GOA grant from the Belgian Government to the VUB AI Lab.

Human Interaction Through the Internet
A website has been created for the experiment (http://talking-heads.csl.sony.fr/). Through this site, anybody who wants can create new agents and follow their progress. Owners of agents can teach them words, so that words already used in human natural languages sneak into the emerging vocabulary. The agents are autonomous and do not necessarily stick to the words given to them but try to adapt to the behavior of the group and invent their own words. Through the website it is also possible to monitor the progress of the experiment: the lexicon being created, the success rate, the coherence among the agents, the complexity of the language, etc. There is a Hall of Fame listing the best speakers and hearers. This motivates humans to take care of their agents thus ensuring that they move to the top in the Hall of Fame.

To express a conceptualisation, agents need a lexicon relating words with meanings. The lexicon must be consultable in both directions (from words to meanings and from meanings to words). It must be able to store synonyms (more than one word for the same meaning) and ambiguities The agents have not been given a lexicon a priori. They have to acquire their own lexicon as a side effect of the game. New words get into a lexicon in two ways: When an agent has no word to express a particular distinction, the agent can create a new one by a random combination of syllables. When an agent hears a word that he does not know, he stores the new word with his own guess of what the meaning could be in the scene being perceived.

Agents then use a hypothesise-and-test strategy to make their lexicon compatible with the rest of the group. They keep a score for every word-meaning pair in their lexicon. When a word has success in the game, the score goes up, and its competitors go down. When the game fails, the score of the used word(s) goes down. This creates an inhibition-excitation dynamics making the lexiconof the individual agent progressively conform to the most successful lexicon of the group. It also ensures that an agent's lexicon keeps adapting if the language changes or if new meanings need to be expressed.

Who controls the voice?

The Preacher and the Chorus

MANUEL FRANQUELO

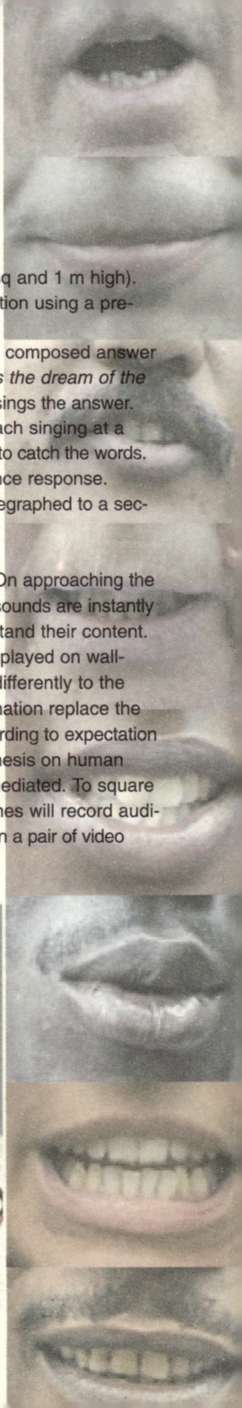

In a space 13 small circuit boards sit on 13 plinths (each 30 cm sq and 1 m high). One, situated slightly away from the others forms a random question using a pre-programmed vocabulary. *Tell me who mediates?...* Pause.
After a few seconds one of the other units formulates a randomly composed answer using the verb from the question. *The noise of the geek mediates the dream of the virus.* -There is a second short pause before the entire assembly sings the answer. Each has a different voice (seven male and six female voices), each singing at a slightly different speed. The mood is ecclesiastical and it is difficult to catch the words. Video cameras positioned around the installation record the audience response. Simultaneously the audio data is converted to Morse code and telegraphed to a second site.

In the second space the experience of the work is very different. On approaching the space sounds of Morse code punctuate the silence. The beeping sounds are instantly recognisable as Morse code despite the fact that few can understand their content. On entering the space, the data is converted back to text and displayed on wall-mounted liquid crystal displays. Visitors to this space react very differently to the audience that engages with the electronic units; Apathy and alienation replace the sense of humour and wonder. The audience response varies according to expectation and prior knowledge. The Preacher and chorus places the emphesis on human interaction and the way information changes its content as it is mediated. To square the circle a number of video surveillance cameras and microphones will record audience response to the work at both venues. This will be displayed on a pair of video monitors in a third space.

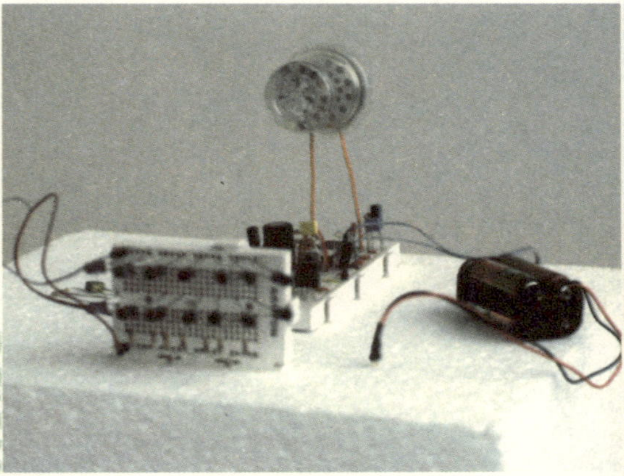

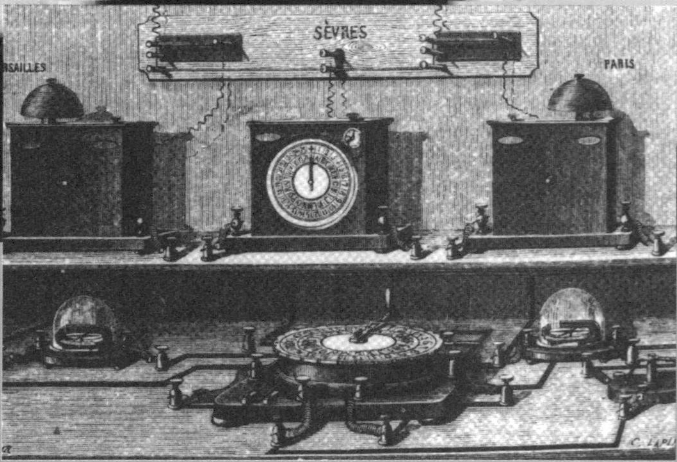

Breton Freres, *Dial Telegraph*
An alternative to the printing telegraph; the letters selected on the transmitter (the horizontal dial) are indicated by the needle on the indicator (the vertical dial) at the receiving station.

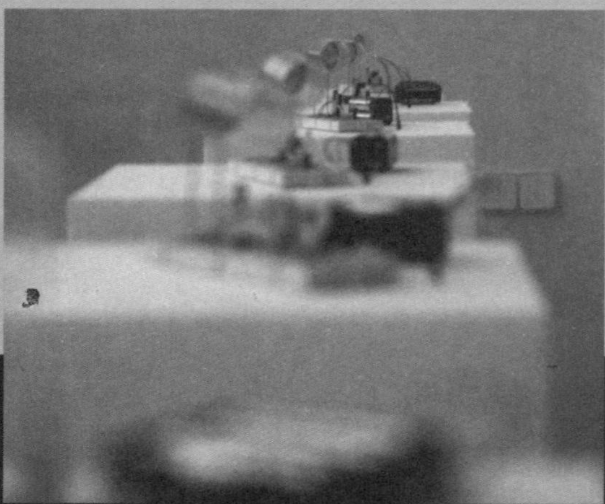

Manuel Franquelo *The Preacher and the Chorus*

Where do answers come from?

"We propose a cannonball express - an institution which, with properly situated artillery stations spaced within range of each other, would fire hollow shells stuffed not with gunpowder but with letters and parcels. They could easily be seen in flight and wherever they landed could be retrieved, unless it was a bog."
Heinrich von Kleist
A Project for a Cannonball Postal Service (1810)

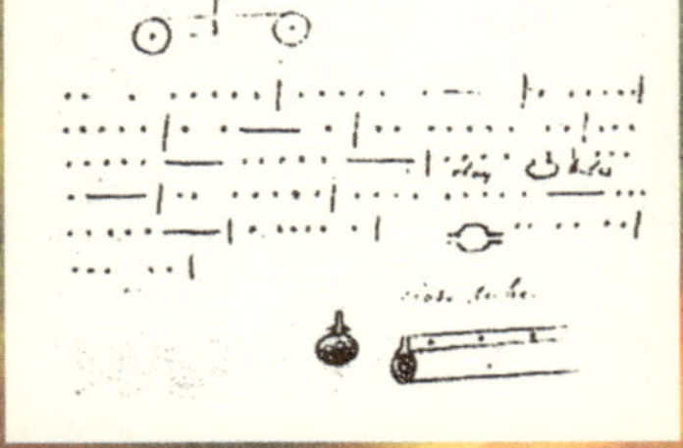

The dots and dashes of electricity flowing down the wire by operator-punched code were commodities — standardised packages with a standardised economic value. As a result, the Victorians learnt new norms for communicating with each other via this novel technology. Clues of meaning that might be visible face-to-face or even in written communication were lost, and alternative means of expression had to be invented. Many found the telegraph and its code an alienating distortion of conversation.

There was a tension within telegraphic culture between openness and secrecy. Many commentators celebrated the way in which telegraphy inaugurated a new era in human interaction across the globe. Instantaneous communication brought everyone closer together, and made the world a smaller, more intimate place. That intimacy had its price, however: early telegraph users felt violated when they suddenly realised that their private communications had to be read by telegraph clerks who translated them into code and communicated them down the wire. Digitalisation distanced them from the means of communication — it erected a barrier between them and the person with whom they aimed to communicate. Morse code and telegraph technology was the province of an expert few who knew the key to translating between Morse and ordinary language. Not everyone was happy to put communication into expert hands. The Morse code's digitisation made a nonsense of the far older codes regulating communication between classes and genders through which Victorians routinely lived their lives. In breaking down barriers, it created new ones.

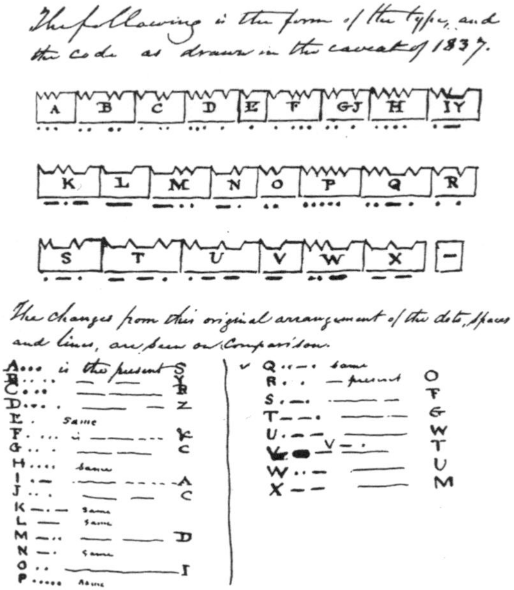

Samuel Morse's first sketch showing the code in three dimensions and as an encoded dot-dash system

Morse Code

IWAN MORUS

Victorian commentators, along with many of their modern counterparts, identified the electric telegraph as one of the greatest triumphs of nineteenth century invention. The ability to send information more or less instantaneously through a wire over massive distances revolutionized ideas about space and time. It was a breakthrough of magical proportions. Pundits waxed lyrical about how the telegraph was "a spirit like Ariel to carry our thoughts with the speed of thought to the uttermost ends of the earth". Beneath the high-flown rhetoric, however, a great deal of hard work and organization was necessary to make the technology work. **Samuel Morse**, inventor of the American version of the telegraph, famously remarked in 1832, "If the presence of electricity can be made visible in any part of the circuit, I see no reason why intelligence may not be transmitted instantaneously by electricity." By the 1830s there were a number of ways of making electricity visible using magnetism, heat, light or chemical reaction. Two more things were needed to make the telegraph viable: the technology to make those signs of electricity's presence visible over long distances, and a way to make those signals intelligible — to turn the twitchings of a needle or random markings on a strip of paper into a language that could be read.

Morse himself played an important role in solving the problem. From the beginnings of his work on the telegraph he visualized his instrument as embodying a code. In its earlier versions, the message was literally notched along a length of wood that was fed through the transmitter. The receiver at the other end duplicated the indentations as a jagged line of long and short peaks along a strip of paper. Only later was the technology modified to produce the familiar dot-dash code we know today.

The early code expressed numbers rather than letters; Morse wanted it to be a cypher as well as a code. He was convinced that the telegraph would be government property and as such he felt sure they would want to keep messages secret. Each number would correspond to a word laid out in a laboriously prepared dictionary. Only those with access to the dictionary cypher would be able to make sense of the code. That plan was later abandoned to produce a code in which combinations of dots and dashes stood for individual letters, though the assigning of combinations to each different letter was neither random nor straightforward. Morse wanted his instrument and the code it embodied to be economical. He spent time visiting printers' shops to find out what letters they used most frequently; the idea was to assign the shortest combinations of dots and dashes to the letters used most often.

The economic imperatives imposed by telegraphic communication on speech had some interesting linguistic consequences. For the first time, the Victorians had to almost literally weigh their words; the cost of sending a message down the telegraph line depended on the message's length. Too prolix a communication could quickly become ruinously expensive. The result, as one Victorian commentator rather ironically noted, was that 'the telegraphic style banishes all forms of politeness.' Morse code and the telegraph were in the process of digitizing speech. Language was being divorced from its original contexts and represented afresh by a new set of symbols.

Manuel Franquelo One of Spain's leading hyper-realist painters, whose paintings are not flat 'photographic' illusions but work a mimetic resonance at all levels. In recent years, his obsessively detailed artistic practice has included proprietory programming and specially designed output devices. Originally trained as an electronic engineer, Franquelo, with German engineer Sven Nebel, recently created a three-dimensional 1:1 scale facsimile of the Altamira caves using the same materials as the original, with an accuracy of within 2 mm.

Iwan Morus Historian of Science at the school of Anthropological Studies, Queens' University Belfast.

Samuel Morse, (1791-1872) Massachusetts painter and telegraphist. After studying art in London, Morse set up the American Academy of Design in New York City, though this great paintings of Congress were denied state support. He was instrumental in introduciing Daguerrotype photography to America. During a transatlantic voyage in 1832 he learnt about the advantages and puzzles of telegraphy, a signal system he studied and perfected between 1835 and 1837. After considerable resistance his system was adopted in the US in 1844. Morse Code was abandoned as the world signal system in 1998.

We see emerging, piecemeal and with the greatest ambiguity, the seeds of a new noise, one exterior to the institutions and customary sites of political conflict. Conceptualising the coming order on the basis of the designation of the fundamental noise should be the central work of today's researchers. The only worthwhile researchers — undisciplined ones. Today, a new music is on the rise, one that can neither be expressed nor understood using the old tools.
Jacques Attali *Noise* (1985)

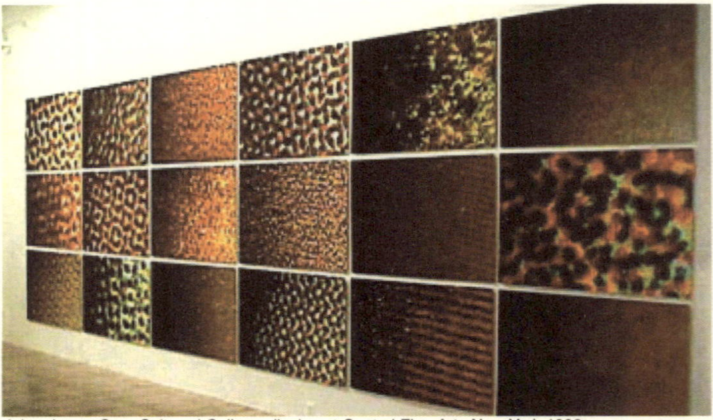

Adam Lowe *Grey Cultured Cells* on display at Central Fine Arts New York 1999.
These micrographs are produced from a single computer generated four-colour blend of neutral grey printed using 18 different printing processes.

What is that sound high in the air?

Disinformation by Design

JOE BANKS

Who knows but that as in a watch, we may hear the beating of the balance, the runing of the wheels, the striking of the hammers, the grating of the teeth and multitudes of other noises; who knows, I say, but that it may be possible to discover the motions of the internal parts of bodies, whether animal, vegetable or mineral by the sound they make. I could proceed further, but methinks I can hardly forbear to blush when I consider how the most part of men will look upon this; but I have this encouragement, not to think all these things utterly impossible, though never so much derided by the generality of men, and never so seemingly mad, foolish, and phantastic, that as thinking them impossible cannot much improve my knowledge, so that believing them possible may, perhaps, be an occasion of taking notice of such things as another would pass by without regard as useless.
Robert Hooke 1635 -1703

It can be productive to look beyond the pejorative associations of the word noise, particularly when defined as communications interference, because doing so exposes listeners to phenomena of surprising complexity and importance. Benoit Mandelbrot's observation of Escher-like self-similarity in the noise peaks of fax-line interference was an important precursor to his discovery of the most complex object in mathematical history. Likewise, the medium of radio offers unprecedented synaesthetic opportunities, expanding perceptual bandwidth across the entire electromagnetic spectrum. AT&T/Bell Telephone engineer Karl Jansky's interception of *galactic radio noise* or *astral static* is the historical basis of the entire field of radio astronomy, and therefore the observational backbone of contemporary scientific cosmology.

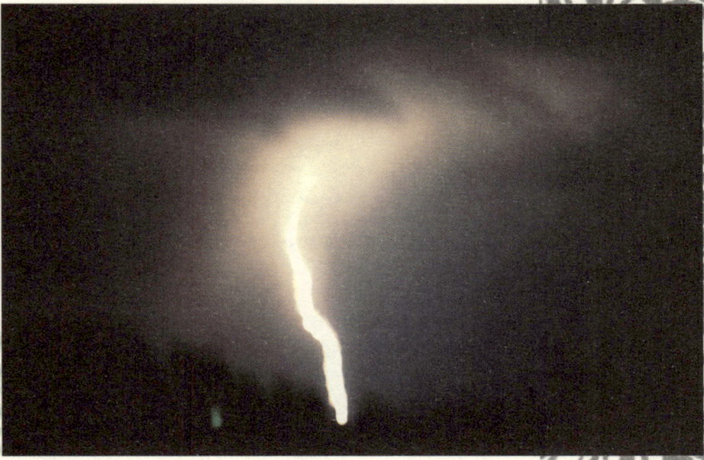

Joe Banks *Theophany*, live in Skiathos 1998

Similarly simple VLF (very low frequency) radio techniques enabled electrical-engineer Heinrich Barkhausen to listen to the progressive magnetisation of individual particles inside iron cores and develop the domain theory of ferromagnetic hysteresis.

During World War I, Barkhausen studied the nocturnal *whistlers* that interfered with German military ECM (electronic counter-measures) the so-called ghosts of artillery shells heard during attempts to eavesdrop on British army field-telephones. After the invention of the first purpose-built whistler-receiving radio at the Cavendish Laboratory, O. Storey confirmed that these whistlers are produced by lightning strikes locking-on to and echoing along the semi-circular field-lines of the earth's magnetosphere in space. The whistlers, hisses, crackles and drones radiated by lightning today are identical to those noises broadcast during the genesis of life on earth - at the electrical ignition of the primordial soup. A strong geographical correlation exists between the intensity of atmospheric interference, as illustrated in radio scientists topographical noise charts, and diversity of species in the tropics. The role of lightning in the fixation of atmospheric nitrogen means that the proverbial Hand of God can, even today, still be detected at the base of all living ecosystems. "The voice of the Lord strikes with flashes of lightning" (Psalms 29:7), so it can be argued that Disinformation's *Theophany* recordings (of local electrical storms) really are the voice of God. Whistlers are also occasionally produced by the EMP (electromagnetic pulses) radiated by atom bombs. In 1998 Theophany was exhibited inside the chapel of a labyrinthine nuclear warfare command centre, which is enclosed in a massive subterranean Faraday cage near Anstruther in Fife, as a symbol of the bewildering technical, theological and political complexities of nuclear war.

In 1936 **Rudolph Arnheim** wrote in his book *Radio* that "in every art it is the most elementary and primitive means that achieve the most profound and beautiful effects". The truth is that many individuals already own machines that can be prompted to receive extraordinary cosmic signals simply by switching them on. The white noise familiar as static on radio and TV is produced by thermal activity within the apparatus, by radio-emissions from lightning, from the Sun, Jupiter or from dying stars, and approximately 2% is contributed directly by the Big Bang. The existence of this microwave background – energy from the Big Bang red-shifted down to radio frequencies by the expansion of the universe - was predicted by Albert Einstein. MIT mathematician **Norbert Wiener** found a statistical model for white noise in Einstein and Jean Perrin's formula for Brownian Motion, and proved that thermal noise is a manifestation of the kinetic activity of free electrons within the molecular lattice of electrical circuits. Decades later, the microwave background was isolated by AT&T/Bell Telephones Arno Penzias and Robert Wilson, using cryogenic amplification techniques to exclude thermal noise and allow direct intercepts of the *echo* of creation itself.

White noise is the ultimate signal for obliterating information, and is often broadcast as electromagnetic camouflage for coded messages and as a weapon of electronic warfare: but we should remember that just like similar natural noise phenomena such as the sounds of surf, wind, fountains and trees, it can be used as acoustic perfume to soften acoustically harsh environments, which is presumably why people articulate sounds like "hush" and "ssh" to signify silence. At low volumes white noise is prescribed

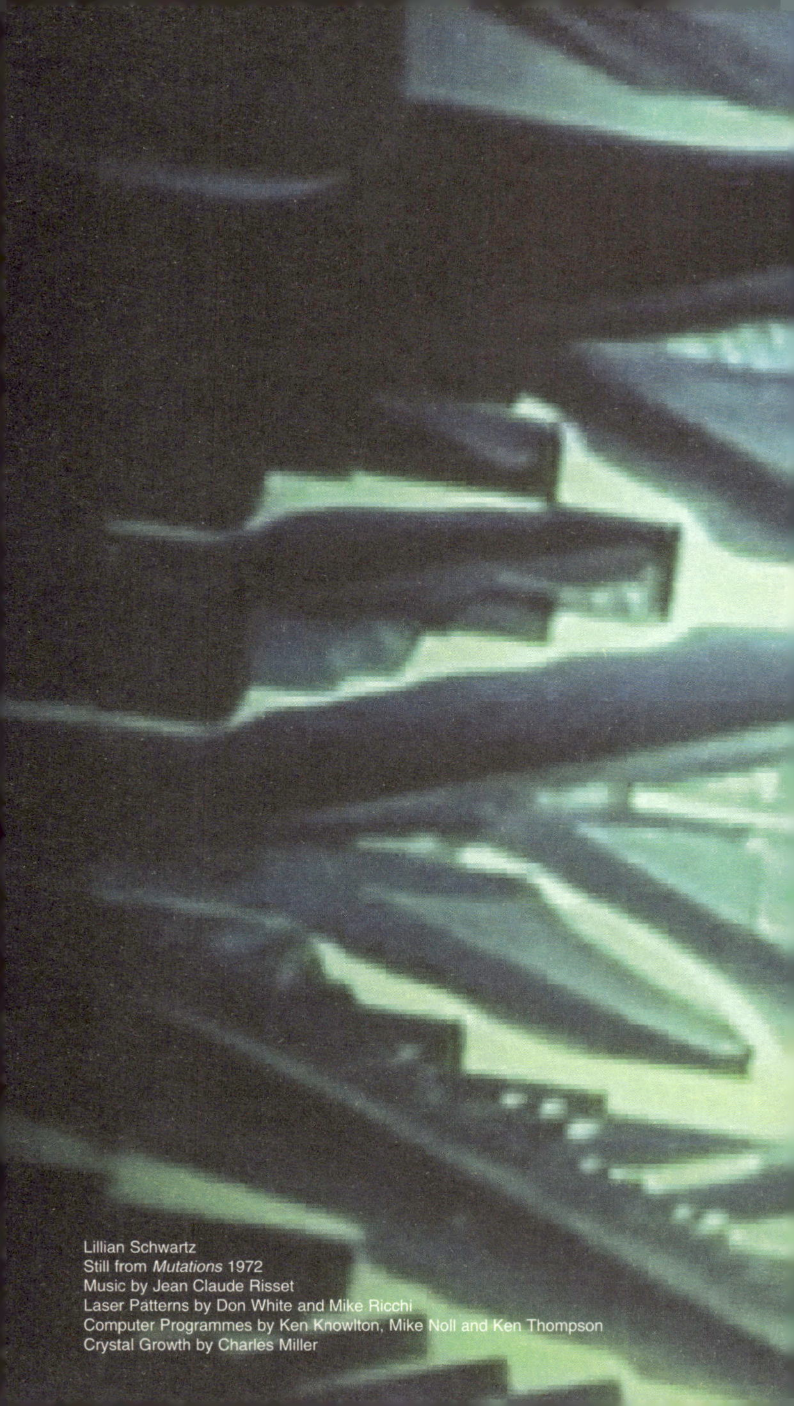

Lillian Schwartz
Still from *Mutations* 1972
Music by Jean Claude Risset
Laser Patterns by Don White and Mike Ricchi
Computer Programmes by Ken Knowlton, Mike Noll and Ken Thompson
Crystal Growth by Charles Miller

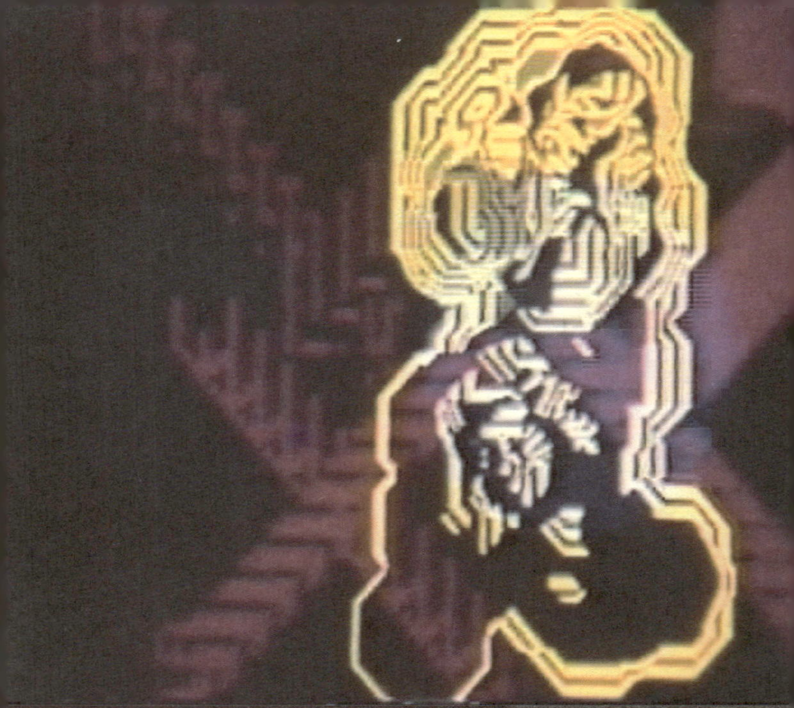

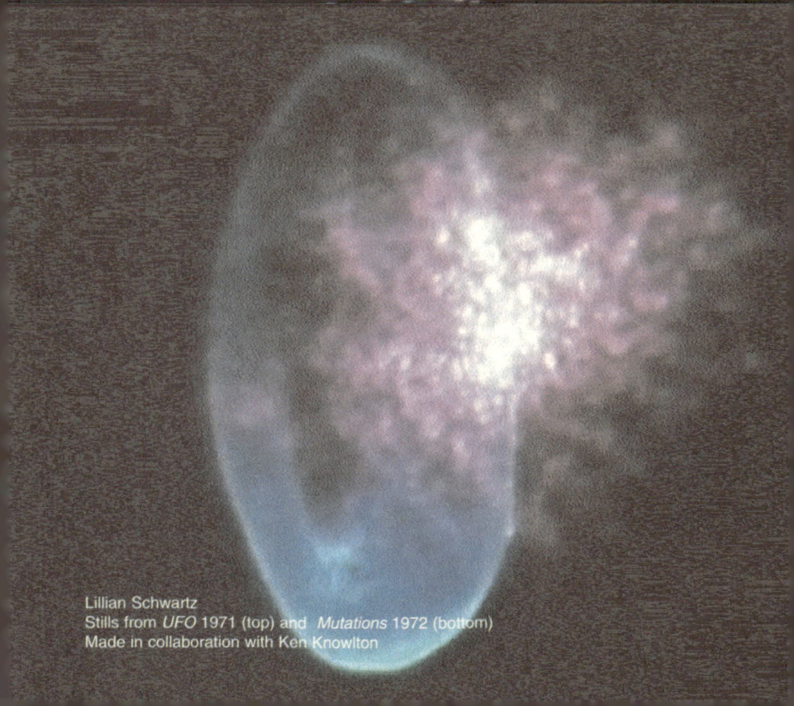

Lillian Schwartz
Stills from *UFO* 1971 (top) and *Mutations* 1972 (bottom)
Made in collaboration with Ken Knowlton

medicinally as treatment for tinnitus. It can also be used to degrade recognisable speech signals and experimentally induce psychoacoustic projections

A noise - the Big Bang - is the archetype of creation itself. Just as in visual language the spark, which is the simplest form of radio transmitter, is the primary signifier of electrical energy, in verbal language the spark is the primordial signifier of creativity.

Disinformation's sub-bass installation *National Grid* takes its source signal either from the ubiquitous ambient VLF field radiated throughout the urban enviroment by electricity pylons and mains circuits, or directly from the outputs of mains transformers. Rhythmic, pulsing sub-bass audio suggests associations with the most primal anthropomorphic phenomenon in music – the rhythms of the human heart, with foetal and infant hypnagogic sense-memories, with seismic activity, the rumble of electric storms (Jimi Hendrix claimed his earliest childhood memory was of a thunderstorm) and even with war. *National Grid* offers live physical evidence of environmental electromagnetic pollution, of beat-frequency effects, the architectural acoustics of its own exhibition space, and a demonstration of the intrinsic musical properties of alternating current. Exploring this arena extends and overturns existing precedents within Western art-music which regard radio primarily as a source of compositional indeterminacy – as a source of random events. In contrast, the central premise of **Disinformation** activity that it is precisely the deterministic aspects of these phenomena that reveal their greatest creative potential.

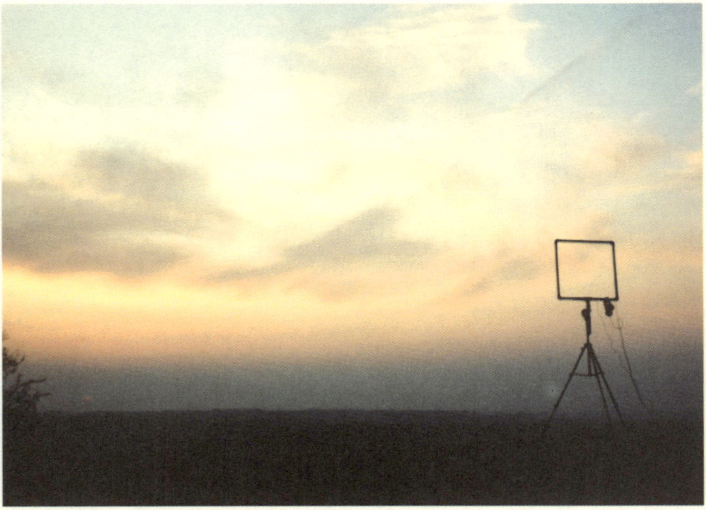

Joe Banks *Ghost Shells*, geomagnetic field recording 1997

Joe Banks Sound artist who produces the Disinformation recordings, installations, texts and performances.

Lillian Schwartz Poineer electronic artist and an early exponent of computer animation. She has had a long-standing association with the Bell Laboratories.

Benoit Mandelbrot Born in Warsaw, he moved to Paris in 1936 and stidied mathematics. Unimpressed by the French prejudice against geometrical diagrams, he worked at California Institute of Technology and then at IBM from 1958. Problems with complex noise in electronic signalling led to early work on fractals, published in book form in 1975. From 1987 Mandelbrot ha been a professor at Yale.

Rudolph Arnheim (b.1904) Psychologist of art, worked at his father's piano factory and at Berlin University in the 1920s. Trained in Gestalt psychology, he was a brilliant film reviewer in Weimar Germany before moving to Rome when the Nazis took power. There he produced an important work on radio as the art of sound in 1936, and responded to the foundation of Cinecitta in 1937. Herbert Read arranged for Arnheim to move to London in 1938, where he translated Dante's *Divine Comedy* and Churchill's radio broadcasts. He arrived in New York in 1940 won a post at Sarah Lawrence College in Bronxville, where he wrote his masterpiece, *Art and Visual Perception'*(1954). He visited Japan, whose artistic culture much affected his attitude to the psychology of expression. He has subsequently been a Harvard professor and a sage in retirement.

Norbert Wiener (1894-1964) Self proclaimed mathematical genius, completed his Harvard doctorate at the age of 19, studied with Bertrand Russell, and became mathematics professor at MIT. Obsessed by disorder, which he saw as evil, he brilliantly theorized Brownian motion, the harmonic analysis of signal systems, and the puzzles of communication theory. In World War II he designed feedback systems for the control of anti-aircraft and bomb delivery systems, thus contributing to the emergence of cybernetics, the theory of regulation and homeostasis on which he published the major work in 1948.

But as we came from Antheil's 'Ballet Mécanique' a woman of our party, herself a musician, made this remark: 'The subway seems sweet after that.' 'Good,' I replied and went on to consider what evidences there were in myself in explanation of her remark. And this is what I noted. I felt that noise, the unrelated noise of life such as this in the subway had not been battened out as would have been the case with Beethoven still warm in the mind but it had actually been mastered, subjugated. Antheil had taken this hated thing life and rigged himself into power over it by his music. The offense had not been held, cooled, varnished over but annihilated and life itself made thereby triumphant. This is an important difference. By hearing Antheil's music, seemingly so much noise, when I actually came upon noise in reality, I found that I had gone up over it.
William Carlos Williams *The Selected Essays of William Carlos Williams*

Think of a number?

BRIAN ROTMAN

At the dawn of the West, Pythagoras taught that the world was constructed from numbers. Two millennia later, Galileo inaugurated modern science with the contention that God wrote the Book of the Universe in the language of mathematics. A century ago, the mathematician Leopold Kronecker asked if mathematics is invented or discovered. He decided it was man-made, with the significant (and much cited) exception of integers, which "were made by God". Certainly, no idea outside religion attracts more mystery and reverence in Western culture than whole numbers: infinite, inexhaustable, the sequence 1, 2, 3 . . . seems miraculous, supernatural. Could they possibly be, extra-human? Divine?

The whole numbers are inseparable in practice —as well as conceptually and semiotically — from counting. True, one can invoke all kinds of numerical magnitudes, trees in a forest, stars in the sky, grains of sand on the beach, without having ever counted them, but the presumption is that they could be counted, that any number of things, however specified, is countable in principle, that any cardinal is always also an ordinal. Certainly, counting is the basis for arithmetic, with addition understood as the repeated adjunction of units, multiplication understood as repeated addition, exponentiation as repeated multiplication, and so on. In other words, without counting arithmetic would not be no more than the comparison of magnitudes.

What, then, is counting? One adds a unit, then another unit, then another, and so on, each time remembering the action by augmenting the recorded store of units or altering a notation (such as the familiar decimal notation, which abbreviates the store). Thus, counting requires one to repeat an action and make a principled record of the repetition. But who or what is supposed to carry out these actions? Who is the agent, the 'one' doing all this repeating and recording?

Each of us can count. It's something we do with our bodies, a pattern of repeated gestures, the making of certain inscriptions or the saying of certain words 'one', 'two', ... 'one hundred and seven', and so on. But our bodies can only count so far: they tire, our attention wanders, we get hungry, alienated, and bored, we die; and so we delegate the task to machines which do not suffer such vicissitudes and can go on counting regardless. But can machines count infinitely far, can they go on counting forever? No, of course not. Machines, however efficient and cleverly designed, whether based on mechanical, electrical, digital, or quantum principles, require energy, occupy space, take time, need to correct for error, fight ever-present noise. And even without error, a machine would eventually appropriate the resources of the entire universe were it to attempt to repeat and record the results of its actions without end.

Only in fantasy, in imagination, can something or someone go on counting for ever.

Only by conjuring extreme idealizations of ourselves, idealized machines capable of perpetual motion or idealized ghost selves free of all demands imposed by the material universe — outside time and space, outside physical law, requiring no labour, effort, or embodied motion — is it possible to make sense of an agency being able to count infinitely far. Outside such a fantasy and its attendant ghost, number is corporeal — embodied, gestural, situated in and derived from the material world (whence its utility); a derivation that makes its origin, then, no more mysterious or divine than any kind of instrumental thought.

But the fantasy of disembodied being, and the endless iteration of the same it makes possible, is too beguiling, and too deeply folded into Western reason to relinquish without a struggle. On the contrary, as both desire and metaphysics, it regulates contemporary techno-science and underpins our thinking about number.

It is what we all accede to — unwittingly and with no cognizance of the implications — when we accept the orthodox mathematical picture of an infinite progression of whole numbers. To replace it with an insistence on the corporeality of the one who counts would be to re-write the connection between number, God, and the body. The result would be a new idea of counting and an arithmetic founded not on the doings of a ghost but on a proxy subject that, however idealized, bore a thread of resemblance to our embodied and contingent presence. To do this would be to take number out of heaven and return it to the noise of the world.

From the result of some preliminary observations, the following points are suggested for enquiry:

1. Generally, whether white paper is as good as lightly printed papers.
2. Whether black ink is preferable to all other coloured inks.
3. Whether that colour both of paper and of ink, which is preferable in strong light, is equally so in a weak light of the same kind.
4. Whether those colours of paper and ink, which have been found most agreeable in daylight, remain so when artificial light is used.
5. Whether colours of paper and ink which are least fatiguing, will not depend on pecularities in the organs of sight of the individuals who make the judgement.
6. Whether the state of general health of the observer may not affect the organ of sight, and render different colours agreeable in different states of health.
7. Whether there are some colours of ink, and some shades of colour of papers, which are most agreeable to the majority.

2° 45'	27° 33'	Num.	0	1	2	3	4	5	6	7	8	9	Diff.
50"	20	9950	9978231	8274	8318	8362	8405	8449	8493	8536	8580	8624	44
	30	1	8667	8711	8755	8798	8842	8885	8929	8973	9016	9060	1 4
	40	2	9104	9147	9191	9235	9278	9322	9365	9409	9453	9496	2 9
	50	3	9540	9584	9627	9671	9715	9758	9802	9845	9889	9933	3 13
	39'	4	9976	0020	0064	0107	0151	0195	0238	0282	0325	0369	4 18
55"	10	5	9980413	0456	0500	0544	0587	0631	0674	0718	0762	0805	5 22
	20	6	0849	0893	0936	0980	1023	1067	1111	1154	1198	1241	6 26
	30	7	1285	1329	1372	1416	1460	1503	1547	1590	1634	1678	7 31
	40	8	1721	1765	1808	1852	1896	1939	1983	2026	2070	2114	8 35
	50	9	2157	2201	2245	2288	2332	2375	2419	2463	2506	2550	9 40
46'	40'	9960	2593	2637	2681	2724	2768	2811	2855	2899	2942	2986	
	10	1	3029	3073	3117	3160	3204	3247	3291	3335	3378	3422	
	20	2	3465	3509	3553	3596	3640	3683	3727	3771	3814	3858	
	30	3	3901	3945	3989	4032	4076	4119	4163	4206	4250	4294	
	40	4	4337	4381	4424	4468	4512	4555	4599	4642	4686	4729	
5"	50	5	4773	4817	4860	4904	4947	4991	5035	5078	5122	5165	
	41'	6	5209	5252	5296	5340	5383	5427	5470	5514	5557	5601	
	10	7	5645	5688	5732	5775	5819	5862	5906	5950	5993	6037	
	20	8	6080	6124	6167	6211	6255	6298	6342	6385	6429	6472	
	30	9	6516	6560	6603	6647	6690	6734	6777	6821	6864	6908	
10"	40	9970	6952	6995	7039	7082	7126	7169	7213	7256	7300	7344	
	50	1	7387	7431	7474	7518	7561	7605	7649	7692	7736	7779	
	42'	2	7823	7866	7910	7953	7997	8040	8084	8128	8171	8215	
	10	3	8258	8302	8345	8389	8432	8476	8519	8563	8607	8650	
	20	4	8694	8737	8781	8824	8868	8911	8955	8998	9042	9086	
15"	30	5	9129	9173	9216	9260	9303	9347	9390	9434	9477	9521	
	40	6	9564	9608	9651	9695	9739	9782	9826	9869	9913	9956	
	50	7	9990000	0043	0087	0130	0174	0217	0261	0304	0348	0391	
	43'	8	0435	0479	0522	0566	0609	0653	0696	0740	0783	0827	
	10	9	0870	0914	0957	1001	1044	1088	1131	1175	1218	1262	
20"	20	9980	1305	1349	1392	1436	1479	1523	1567	1610	1654	1697	
	30	1	1741	1784	1828	1871	1915	1958	2002	2045	2089	2132	
	40	2	2176	2219	2263	2306	2350	2393	2437	2480	2524	2567	
	50	3	2611	2654	2698	2741	2785	2828	2872	2915	2959	3002	
	44'	4	3046	3089	3133	3176	3220	3263	3307	3350	3394	3437	43
25"	10	5	3481	3524	3568	3611	3655	3698	3742	3785	3829	3872	1 4
	20	6	3916	3959	4003	4046	4090	4133	4177	4220	4264	4307	2 9
	30	7	4350	4394	4437	4481	4524	4568	4611	4655	4698	4742	3 13
	40	8	4785	4829	4872	4916	4959	5003	5046	5090	5133	5177	4 17
	50	9	5220	5264	5307	5351	5394	5438	5481	5524	5568	5611	5 22
30"	45'	9990	5655	5698	5742	5785	5829	5872	5916	5959	6003	6046	6 26
	10	1	6090	6133	6177	6220	6263	6307	6350	6394	6437	6481	7 30
	20	2	6524	6568	6611	6655	6698	6742	6785	6829	6872	6915	8 34
	30	3	6959	7002	7046	7089	7133	7176	7220	7263	7307	7350	9 39
	40	4	7393	7437	7480	7524	7567	7611	7654	7698	7741	7785	
35"	50	5	7828	7871	7915	7958	8002	8045	8089	8132	8176	8219	
	46'	6	8262	8306	8349	8393	8436	8480	8523	8567	8610	8653	
	10	7	8697	8740	8784	8827	8871	8914	8958	9001	9044	9088	
	20	8	9131	9175	9218	9262	9305	9349	9392	9435	9479	9522	
	30	9	9566	9609	9653	9696	9739	9783	9826	9870	9913	9957	
			0	1	2	3	4	5	6	7	8	9	

2° 45′	27° 38′	Num.	0	1	2	3	4	5	6	7	8	9	Diff.
30″	20	9950	9978231	8274	8318	8362	8405	8449	8493	8536	8580	8624	44
	30	1	8667	8711	8755	8798	8842	8885	8929	8973	9016	9060	1 4
	40	2	9104	9147	9191	9235	9278	9322	9365	9409	9453	9496	2 9
	50	3	9540	9584	9627	9671	9715	9758	9802	9845	9889	9933	3 13
	39′	4	9976	•020	•064	•107	•151	•195	•238	•282	•325	•369	4 18
35″	10	5	9980413	0456	0500	0544	0587	0631	0674	0718	0762	0805	5 22
	20	6	0849	0893	0936	0980	1023	1067	1111	1154	1198	1241	6 26
	30	7	1285	1329	1372	1416	1460	1503	1547	1590	1634	1678	7 31
	40	8	1721	1765	1808	1852	1896	1939	1983	2026	2070	2114	8 35
	50	9	2157	2201	2245	2288	2332	2375	2419	2463	2506	2550	9 40
46′	40′	9960	2593	2637	2681	2724	2768	2811	2855	2899	2942	2986	
	10	1	3029	3073	3117	3160	3204	3247	3291	3335	3378	3422	
	20	2	3465	3509	3553	3596	3640	3683	3727	3771	3814	3858	
	30	3	3901	3945	3988	4032	4076	4119	4163	4206	4250	4294	
	40	4	4337	4381	4424	4468	4512	4555	4599	4642	4686	4729	
5″	50	5	4773	4817	4860	4904	4947	4991	5035	5078	5122	5165	
	41′	6	5209	5252	5296	5340	5383	5427	5470	5514	5557	5601	
	10	7	5645	5688	5732	5775	5819	5862	5906	5950	5993	6037	
	20	8	6080	6124	6167	6211	6255	6298	6342	6385	6429	6472	
	30	9	6516	6560	6603	6647	6690	6734	6777	6821	6864	6908	
10″	40	9970	6952	6995	7039	7082	7126	7169	7213	7256	7300	7344	
	50	1	7387	7431	7474	7518	7561	7605	7648	7692	7736	7779	
	42′	2	7823	7866	7910	7953	7997	8040	8084	8128	8171	8215	
	10	3	8258	8302	8345	8389	8432	8476	8519	8563	8607	8650	
	20	4	8694	8737	8781	8824	8868	8911	8955	8998	9042	9086	
15″	30	5	9129	9173	9216	9260	9303	9347	9390	9434	9477	9521	
	40	6	9564	9608	9651	9695	9739	9782	9826	9869	9913	9956	
	50	7	9990000	0043	0087	0130	0174	0217	0261	0304	0348	0391	
	43′	8	0435	0479	0522	0566	0609	0653	0696	0740	0783	0827	
	10	9	0870	0914	0957	1001	1044	1088	1131	1175	1218	1262	
20″	20	9980	1305	1349	1392	1436	1479	1523	1567	1610	1654	1697	
	30	1	1741	1784	1828	1871	1915	1958	2002	2045	2089	2132	
	40	2	2176	2219	2263	2306	2350	2393	2437	2480	2524	2567	
	50	3	2611	2654	2698	2741	2785	2828	2872	2915	2959	3002	
	44′	4	3046	3089	3133	3176	3220	3263	3307	3350	3394	3437	43
25″	10	5	3481	3524	3568	3611	3655	3698	3742	3785	3829	3872	1 4
	20	6	3916	3959	4003	4046	4090	4133	4177	4220	4264	4307	2 9
	30	7	4350	4394	4437	4481	4524	4568	4611	4655	4698	4742	3 13
	40	8	4785	4829	4872	4916	4959	5003	5046	5090	5133	5177	4 17
	50	9	5220	5264	5307	5351	5394	5438	5481	5524	5568	5611	5 22
30″	45′	9990	5655	5698	5742	5785	5829	5872	5916	5959	6003	6046	6 26
	10	1	6090	6133	6177	6220	6263	6307	6350	6394	6437	6481	7 30
	20	2	6524	6568	6611	6655	6698	6742	6785	6828	6872	6915	8 34
	30	3	6959	7002	7046	7089	7133	7176	7220	7263	7307	7350	9 39
	40	4	7393	7437	7480	7524	7567	7611	7654	7698	7741	7785	
35″	50	5	7828	7871	7915	7958	8002	8045	8089	8132	8176	8219	
	46′	6	8262	8306	8349	8393	8436	8480	8523	8567	8610	8653	
	10	7	8697	8740	8784	8827	8871	8914	8958	9001	9044	9088	
	20	8	9131	9175	9218	9262	9305	9349	9392	9435	9479	9522	
	30	9	9566	9609	9653	9696	9739	9783	9826	9870	9913	9957	
			0	1	2	3	4	5	6	7	8	9	

Charles Babbage's *Specimen of logarithmic tables printed with different coloured inks on variously coloured papers* (1831) involved the same two pages of Babbage's logarithm tables printed in ten colours on 151 colours of paper, then bound in 20 unique volumes. The complete set is now in the Crawford Library of the Royal Observatory, Edinburgh.

The object of the experiment for which these volumes were printed, was to ascertain the colours of the inks and the tints of the papers least fatiguing to the eye. For that purpose one hundred and fifty one differently coloured papers were chosen, and ten different colours of ink were employed.

With respect to the papers, it was not easy to procure them in sufficient variety and in proper sizes; many have been chosen which obviously would not succeed; but as the additional expense was not great, it was esteemed desireable to print one on every coloured paper which could be purchased in London.

It was found difficult to procure ink of a pure colour: ten varieties have been employed(light blue, dark blue, light green, dark green, olive, yellow, light red, dark red, purple and black).

The work has been bound in twenty-one volumes; the first twenty of these consist of sets of two volumes each. Each set contains about one hundred and forty different coloured papers, on each leaf of which the same two pages of logarithms are printed. As far as possible the two volumes of each set ought to be identical, but owing to accidents in the printing this is not always the case. On each separate coloured paper is a number written in ink. When these numbers are interrupted, it is to be understood that the papers corresponding to the intermediate numbers are wanting. The same number always indicates the same paper throughout all the volumes. The twenty first volume contains specimens of the same printing in gold, silver, and copper upon vellum and variously coloured papers. It rarely happened that more than two leaves of the same paper were printed upon, so that when one was spoiled, after they had been worked off, it was impossible to replace it. This accounts for the occasional deficiencies, and for the fact that very few duplicates of any paper remain.

The reason for having two sets of each differently coloured ink was, that comparisons might be instituted by laying open, side by side, the same table printed with the same ink, but on differently coloured paper. When comparisons between inks of different colours are made, the two required volumes may be laid open either at the same or at differently coloured papers. The question is whether there are some colours of ink, and some shades or colour of papers, which are most agreeable to the majority.

Brian Rotman On the faculty of the Ohio State University. He has a joint appointment in the Division of Comparative Studies and at the Advanced Computer Center for Arts and Design.

Charles Babbage (1791-1871) A banker's son. After precocious mathematical work in Cambridge he lived on a private income, married well, and settled in Marylebone as technical consultant and public whistle-blower. He offered advice on railway design, insurance fraud, annoying buskers, science exhibitions, cryptography and tax reform. From 1820 until 1848 he tried to design, fund and build a series of increasingly ambitious calculating machines. When Lucasian professor of mathematics at Cambridge he wrote a definitive study of the factory system. His evening parties were an indispensable part of the London scene; in 1846, to try out his clever new stage-lighting system, he produced a sound and light show at Her Majesty's theatre on the theme of geological stratigraphy. In his autobiography he showed 'what peculiarities of mind enabled me to accomplish what even the most instructed in their own sciences deemed impossible'.

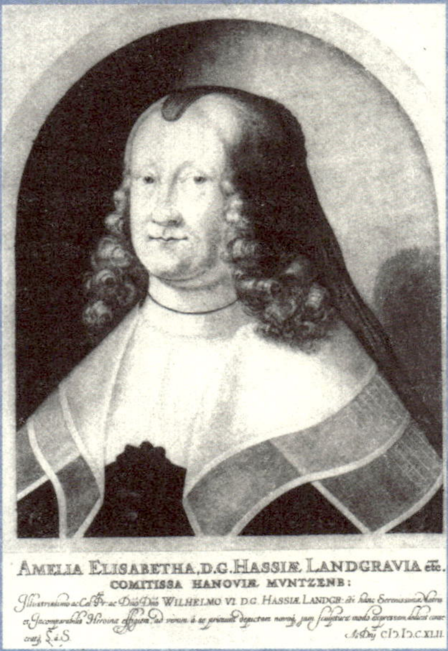

Ludwig Von Siegen *Portrait of the Landgravine of Hesse* 1642 Mezzotint
In 1642, the year Pascal invented the first computer, Ludwig Von Siegen produced the first mezzotint by using a roulette to cover a plate with tiny dots which can be burnished to produce gradations of tone. The inspiration came from observing the fact that pits in the barrel of his gun caused by rust held dirt in a different way from the unpitted surface.
In a letter to his patron he noted; "...and if in some parts this work seems to be done with hatching, it is notwithstanding, entirely dotted.."

What difference does difference make?

The Difference Engine Revisited

BRUCE STERLING

The most remarkable aspect of the Difference Engine is, of course, its abandonment. Disowned by the government that financed it, despaired of by its baffled builders, it even suffered the final insult of being spurned by its own creator, as the mere rough draft of some more high-flown concept. The dead Engine had to settle in the dustiest garage of technical history, a brassy footnote for pop-science charlatans like Edgar Allen Poe.

The device's Gothic science-fictionality made it impossibly appealing to William Gibson and myself when we co-wrote our 1991 novel, *The Difference Engine*. The novel is haunted by the highly unsettling presence of Charles Babbage, who, in our fiction, rises to the dazzling world preeminence he failed to win in reality. The book is also graced by his colleague Ada, the Marianne of the Cyber Revolution, an iconic muse of computation.

Ada is a far more approachable woman than her mythography would lead one to believe. To judge by her letters, she was astonishingly sane, sweet-tempered and sensible. Her father was Lord Byron, the century's leading poet maudit, whose divine discontent was quite deliberately beyond anyone's ability to satisfy. And her grievous mother, a stuffy bluestocking, emotionally traumatized by a great artist, who treasured her resentment to her last breath.

Ada, however, was never bad, mad or dangerous to know. Iconic status as the world's first computer programmer was the farthest thing from the woman's mind. She was a kindly, tactful, somewhat well-to-do, intellectually active British wife and mother. Were she to show up today in the Cambridge Museum of Science, perhaps with a tot in tow, she'd be very much in her element and at ease.

Ada involved herself with Babbage out of personal kindness. Here was a woman who never knew her own father, meeting a much older man, brilliant but misunderstood. Babbage aspired to Byronic eminence, but found a dusty vitrine instead. Rather than becoming the equal of Newton — or perhaps more aptly Karl Marx — Babbage was the world's first victim of vaporware.

Ada's peppy public-relations couldn't save him, however. His Engine was shunted off the iron rails of Victorian progress into a sideshow netherworld. Babbage slowly faded from sage to scarecrow. Once he'd aspired to purge the landed aristocracy, boldly replacing them with industrial cognoscenti, a technocracy of go-getting supernerds who (because they could comprehend Babbage's plans) were inherently fit to master the universe. But the weird donnish whimsy that had once invented a cosmology for cheesemites thickened and soured into the crank eccentricity of

Babbage's last, painful years. He ended as a migraine-crippled curmudgeon, thundering at hurdy-gurdy men.

Ada is not the mother of the computer revolution. She wasn't looking for the job, she was not up for it, and worst of all, she was horribly struck down in the prime of her life. To die as Ada did, of a wasting sexual cancer in the midst of Victorian prudery, is a fate that scarcely bears contemplation. Add to that opium habits, huge gambling debts, and a scolding mother at her bed of pain. Really, it would crack a heart of stone.

The first brass spring of computation was a withered spring, a metal bud that bloomed almost unseen and lodged in its own rust. But as I write these words in Seattle Airport, I can see modern Adas by the score. Freed at last from corsets, gloves, petticoats, and ladylike restraint, they're a queenly conquering army of yuppie geekettes. Like as not they're writing press releases, which extol and explain some postindustrial gizmo that no one but a Babbage understands.

Most Ada-like of all, these women are aristocrats, because they possess stock options sailing into the financial stratosphere. If there's truly a link between her and us, it's not between the mechanical worlds of brass and silicon. That link is in human failing and human vulnerability. Ada's dark triumvirate of laudanum, cancer and gambling is still very much with us today, as some high-flyer's private nightmare of AIDS, substance abuse, and stock market bubbles.

Because it was never just about the machine, you see. There was once flesh and blood behind that wondrous gizmo.

Take heed, O traveller; take pity.

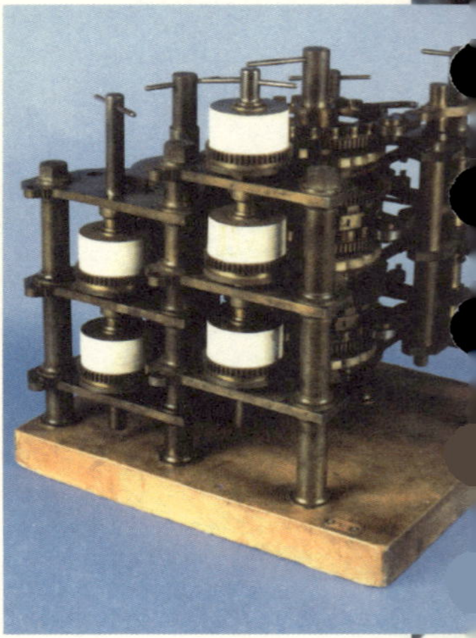

Charles Babbage Difference Engine, 1822 prototype
The Whipple Museum of the History of Science, University of Cambridge

Lynn Hershman, *Difference Engine 3.*
An interactive work in the collection of the ZKM Media Museum, Karlsruhe,
The works depict the increasingly blurred boundary between the real and the virtual world using the architecture of the museum as a three dimensional template and viewers themselves as the interface. "Avatars" of viewers are "born" as they approach any of the three bi-directional browsing units: quickcams embedded in these units capture an image of the person standing before it, each of which is assigned a number representing the time in seconds when the viewer approached the unit. Thus numbered, the viewer's paraphysical "avatar" embarks on a journey through a 3D representation of the museum, then moves on to a "Purgatory" where it cycles continuously together with 30 other avatars. Eventually, the avatars are permanently archived on the internet where their image can be called up via their identity number.

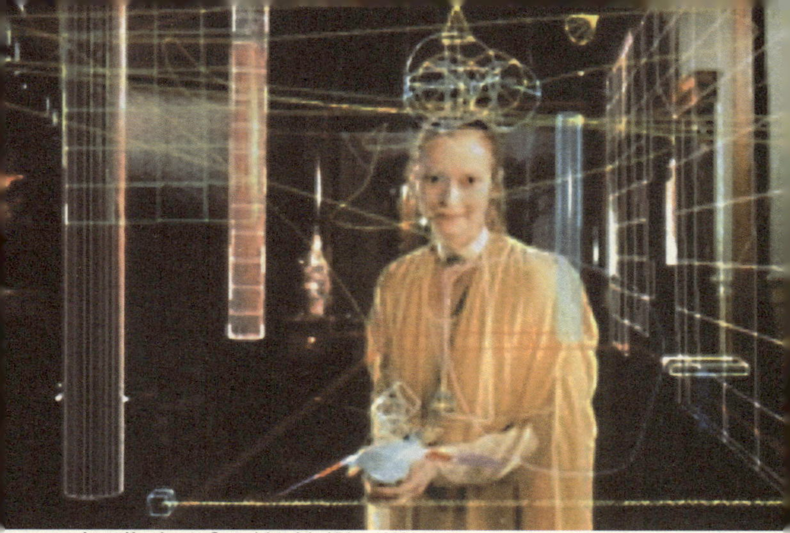

Lynn Hershman *Conceiving Ada*, Video 1998
courtesy of the artist and ZKM
Tilda Swinton in computational space.

At the end of his life Charles Babbage reminisces about the Difference Engine:

"This much abused Difference Engine is a being of sensibility, of impulse, and of power. It can deal with the smallest quantities, nay, it feels even for zeros. It is consious of the presence of a negative quantity, and it is not beyond its ken to forsee the existance of impossible ones"
Passages from the Life of a Philosopher 1864

At the end of her life Ada Lovelace writes to her mother:

"You will not even despair of my being in time an autocrat, in my own way, before whose marshalled regiments some of the iron rulers of the Earth may even have to give way.... I have the hope that they will be the most harmoniously disciplined troops - consisting of vast numbers and marching in irresistable power to the sound of music. Is not this very mysterious? Certainly my troops must consist of numbers, or they can have no existence at all. But then, what are numbers? There is a riddle."
from *The Letters of Lord Byron's daughter*, ed. Betty Alexandra Toole 1992

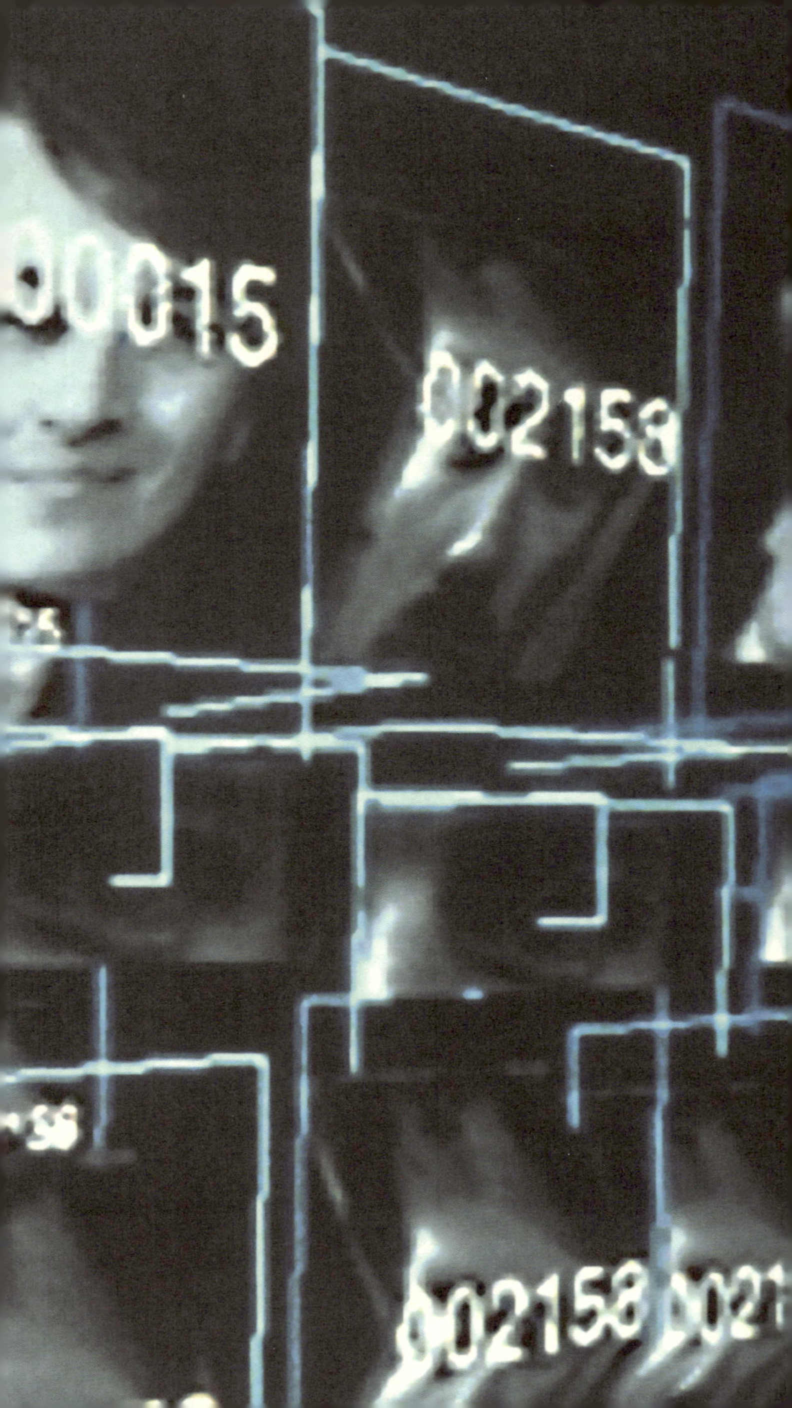
00015
002158
002158

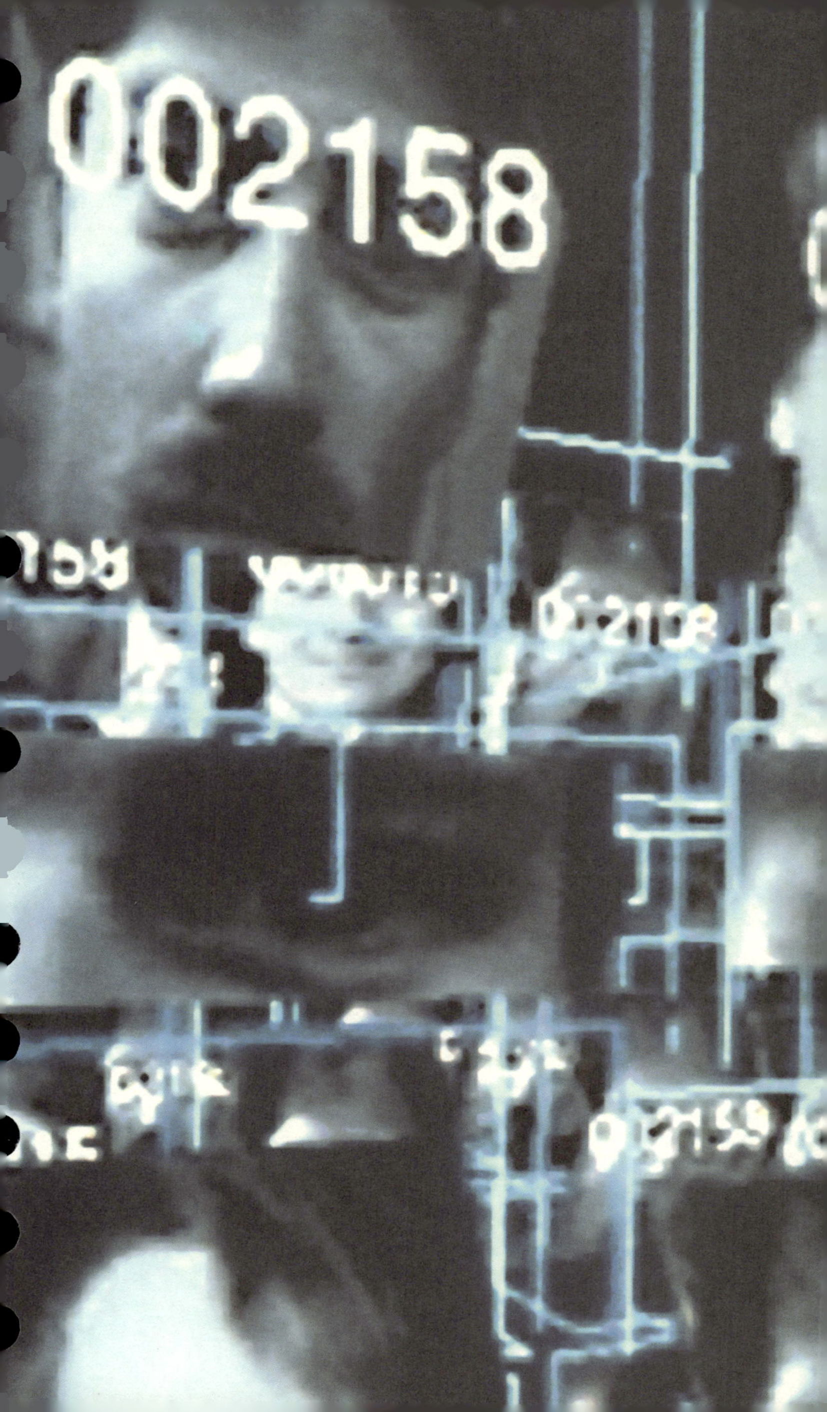
002158

Bruce Sterling Co-author of The Difference Engine Together with Gibson, he is considered one of the fathers of "cyberpunk" literature.

Lynn Hershman Media artist working in San Francisco. This year the interactive jury at Ars Electronica in Linz selected her *Difference Engine 3* for The Golden Nica Award.

Charles Babbage (1791-1871) A banker's son. After precocious mathematical work in Cambridge he lived on a private income, married well, and settled in Marylebone as technical consultant and public whistle-blower. He offered advice on railway design, insurance fraud, annoying buskers, science exhibitions, cryptography and tax reform. From 1820 until 1848 he tried to design, fund and build a series of increasingly ambitious calculating machines. When Lucasian professor of mathematics at Cambridge he wrote a definitive study of the factory system. His evening parties were an indispensable part of the London scene; in 1846, to try out his clever new stage-lighting system, he produced a sound and light show at Her Majesty's theatre on the theme of geological stratigraphy. In his autobiography he showed 'what peculiarities of mind enabled me to accomplish what even the most instructed in their own sciences deemed impossible'.

Ada Lovelace (1815-1852) Daughter of Lord Byron and Annabella Milbanke, she met Charles Babbage in 1833, then after strenuous studies with leading London mathematicians translated and annotated a major essay on Babbage's analytical engine in 1843. Lovelace experimented with mesmerism and other fashionable medical and philosophical pursuits, suffered several nervous crises, and in 1851 became involved in a disastrously unsuccessful gambling syndicate. After a long illness, forwhich she was prescribed heavy laudanum doses, she died of cervical cancer the following year.

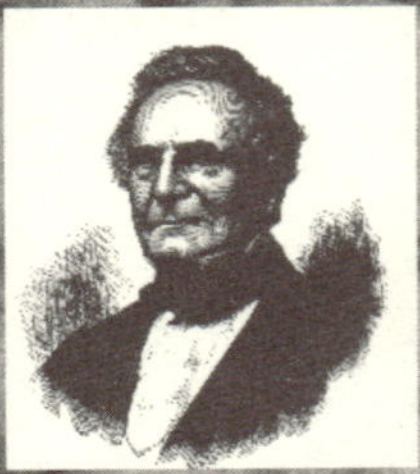

Charles Babbage
(1792 - 1871)
English mathematician and inventor

The right hemisphere of Charles Babbage's brain.
Collection of the Royal College of Surgeons, London
The brain of Charles Babbage, removed by Sir Thomas Smith was placed in the care of the Hunterian Trustees where it has remained ever since.
'There is no doubt that Mr. Babbage was a very profound thinker, that his mentation carried with it complete fixation of attention (often to the exclusion of domestic duties) and that he was able to resolve complex conditions by an unusual power of forming wide concepts.
From *Description of the Brain of Mr Charles Babbage, F.R.S.* by Sir Victor Horsley 1907

Why is it better to give than exchange?

<THE::CYBER.COM/MUNIST::MANIFESTO>

RICHARD BARBROOK

At the beginning of the twenty-first century, the prophets of American neo-liberalism are heralding the imminent arrival of the digital utopia. They believe that the noise and confusion of industrial production are being replaced by friction-free trading within the perfect markets of cyberspace. They claim that an elite of entrepreneurs, inventors and ideologues are pioneering a digital lifestyle which will eventually become available to everyone. These right-wing gurus even measure our progress towards the privatised future through increases in the ownership of new technologies: computers, mobiles, decoders and Net connections. Ironically, this neo-liberal futurism echoes the preconceptions of Soviet communism. During the 1930s, Josef Stalin similarly measured progress towards utopia through the rising output of modern products: steel, cars, tractors and machine-tools. In the former Soviet Union, the enlightened minority was also leading the ignorant masses towards eventual emancipation. Most notoriously, the Stalinists used the promise of future liberation to justify the forcible silencing of the noise of dissent. Although the Soviet Union has long disappeared, the ideologues of American neo-liberalism are still inspired by the Stalinist version of communism.

vanguard party	digerati
The Five-Year Plan	The New Paradigm
boy-meets-tractor	nerd-meets-Net
Third International	Third Wave
Moscow	Silicon Valley
Pravda	Wired
party line	unique thought
Soviet democracy	electronic town halls
Lysenkoism	memetics
society-as-factory	society-as-hive
New Soviet Man	post-humans
Stakhanovite norm-busting	overworked contract labour
purges	downsizing
Russian nationalism	Californian chauvinism

According to most politicians, executives and pundits, intellectual labour within the Net must be enclosed into commodities and protected by copyright. However, the scientists who invented computer-mediated communications were working within the academic gift economy. As a consequence, they embedded the free distribution of information within the technical structures and social mores of the Net. Over time, the charmed circle of users has slowly grown from scientists through hobbyists to the general public. Crucially, each new member doesn't just observe the technical rules of the system, but also adheres to certain social conventions. Without even thinking about it, people continually circulate information between each other for free. By giving away their own personal efforts, Net users always receive the results of much greater amounts of labour in return from others. Although many on-line activities are trivial, some collaborations are now creating very sophisticated products, such as the Linux operating system and interactive music pieces. Net users are now developing a much more efficient and enjoyable way of working together: cyber-communism.

commodity	gift
enclosure	disclosure
copyright	piracy
fixed	fluid
product	process
proprietary	open source
digital encryption	free download
original recording	latest remix
scarcity	abundance
alienation	friendship
market competition	network communities
e-commerce	cyber-communism

For those nostalgic for ideological certainty, there can be no compromise between these contradictory visions of the Net. The digital future must be homogeneous and unsullied. However, it is impossible to expel noise and disturbance from cyberspace. Already the synthesis of dialectical opposites is happening for pragmatic reasons. The low cost of entry into e-commerce depends upon the absence of proprietary barriers within the Net. The rapid expansion of the hi-tech gift economy is facilitated by hardware and software sold by large companies. Above all, Net users always adopt the working methods which are most beneficial to their own interests. While sometimes engaging in e-commerce, they often prefer to collaborate within the hi-tech gift economy. Many social activities have long been organised by voluntary labour and with donated resources. Now, with the advent of the Net, this gift economy is hybridising with market competition at the cutting-edge of modernity. Living within a prosperous society, many people will work solely to gain the respect from their peers for their digital artefacts. During the last two hundred years, the intimate bonds of kinship and friendship have simultaneously inhibited and underpinned the impersonal relationships needed for market competition. The modern has always co-existed with the traditional. Now, within cyberspace, the exchange of commodities is being both intensified and prevented by the circulation of gifts. The modern must synthesise with the hyper-modern. Far from needing leadership by a heroic elite, ordinary people are now successfully constructing their own utopia. In the age of the Net, cyber-communism is becoming an everyday experience. The digital future is a noisy festival.

The Dialectics of Cyber-Communism

The Positive:	work-as-commodity e-commerce reactionary modernism
The Negation:	waste-as-gift potlatch revolutionary anti-modernism
The Negation of the Negation:	work-as-gift network communities revolutionary modernism

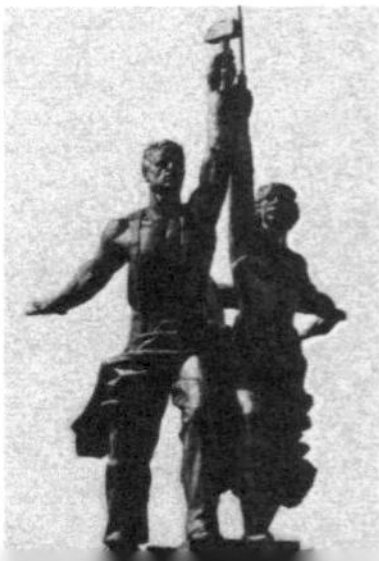

Worker and collective farm woman
Mukhina 1937
Made for the Soviet Pavilion Paris
International Exhibition

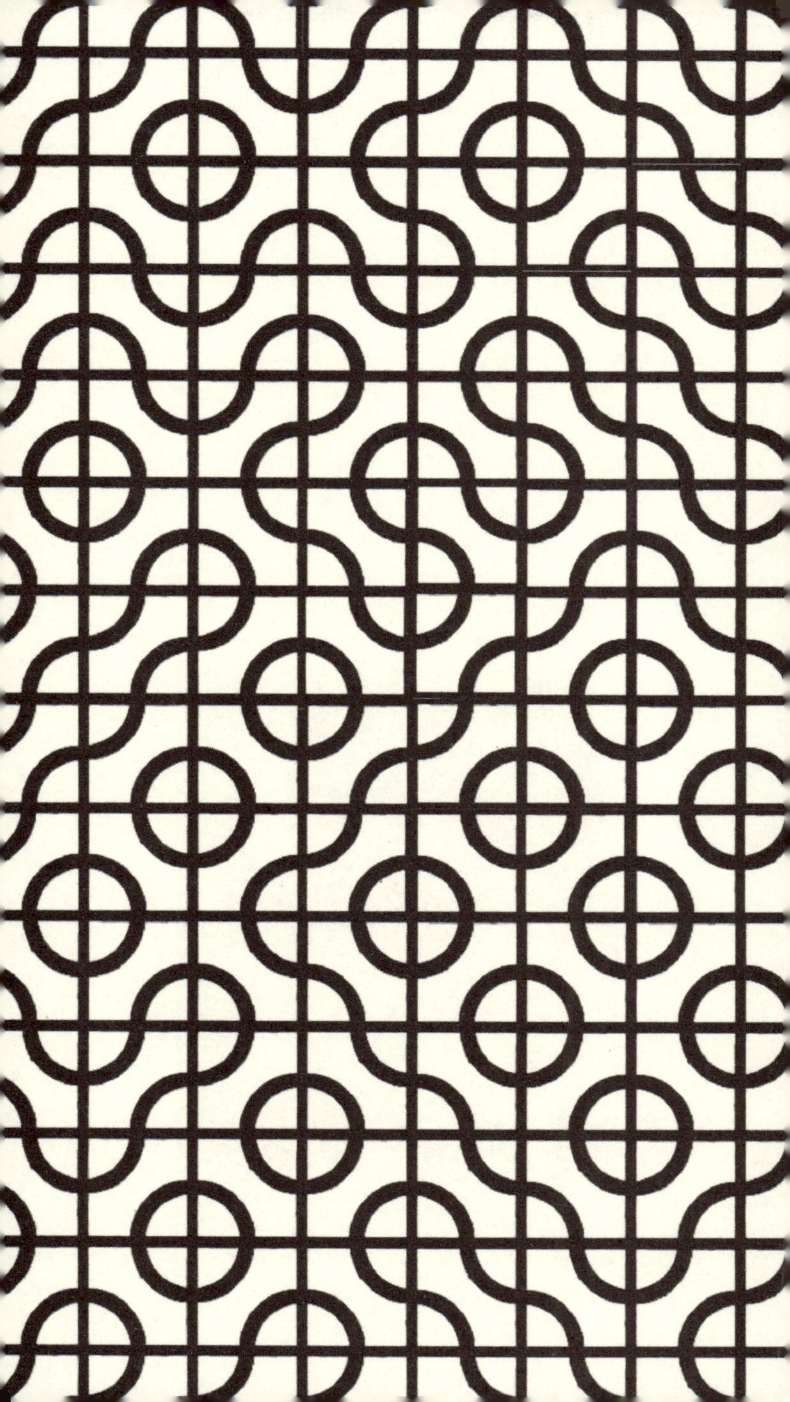

research, eventually stepping from an Ecology of Mind to "an epistemology of the sacred" – speculation on the patterns that connect biological evolution and the development of thought. Bateson made cybernetics' curiosity about the Mind of God explicit. The current next big thing in American popular psychology, Neuro-Linguistic Programming, acknowledges its debt to Bateson. Familiar with Gestalt psychology, its founders, Grinder and Bandler, met him at the West Coast eco-new-age-retreat, Esalen. Practitioners of NLP associate a past emotion (enthusiasm, willingness to buy) to the present situation; they take the words and imagery you use and feed them back to you, using your own "modalities" to rework your assumptions. Applying principles of hypnosis, they "reprogram" the commands that have been programmed over the course of your life. American late-night television is crowded with "infomercials" hustling this "new science of excellence". The current crown prince is the 6 foot plus motormouth Anthony Robbins whose best seller promises *Unlimited Power*: attendees of his expensive seminars walk across coals and say "YEAH! I can do it!" with an unstoppable gleam in their eyes. This interpersonal technology has saturated entertainment, politics, and management policy.

Most of these soft technologies are given the hard sell on the World Wide Web. Is the cybernetic age bringing us closer together, or are we simply getting fed, in a new format, the same old promise of total control?

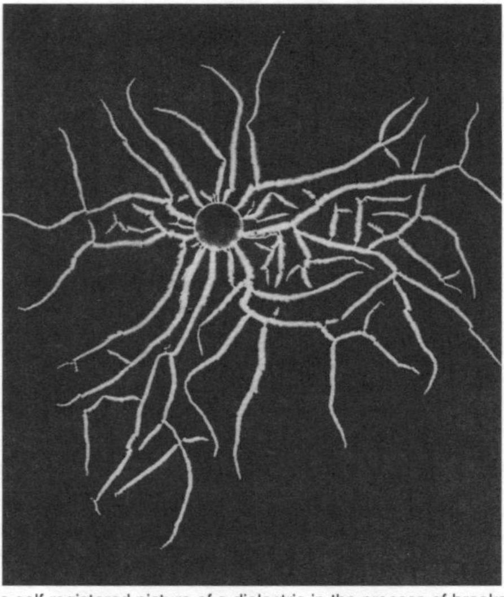

"This...is the self registered picture of a dielectric in the process of breakdown. The mathematics of breakdown is as important as it is unfamiliar even to the average physicist. It is closely allied to the mathematics of crackle finish... The significance of the processes of breakdown is great not only in physics, but even in the study of sociological processes."
Norbert Weiner *The New Landscape in Art and Science* 1956

Cybernetics and the Mind of God

JOHN TRESCH

Cybernetics means control. Literally. The term was coined from the Greek word for "governor" (*kybernetes*). What did its inventors, Norbert Wiener and his pals at MIT, want to control? What didn't they want to control, more like. At the start, they would have been happy just figuring out how to keep a missile following a jet plane that was smart enough to change course. But after World War II, Wiener moved beyond trying to understand— and control— missiles: he started talking about physiology, logical processing in a mechanised brain, and finally, individuals and societies. After *Cybernetics*, he wrote a book called *The Human Use of Human Beings*. By modelling natural interactions as self-regulating machines - as systems that maintain themselves in a steady state by constantly monitoring their own inputs and outputs - cybernetics offers a peculiarly twentieth-century version of the promises of the scientific revolution: to know is to control, to attain god-like powers over nature, oneself, and other people. Norbert made himself into the prophet of the cybernetic world-view. Other prophets (and some would-be messiahs) have kept this message alive. Just after *Cybernetics* appeared, a similar book promising a new way of seeing the world was published. This book was not the work of a scientist, but of a science-fiction writer, and if we are to believe his followers (which is not necessarily a great idea), his book has vastly outsold *Cybernetics:* the author was Lafayette Ron Hubbard, and the book was *Dianetics*. Hubbard borrowed more than the technical ring of his title from Wiener: notions like the "ARC" of Affinity, Reality and Communication, are essentially cybernetic theories of interaction. The Church of Scientology has a number of, to put it lightly, "control issues". Following orders legislated by Hubbard before his quiet death as a paranoid hermit, members of the Church, dedicated to "Clearing the Planet" of humans who have not yet forked out to receive the message, keep huge files on members and non-members, suing and harassing anyone who speaks against them. Please don't quote me on this.

Not long afterwards, another book appeared that took cybernetics as the answer to everyone's problems, a book with a title that if it didn't exist would have to be invented: *Psycho-cybernetics*, by Maxwell Maltz. Dr. Maltz was a plastic surgeon who was convinced that more could be accomplished with a dose of good old fashioned all-American positive thinking than with a nip or a tuck. The key cybernetic loop was that improving your self-image would improve other people's image of you, and so on, and so on – a slightly more technical version of "you have to be a friend to make a friend", or even "do unto others as you would have them do unto you". A golden Catch-22.

The flipside of this version of "positive feedback" is the double bind, where the frame of a message contradicts the message's content, like when a parent beats a child and calls it an expression of love. Such classics of intrafamilial crazy-making were studied by Gregory Bateson, prodigal son of English genetics and William Bateson. The younger Bateson applied cybernetic concepts to psychology, looking at how presuppositions about the nature of relationships affect communication. He also brought his cybernetic perspective back to his earlier anthropological and zoological

Richard Barbrook, Hypermedia Research Centre, University of Westminster.

John Tresch A doctoral student in Cambridge and Paris.

Piers Wardle's preoccupation with certain aspects of visual noise and the determinism inherent in chaos mechanics led him to the doors of a psychiatric institution in the late eighties. Since then he has adhered to a rigorous regimen of artistic anonymity which has met with remarkable success so far.

Norbert Wiener (1894-1964), self proclaimed mathematical genius, completed his Harvard doctorate at the age of 19, studied with Bertrand Russell, and became mathematics professor at MIT. Obsessed by disorder, which he saw as evil, he brilliantly theorized Brownian motion, the harmonic analysis of signal systems, and the puzzles of communication theory. In World War II he designed feedback systems for the control of anti-aircraft and bomb delivery systems, thus contributing to the emergence of cybernetics, the theory of regulation and homeostasis on which he published the major work in 1948.

For Marx, music is the 'mirror of reality'; for Nietzsche, the 'expression of truth'; for Freud, a 'text to decipher.' It is all of that, for it is one of the sites where mutations first arise and where science is secreted: 'If you close your eyes, you lose the power of abstraction' [Michel Serres].
Jacques Attali, *Noise: The Political Economy of Music*

Overleaf: Piers Wardle preliminary drawing for *Zero Sum for Everybody* 1999

Crowd at KCC Sound System Notting Hill Carnival 1999
Photographer Richard Barbrook

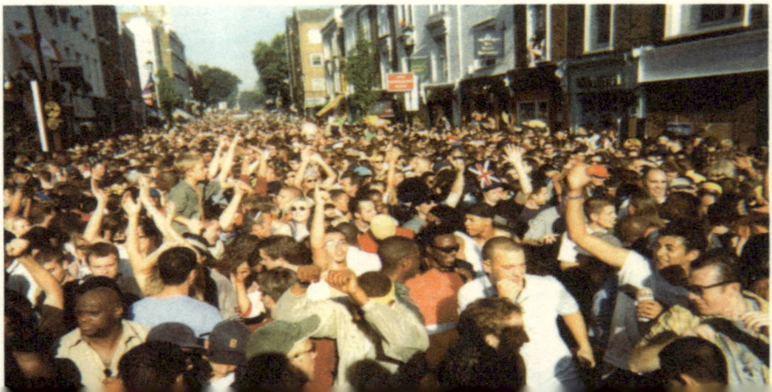

Where in the World are we?

The Cosmic Background Explorer (COBE) Map of the Whole Sky

MALCOM LONGAIR

The map of the whole sky created from observations made by the **Cosmic Background Explorer** (COBE) is one of the most remarkable astronomical images ever produced. The false colour picture shows the whole sky as observed in the millimetre waveband in an equal area projection. The map is presented in what are known as galactic coordinates, meaning that the plane of our own Galaxy, the Milky Way, lies along the centre of the picture, with the centre of our Galaxy in the very centre of the picture. The bright red band lying along the centre of the picture is the emission of our own Galaxy, mostly the emission of cool dust and high energy particles in the interstellar medium.

For studies of the origin of the Universe, the remarkable features are the low intensity ripples in brightness seen in directions away from the Galactic plane. These tiny fluctuations provide a picture of the Universe on the large scale as it was when it was only about 300,000 years old, a very early stage in its evolution compared with its present age which is about 12,000,000,000 years. This *fossil* radiation provides the earliest picture of the Universe we can hope to obtain and is of the greatest importance for understanding how galaxies and the Universe as we know it came about.

How was the picture created? We take for granted the incredible images obtained by telescopes such as the Hubble Space Telescope. Technically speaking, these are all composed of millions of individual picture elements, or pixels, each carrying information about the intensity and spectrum of the radiation incident upon that element of the detector. In the case of the Hubble Space Telescope, the picture elements are tiny, about 0.1 arc seconds, matching the resolving power of the telescope. The same principles apply to COBE, although COBE observations are made at a millimetre wavelength of about 6 mm. At this wavelength, radio techniques are used to map of the sky, the COBE telescope itself resembling a small satellite dish. The wavelength is so long and the telescope so small that the angular resolution of the telescope was only about 7º. The Moon subtends an angle of about half a degree on the sky and so it can be appreciated that the COBE satellite could only create a rather low resolution map of the whole sky. The signal to be detected is

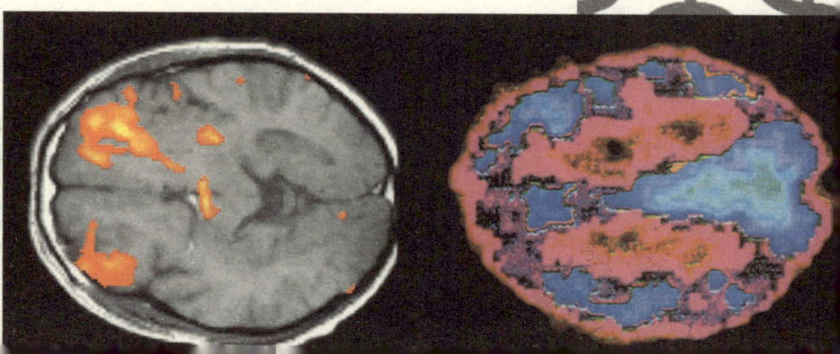

only a very tiny fraction of the total brightness of the sky at these wavelengths. The observations were made by continually switching between patches of sky separated by 60º. The satellite had to point away from the Earth and be shielded from the Sun. Despite these constraints, by observing for four years, the whole sky was covered many times with excellent sensitivity. The sky map was reconstructed from the differences in intensity measured as the axis of the telescope drifted slowly over the sky.

The end product was a total intensity map of the sky at three millimetre wavelengths. A key consideration for making such a map is the necessary number of pixels to ensure that as much information as possible can be extracted from the observations. One might think we would want to sample on as fine a grid as possible, but that is not necessary: information theory tells us that we need only sample at two points per resolution element in any direction to obtain all the information we can obtain. This criterion determines the number of pixels needed for any observation. Over the whole sky, there are only 6144 independent pixels in the COBE map.

The problem was that the NASA astronomers were searching for signals in the COBE data which were at an intensity level of only about 1/100,000 of the total radiation. Therefore, the calibration of the intensities measured on the map had to be extraordinarily precise. Just like peeling layers of an onion, the astronomers had to remove layer after layer of potentially confusing radiation before they could assuredly detect the tiny cosmological signals they sought.

The initial calibrated map looks very smooth indeed, *fossil* radiation from the Big Bang itself. If one looks at the ripples on that smooth radiation at 1/1000 of the total intensity, the radiation looks hot in one direction and cold in the opposite direction. This perfect dipole structure in the radiation intensity is due to the motion of the Earth with respect to a system of coordinates in which the radiation would be completely uniform - the Doppler effect. The intensity at each pixel of the map had to be corrected for the motion of the Earth.

To find the tiny cosmological fluctuations, the astronomers had to dig even deeper by a factor of 100. At that level, the plane of the Galaxy is very bright but, at last, real cosmological ripples are seen away from the Galactic Plane. Eliminating the Galactic plane leaves only 3881 independent pixels. Even then, the level of the signal is tiny. The great achievement of the mission was that the telescope and its detectors were sufficiently stable to detect a real signal, only 1/100,000 of the total intensity of the background.

A seletion of images from the Cobe Satellite
The microwave sky, recorded by the COBE satellite, made from 6144 pixels, may give new insights into our understanding of the universe

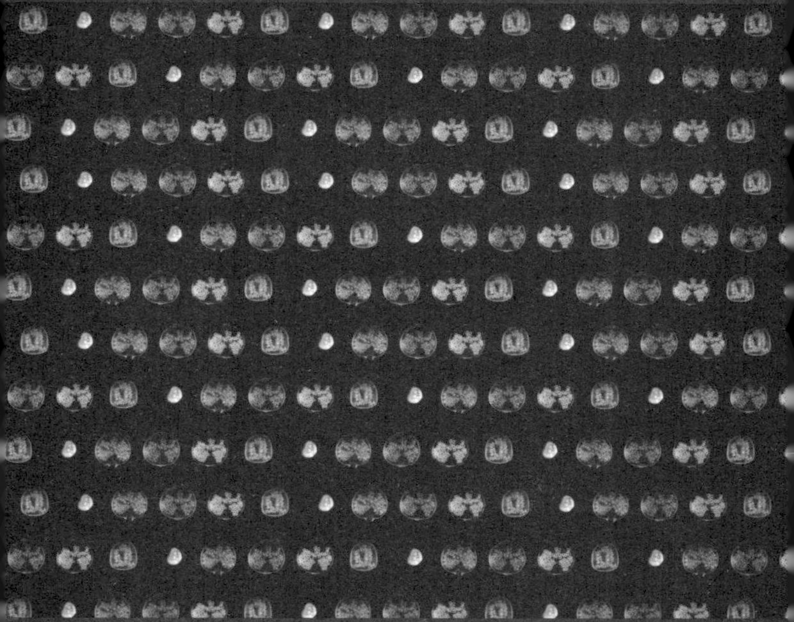

Catherine Wagner *Pomegranate* 1998
Iris print 32x44ins
Courtesy Fraenkel Gallery (San Francisco) and Jack Shainman Gallery (New York)

A cross section of a single pomegranate.
The cross section pattern was repeated so as to form an analogue of the replication of the cells. The image was made at the Weizman Institute in Tel Aviv where Catherine Wagner has been a visiting artist. During this time she has produced a body of images including a series of images of vegetables scanned on an fMRI Scanner.

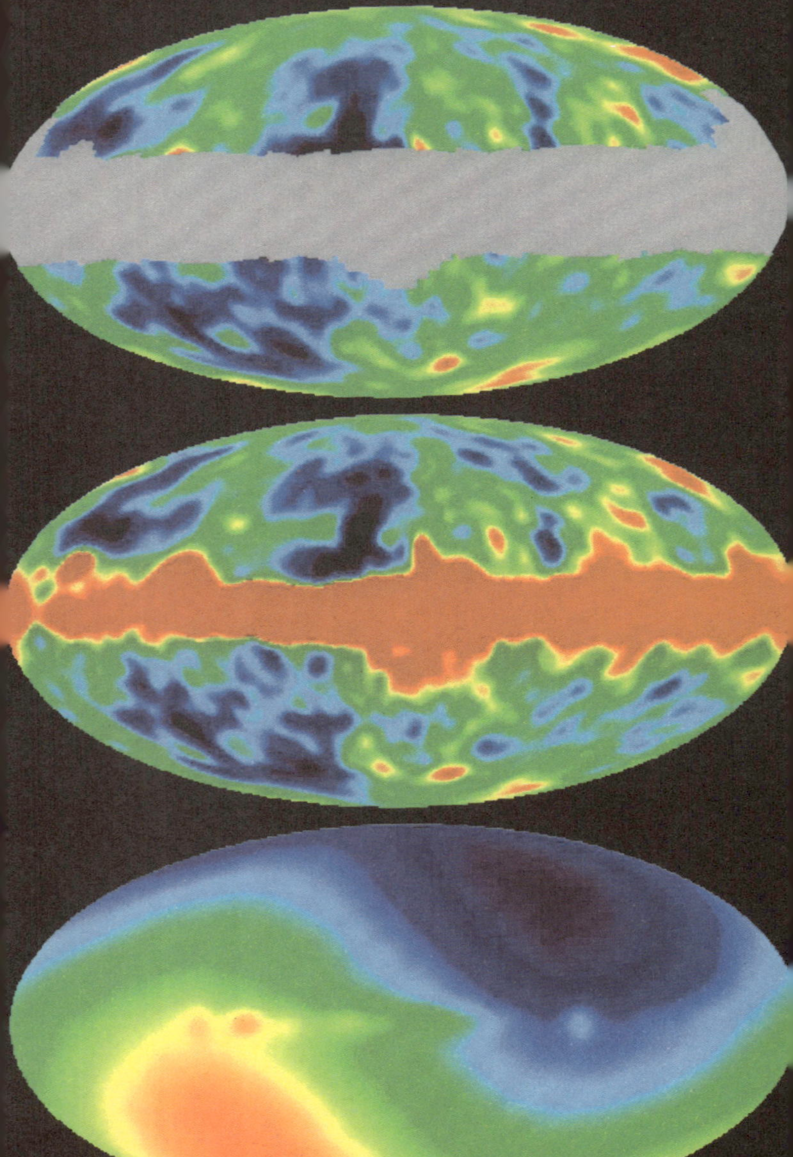

In fact, the tiny ripples observed away from the Galactic plane are only a few times the instrumental noise. Averages can, however, be taken over all 3881 independent pixels to obtain a real cosmological signal of very high significance. It is astounding to think that these 3881 pixels provide us with the best map of the largest structures we can observe in the Universe at epochs long before the galaxies existed. The next generation of space observatories to study the Cosmic Microwave Background Radiation, the NASA MAP and the ESA Planck missions, will provide much more information about the crucial fine-scale structure in the radiation - these will reveal much more about the physics of the very, very early Universe.

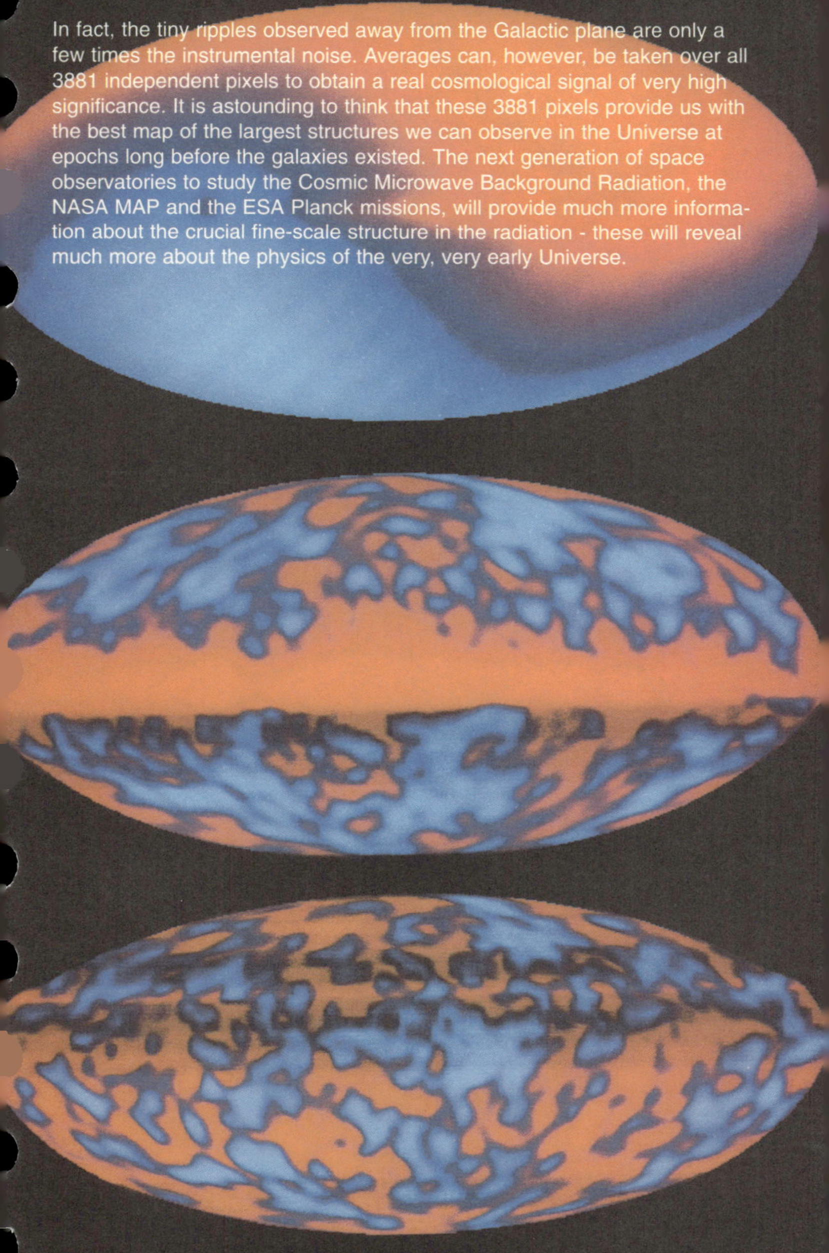

Malcolm Longair is head of the Cavendish Laboratory and Jacksonian Professor of Natural Philosophy, University of Cambridge.

Catherine Wagner An artist working in San Francisco. She is the recipient of a Visual Arts Fellowship from the San Jose Museum of Art and is currently working at the Weizman Institute in Israel.

John Tchalenko and Humphrey Ocean Their collaboration started in 1991 with *Double Portrait* which led to in depth research into the drawing process. This work included eye hand coordination and brain scanning studies.

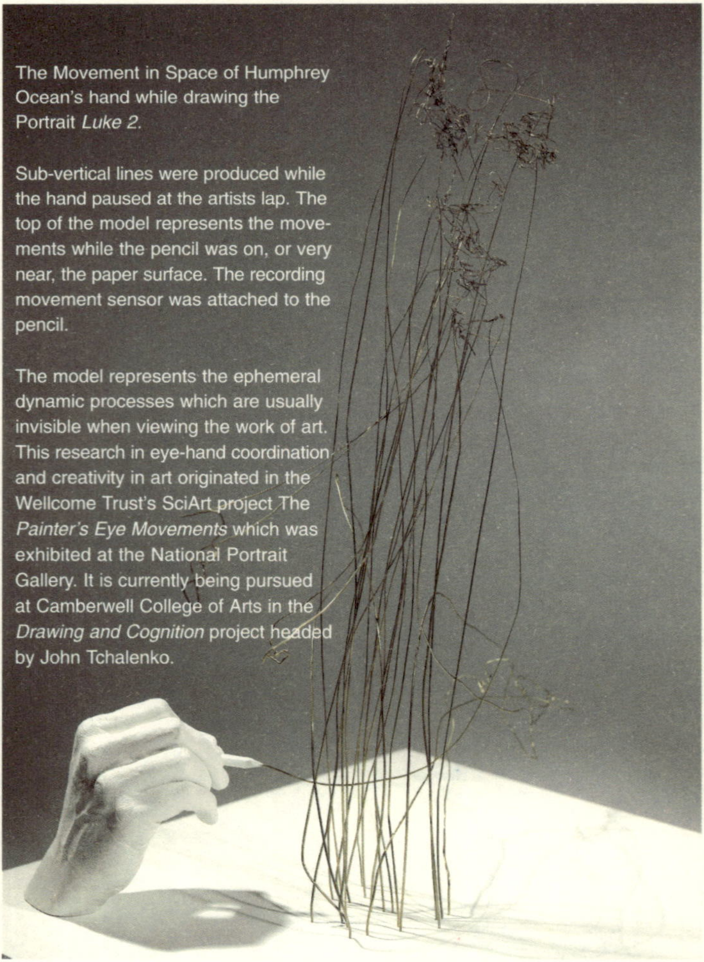

The Movement in Space of Humphrey Ocean's hand while drawing the Portrait *Luke 2.*

Sub-vertical lines were produced while the hand paused at the artists lap. The top of the model represents the movements while the pencil was on, or very near, the paper surface. The recording movement sensor was attached to the pencil.

The model represents the ephemeral dynamic processes which are usually invisible when viewing the work of art. This research in eye-hand coordination and creativity in art originated in the Wellcome Trust's SciArt project The *Painter's Eye Movements* which was exhibited at the National Portrait Gallery. It is currently being pursued at Camberwell College of Arts in the *Drawing and Cognition* project headed by John Tchalenko.

What sort of noise does a map make?

Determining the Distance

JERRY BROTTON

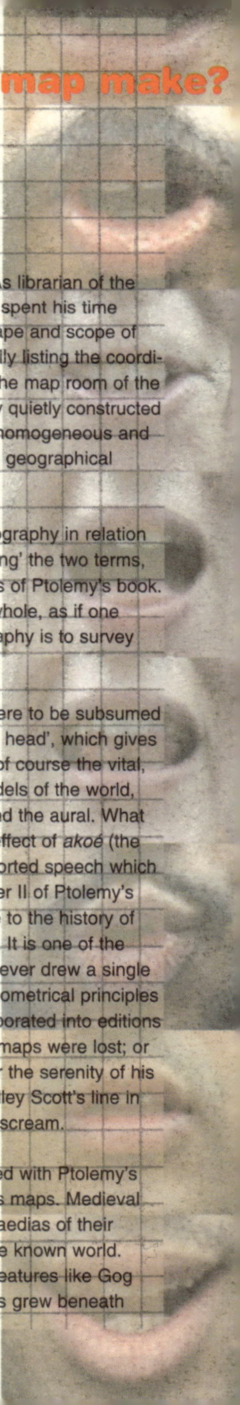

Claudius Ptolemy, so-called father of geography, hated noise. As librarian of the fabled library of Alexandria in the second century A.D., Ptolemy spent his time compiling the raw data for his *Geographia*, which defined the shape and scope of the classical world, the Greek *ecumene* (or 'living space'), carefully listing the coordinates of over 8,000 locations. From his 'centre of calculation' in the map room of the vast library at Alexandria, the still point in a turning world, Ptolemy quietly constructed a projection of the world built upon the fantasy of empty, silent, homogeneous and infinitely extendible space. For Ptolemy, the basic element in his geographical investigation was not the line, but the abstract point.

In Book One of the *Geographia* Ptolemy defined the task of Geography in relation to the more localised nature of Chorography by literally 'embodying' the two terms, an approach that was vividly taken up by Renaissance illustrators of Ptolemy's book. The end of Chorography is to deal separately with a part of the whole, as if one were to paint only the eye or the ear by itself. The task of Geography is to survey the whole in its just proportions, as one would the entire head.

For Ptolemy, the deception of the eye and the noise of the ear were to be subsumed into the silent interior reflection of the mind encased in 'the entire head', which gives shape to the world 'in its just proportions'. Travellers' tales were of course the vital, raw material which allowed Ptolemy to make his geometrical models of the world, but they were themselves prey to the vicissitudes of the visual and the aural. What Ptolemy feared more than anything else was the contaminating effect of *akoé* (the Greek for 'hearsay'), the noise of the aural and the babble of reported speech which attended accounts of those who travelled to distant lands. Chapter II of Ptolemy's first book makes clear his unease at the need to make 'reference to the history of travel', but only in 'determining the distance between two places'. It is one of the great ironies of the history of geography that its founding figure never drew a single map. Whilst the *Geographia* provides detailed accounts of the geometrical principles of projecting the world on a plane surface, maps were only incorporated into editions of the book from the late thirteenth century. Perhaps the original maps were lost; or perhaps Ptolemy feared the the noise that he knew would shatter the serenity of his silent global geometry. He would undoubtedly have endorsed Ridley Scott's line in the publicity for his film *Alien* that in space, no one can hear you scream.

Subsequent medieval and early Renaissance geography struggled with Ptolemy's legacy, keen to reduce the noise of the world to the margins of its maps. Medieval *mappae-mundi*, in their attempt to offer comprehensive encyclopaedias of their world, placed troublesome noise on its borders, at the edge of the known world. Geographical noise metamorphosed into monsters, fantastical creatures like Gog and Magog, Anthropophagi (or cannibals), and men whose heads grew beneath their shoulders. So loud did the clamour of the expanding world become that **Mandeville's** fabled *Travels*, and **Hartmann Schedel's** monumental *Nuremberg Chronicles* became obsessed with the monsters projected just over the horizon.

The seventeenth-century desire for order and classification once more consigned the troubling noise of these other voices to the margins of the geographical imagination, and in some cases even drove them off the map. Early European callers at the tip of Southern Africa, the Cape of Good Hope, were particularly disgusted with the local inhabitants they encountered, the Khoikhoi. Angered at the refusal of the Khoikhoi to trade, Dutch and English travellers repeatedly condemned the local inhabitants as lazy, uncivilised, dirty and possessing disgusting eating habits, which seemed to revolve around the eating of half-cooked animal intestines discarded by the Europeans. One English caller claimed in 1608 that 'I think the world doth not yield a more heathenish people and more beastlie', whilst a French caller opined that 'the inhabitants of the country towards the point of the Cape are, I believe, the most miserable savages which have been discovered up to now.' The focus of all this attention was the peculiar diet of the Khoikhoi. 'In the time of our being there,' claimed one disgusted Englishman, 'they lived upon the guts and filth of the meat which we did cast away'. The Khoikhoi consumed what the Europeans deemed useless; yet they also ignored what the Europeans considered valuable. As a result they were labelled abject, or, in the words of one exasperated English traveller, 'noysome'. Dirt and noise are conflated in the disgusted and exasperated reactions of the Europeans to the Khoikhoi. Sure enough, the margins of mid-seventeenth century maps of Africa are made up of vignettes of miserable, intestine-chewing Khoikhoi, abject, 'noisy' interference on the emerging map of the world defined by European norms of what it meant to be civilised.

If dirt, as anthropology has taught us, is in fact simply matter out of place, then one response is to brush it away; similarly, one way to eradicate noise is to silence and remove the object from which the disturbance emanates. Throughout the eighteenth and nineteenth centuries the Khoikhoi were slowly but systematically exterminated by European colonists at the Cape. It was even possible during the nineteenth century to purchase a licence to hunt and shoot the Khoikhoi like animals. Ptolemy's *Geographia* was not responsible for the ultimate genocide of Khoikhoi, but the tradition that it established suggests that we label and silence noise at our peril.

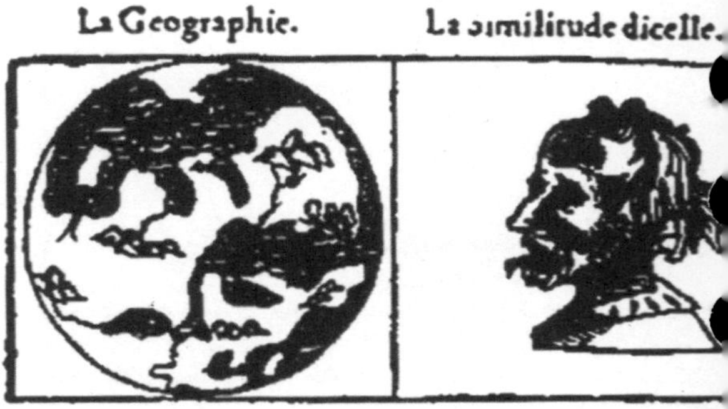

Petrus Apianus, *Cosmographia* (Paris, 1551).
The comparison between Geographie and Chorographie, so important to Ptolemy, was a popular subject with C16th authors.

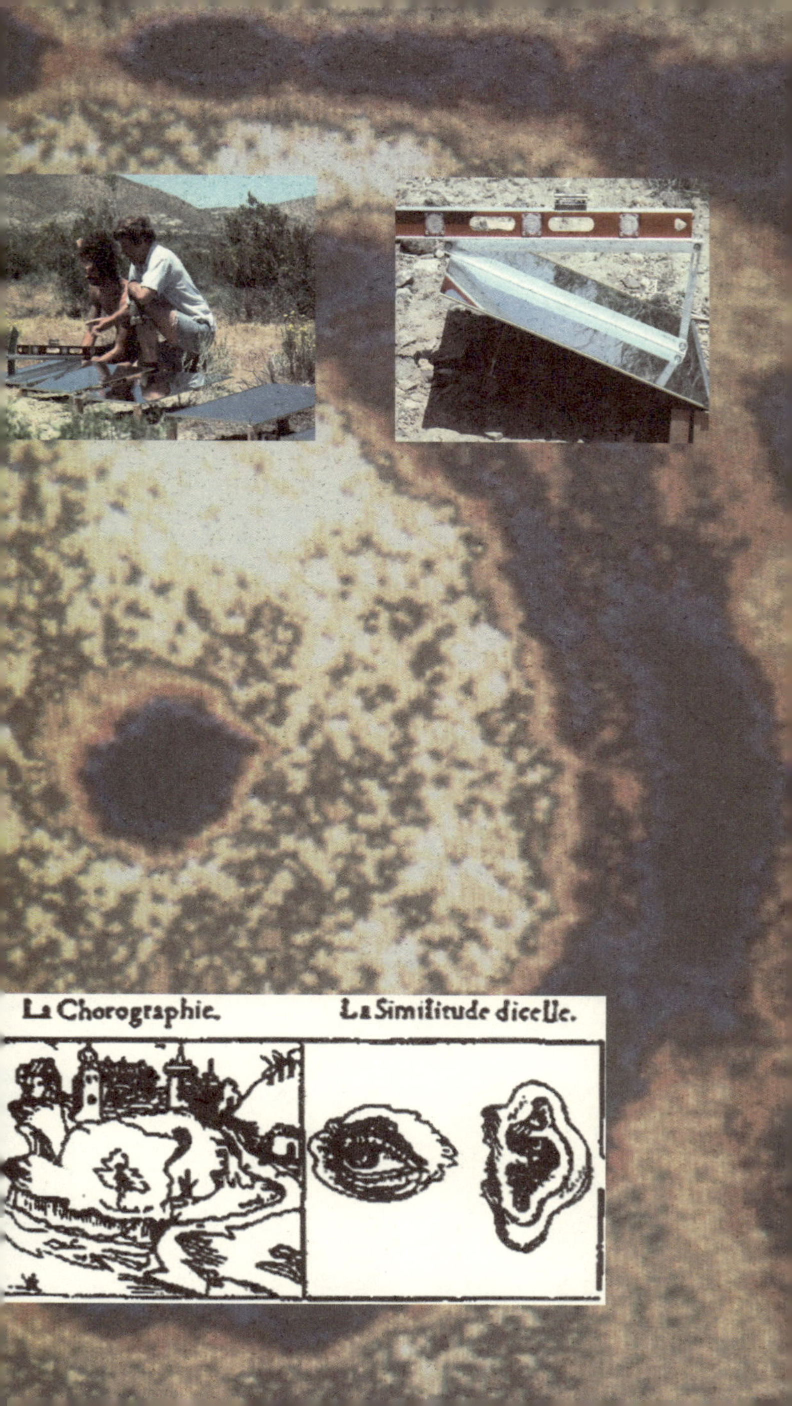
La Chorographie.
La Similitude dicelle.

The Micro and Macro Eye

In 1980, following the successful exhibtion of his 300m-long structural kites at the London ICA (and various museums in Europe) Tom Van Sant began work on his Micro and Macro Eyes. The project grew from a discussion with Richard Feynman, and resulted in two images of an eye, one 100,000 times reduced and the other 100,000 times magnified. Neither existed for more than 10,000 th of a second. They were recorded on an electron microscope and a landsat satellite respectively. The Micro Eye was produced at Cornell University; the Macro Eye was made by Tom Van Sant and friends in the desert north of Los Angeles.

The inspiration behind the project was a fusion of two very different notions: Feynman's ideas on nanotechnology, and Van Sant's observations on sunlight reflecting off mirrored buildings in Los Angeles. Feynman asked, how small can writing or numbers be made? what is the ultimate limit of scale? Marks can't go smaller than an atom -or can they?. And the inverse of how small is, of course, how big? Van Sant realised he could produce images on both a micro and macro scale using the same principle of "burning out pixels". He would use mirrors to reflect sunlight from the surface of the earth back up to a Landsat satellite, burning out a cluster of pixels to produce a clearly discernible eye on the Landsat image. He did this by placing 24 two-foot square mirrors in the desert north of Los Angeles. The mirrors were positioned using accurate measurements, a compass and spirit level, so that they reflected the sun at exactly the time the satellite passed overhead. This was done in part by calculation and in part by trial and error. After several attempts all mirrors were positioned at the correct angle to form the Macro Eye. Only one mirror failed to register on the Landsat image - Van Sant later discovered that a rabbit had jumped onto the mirror, changing its position.

Van Sant's drawing to indicate the position and angle of the mirrors in the desert.

For the Micro Eye, a laser beam was directed at a salt crystal cutting a trough into its surface. The distance across the picture is about 100 atoms.It was done at Cornell University and the team of engineers were disappointed that Van San had not produced an image even smaller as the theoretical limit at the time was about 50 atoms across. The flaw visible on the left-hand side of the image was probably caused by vibrations produced as a truck drove past the laboratory, shaking the apparatus. The laser-cut grain of salt was then imaged using an electron microscope. In the process of recording the image the drawing was destroyed.

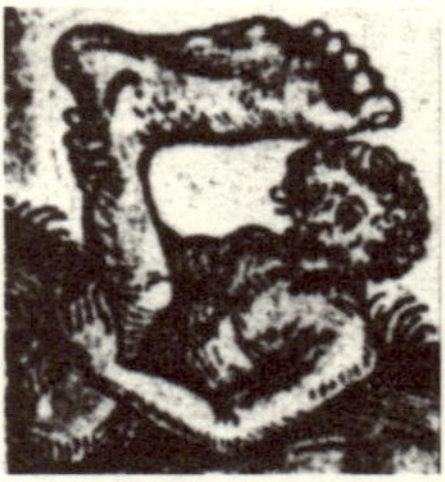

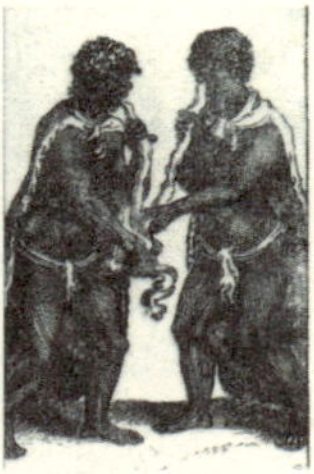

Two examples of the people who inhabit lands at the edge of the cartographic imagination. A figure from Schedel's *Nuremburg Chronicle* (1493) and a pair of intestine eating Khoikhoi from Blaeu's *Map of Africa* (1630)

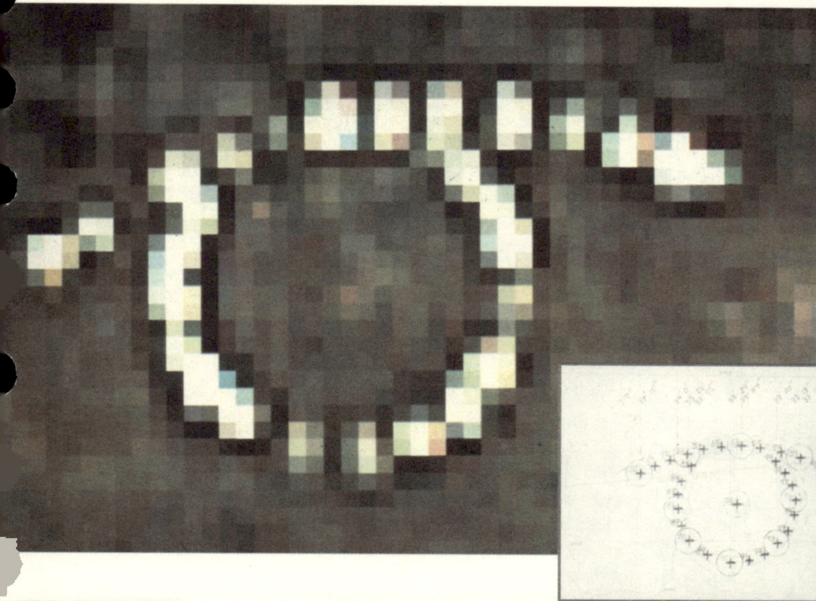

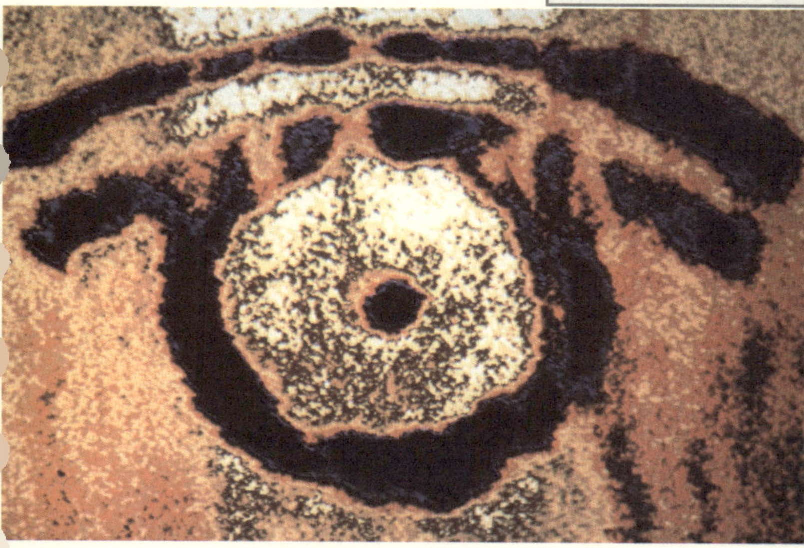

Top;Van Sant's *Eye* recorded on the Landsat in 1980.
(The eye measures approximately 2.5 kilometers from one side to the other.)
Bottom;Van Sant's *Eye* recorded on a grain of salt at about 100 atoms wide

Jerry Brotton Lecturer in English at Royal Holloway College, University of London.

Tom Van Sant Artist based in Santa Monica and director of the Geosphere Project. Initially known in Europe for his work with kites he is now best known for the *World Without Clouds* and other projects that cross between art and science.

Claudius Ptolemy A mathematician working in second century Alexandria. His earliest work, thirteen books on the motion of the planets, was known as *The Greatest*. He composed guidelines for builders of planetary machines, mathematical principles of music and optics, and the fundamental theory of astrology. His work on geography, which counted longitude from the Canary islands, remained a crucial text on map projection long after its many errors were well known. Ptolemy's maps were reconstructed in Constantinople in the thirteenth century; translated into Latin early in the fifteenth century, and first printed as a deluxe deition in 1475.

Sir John Mandeville did not exist. Travel stories allegedly written by an English knight of this name first appeared in the 1370s, and outsold Marco Polo: Columbus consulted them avidly. *Mandeville's Travels* imagine their author leaving England in 1322, and after offering a guidebook for pilgrims to Jerusalem, then tell stories of eastern lands where everyone is naked and those where everyone has two heads. Mandeville drinks from the fountain of youth and finds sheep growing on trees in central Asia. Much of the reliable part of the work is simply plagiarised from Franciscan monks who made it to the Orient. But *Mandeville's Travels* often describe its own author voyaging in company with the author of the work being plagiarised.

Hartmann Schedel A Nuremberg humanist who wrote a history of the world, the so-called *Nuremberg Chronicle*, published in 1493. Gorgeously illustrated with Ptolemaic maps and images of nations and lands, placing Nuremberg (and, sometimes, Jerusalem) at the centre of things, Schedel's work divides history into seven ages. The seventh age, the coming of the Antichrist and the Last Judgment, is followed by pages deliberately left blank.

Peter Apian (1495-1552) A Vienna mathematics professor eminent for his map workshop. His world map of 1522 was one of the first to carry the word *America*.

Richard Feynman (1918-1988) American theoretical pyhsicist and bongo drum player. He worked at Los Alamos on the atomic bomb and in 1965 won the Nobel prize for his reformulation of quantum electrodynamics. In late 1959 he delivered a famous lecture; *There is Plenty of Room at the Bottom* on the possibilities of nanotechnology through digitisation He observbed that the *Encylopedia Britannica* could be written on a cube of material one two-hundredth of an inch wide - " the barest piece of dust that can be made out with the human eye".

"Their noise be our instruction."

William Shakespeare, *Coriolanus*, I.iv.22

A moment of inspiration?

The Chamber of Clouds

PETER GALISON

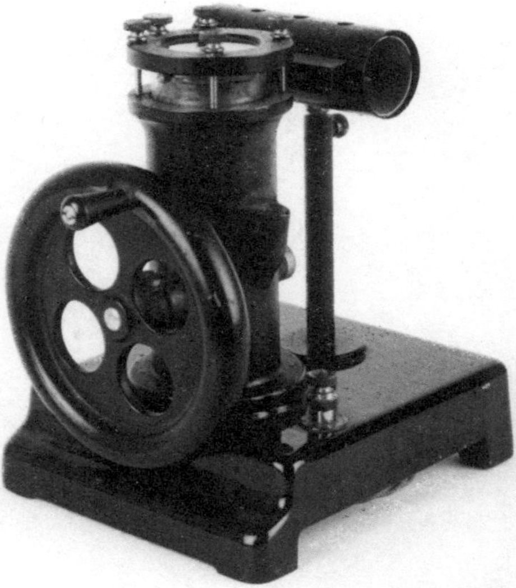

A simplified cloud chamber built in 1926 by Cambridge Scientific Instrument Company for use by schools
Whipple Museum of the History of Science, University of Cambridge

Because the cloud chamber helped launch the microphysical study of nature, because in various forms it led to such later instruments as the nuclear emulsion stack or the bubble chamber, we see it as an analytical device. **C.T.R. Wilson** is thus remembered as an experimentalist behind our twentieth century visualisation of the very small. It was in cloud chambers that a myriad of elementary particles — including the positive electron — first made their appearance. There is much to recommend such a picture of the cloud chamber as analytical tool, yet half our image is still missing.

Another aim was not to dissect nature but to reproduce it. Recreating, in miniature, dramatic natural phenomena — glaciers, jungles, volcanoes — was a Victorian preoccupation. Science museums re-instantiated, in the safety of London, the geology of Britain, captured the flora of Africa and Amazon, put the world under glass. Photography participated in this reproduction, and young Wilson, instructed by his Foreign Service brother, wandered across the Scottish highlands photographing the craggy heights in fog and cloud. During his apprenticeship at the weather outpost atop Ben Nevis, Wilson saw unfamiliar meteo-optical phenomena: Bishop's Rings, powerful frightening lightning bolts. In the safety of the observatory, he also found an inverted bowl-like device designed by a former engineer that used dust to precipitate water and so make miniature rain. Returning from Ben Nevis, Wilson wanted to miniaturise thunderstorms and optics inside such a glass bubble.

Using his old camera and the vocabulary of meteorology, he described his prizes inside the chamber: fog, rain, and mist. Hence we need to see double: Wilson's cloud chamber is both a new space that launched an analytic tradition in physics and at the same time a space of reproduction. The camera nebulosa, so to speak, joined other recreational "chambers": the camera obscura, the camera lucida and today's camera.

By combining mimetic and analytic traditions, Wilson produced an instrument that immediately captured both scientific and public attention. Buyers across the world eagerly seized upon the commercial cloud chamber manufactured under Wilson's watchful eye by the Cambridge Scientific Instrument Company, even as cosmic-ray physicists in California, France, Russia and Japan began to perfect ever more optically reliable ways of making the invisible visible. Reflecting on the vivid images the instrument provided, physicist-philosopher Percy Bridgman, whose austere test of scientific meaning demanded operational proof, once declaimed that the Wilson chamber actually defined "the operational meaning of reality."

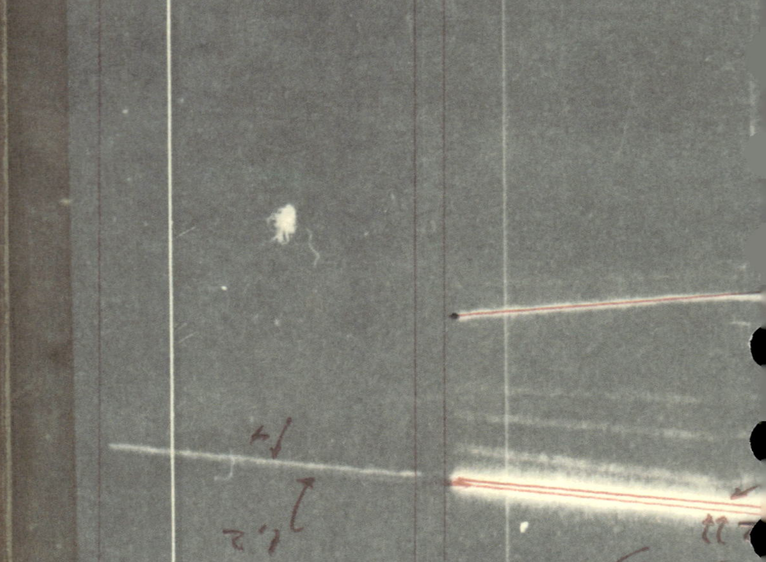

A bubble chamber photograph of a charm event produced by Dr D Tovee
In a charm event a neutrino interaction produces a charmed particle that then decays - a charmed particle is one that contains a charmed quark.

"The experimental physicist must be a jack-of-all-trades, a versatile but amateur craftsman. He must blow glass and turn metal, though he could never earn his living as a glass-blower nor even be classed as a skilled mechanic; he must carpenter, photograph, wire electric circuits and be a master of gadgets of all kinds; he may find invaluable a training as an engineer and can profit always by utilising his gifts as a mathematician. In such activities he will be engaged for three quarters of his working day. During the rest he must be a physicist, that is, he must cultivate an intimacy with the behaviour of the physical world."
P.Blackett

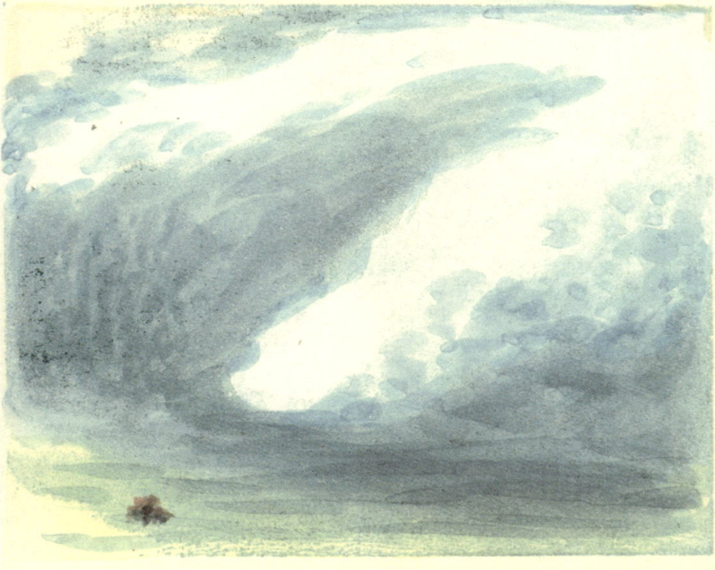

Clouds according to Turner's Principle from *Colour as a Means of Art* by Frank Howard 1838
This book, with colour lithographs, discusses the abstract principles behind great artists' use of colour and composition.
Constable's Cloud studies, commissioned by Luke Howard, were the first observationally accurate representations of clouds.

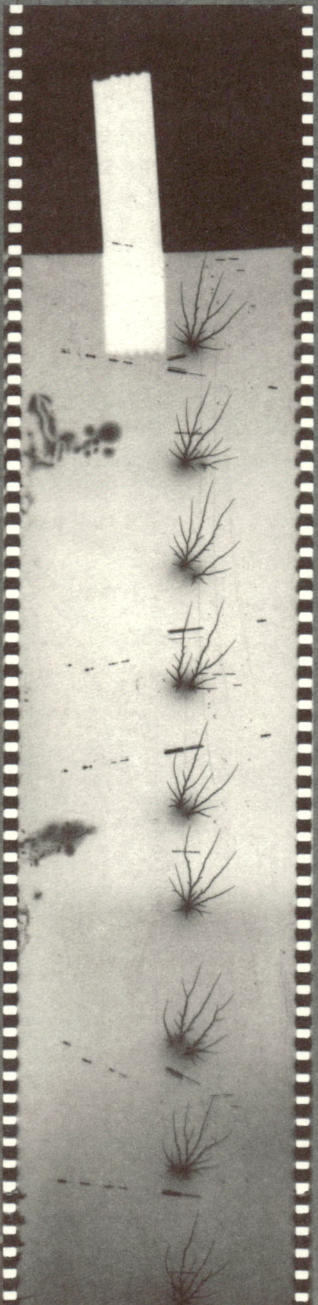

A film strip showing bubble chamber activity recorded at Fermilab.
The sparks that dominate the image were caused by a fault in the camera releasing an electrical discharge that exposed the film. The required data are the small scratch-like lines moving horizontally across the film. Everything else is noise.

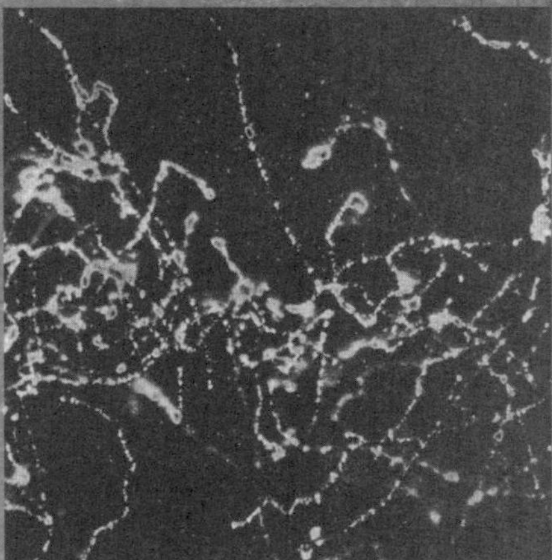

A photograph of X ray tracks recorded on Wilson's original cloud chamber showing the effects of altering the expansion ratio.
Reproduced from *C.T.R.Wilson and the Cloud Chamber 1894-1951* issued by Cambridge Instrument Company 1952
Collection of the Whipple Museum of the History of Science, University of Cambridge.

Peter Galison The Mallinckrodt Professor of the History of Science and Physics at Harvard University

C.T.R.Wilson (1869-1929) Son of a Scottish sheep farmer and in turn a Manchester medic, Bradford school teacher, photographer and meteorologist.
After experiences of lightning storms and the effects of sun through mist atop Ben Nevis, Wilson joined the Cavendish laboratory in 1895 and at once designed a cloud chamber artificially to produce condensing droplets. As Jacksonian professor at Cambridge, he was a dreadful lecturer, specialising in almost invisible marks on the blackboard, but promoted work to improve and automate the chamber, especially to spot the effects of disintegrating nitrogen nuclei with fast alpha particles. Wilson worked on condensation physics and atmospheric electricity, until in 1934 he retired and returned to highland mountaineering

Patrick Blackett (1897-1974) After naval service in the first world war, Blackett worked at Cambridge on Wilson's cloud chambers. In 1932, with G.P.S.Occhialini, he improved the chamber's design, and the following year used the device to demonstrate the production of pairs of electrons and positrons from gamma rays. In 1933 Blackett moved to Birkbeck College, London and then in 1937 took over the Manchester Physics Department where he continued cosmic ray research. During the Second World War he ran the operations research group fighting against U boats and after the war became head of Imperial College London. A convinced socialist, Blackett wrote widely on atomic energy and eventually became scientific advisor to the Labour Government of 1964-70.

Dr D.Tovee Reader in Physics at the Department of Physics and Astronomy, University College, London

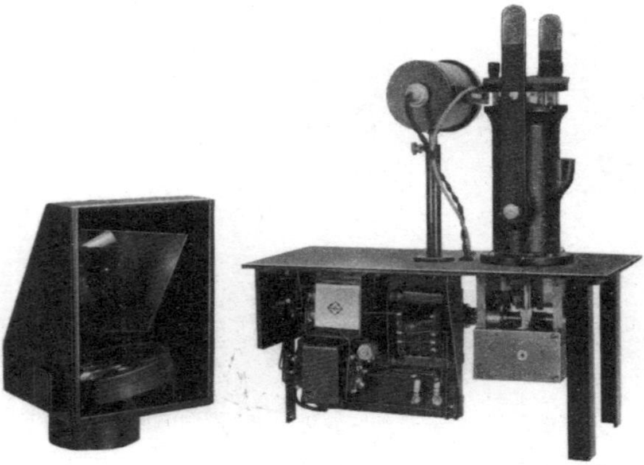

Cambridge Recriprocating Cloud Chamber for the 1951 Festival Exhibition London
C.T.R.Wilson and the Cloud Chamber 1894-1951 issued by Cambridge Instrument Company
Collection of the Whipple Museum of the History of Science, University of Cambridge.

This cloud chamber was specially built for exhibition in the Atomic Science Section of the Dome of Discovery at the South Bank and was on display for the full five months, during which time it continuously produced, for visual observation, nearly six million sets of alpha tracks

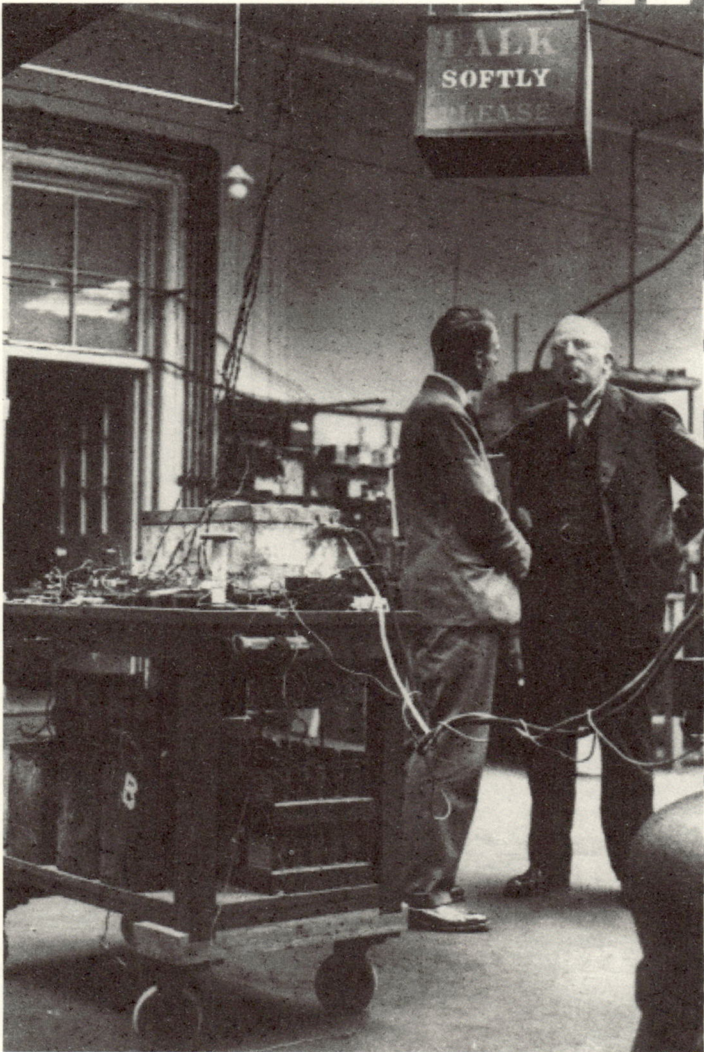

Talk Softly Please

noise

Talk Softly Please!

The Scale-of-Two Counter

JEFF HUGHES

Designed and constructed in 1931 by **Charles Eryl Wynn-Williams** (1903-1979) at the Cavendish Laboratory, Cambridge, the scale-of-two counter was used to count sub-atomic particles in nuclear disintegration experiments. It was the first practical digital electronic counting device, and played a crucial role in the development of nuclear physics. It opened the way to the digital electronic computers developed during and after the Second World War.

Until the late 1920s, atomic and sub-atomic particles were counted through a microscope by the flashes resulting from their impacts on a phosphorescent screen. The experiments were tedious, difficult and often unreliable, requiring a darkened room and teams of skilled observers who could only count small numbers of particles over short periods of time. Nevertheless, it was with this method that **Ernest Rutherford** and his students discovered the atomic nucleus at Manchester in 1911, and with which they began to chart its structure at the Cavendish Laboratory in the 1920s. As other laboratories began to compete with the Cavendish in nuclear research, however, it became increasingly difficult to maintain the viability of the scintillation counting technique as different laboratories tended to use different protocols in their experiments.

Against this background of confusion and controversy, Wynn-Williams, a young Welsh postgraduate student at the Cavendish, began to explore alternative, electronic methods of counting particles. He was able to exploit recent developments in the booming radio industry. With the rise of wireless broadcasting in the 1920s and the rise of a mass market for wireless sets, proprietary valves became increasingly cheap, reliable and available. Just as they acted in a wireless set to amplify an electrical impulse to produce a signal, so they could be used with suitable circuitry in the physics laboratory to amplify the tiny electrical current produced by a sub-atomic particle into a measurable form - usually an audible `click' in a headset or the kick of a galvanometer needle. These clicks or kicks could then either be counted directly or photographed on a moving film and analysed later. A skilled wireless enthusiast himself, Wynn-Williams constructed the Cavendish's first valve amplifier in 1927, using proprietary radio components.

With this new device, up to 500 particles per minute could be recorded – a significant improvement over the scintillation technique. Problems remained, however. It was still laborious and tiring to count tens of thousands of kicks, either directly or from a 400-foot long paper film, and silence had to imposed in the laboratory during experiments so as not to disturb the sensitive valve amplifier and create spurious counts. Wynn-Williams and others therefore continued to modify and improve the apparatus, building in a mechanical counter to record the number of particles. For large numbers of particles, however, the speed of counting was limited by the speed of the mechanical counter. In 1930 researchers in the Cavendish began to exploit a new kind of valve - the thyratron, recently invented by researchers at General Electric,

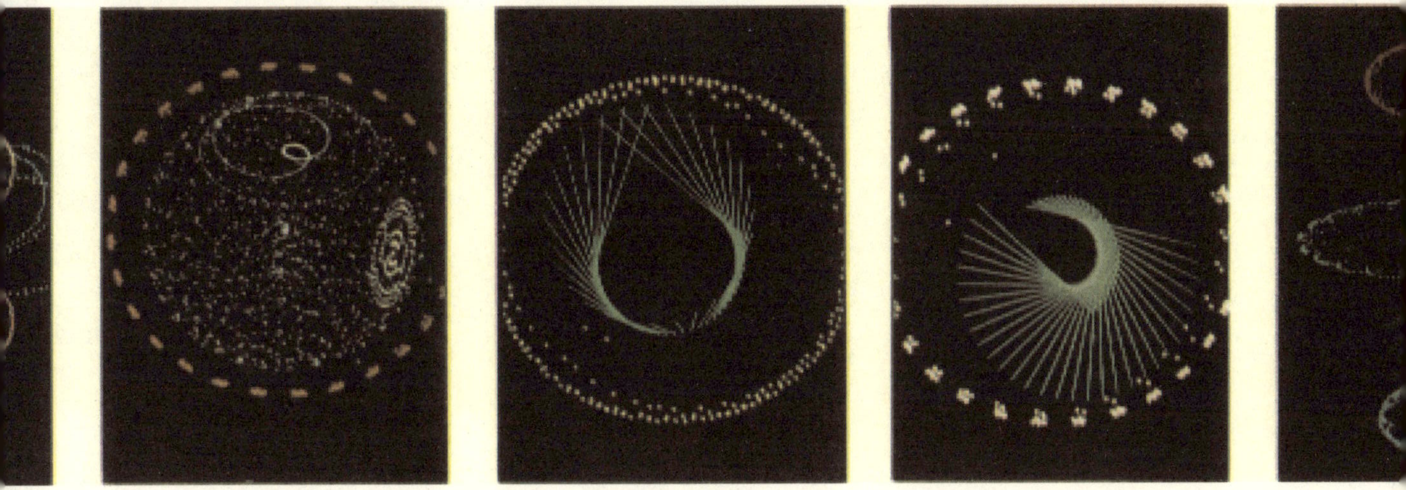

Whitney Bros *Permutations* 1967

Stanley W. Anquist Hydraulic digital computing circuit 1967

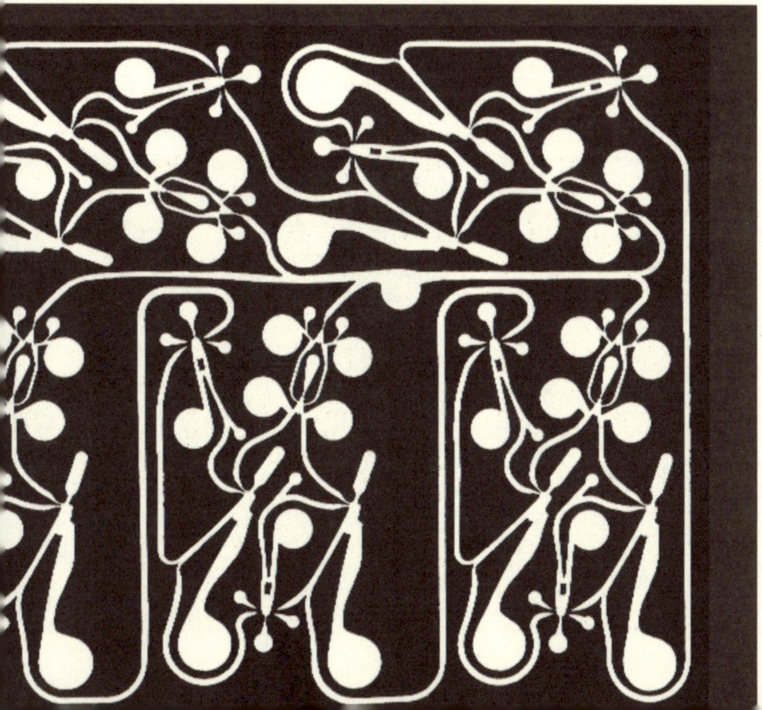

Stan Vanderbeek *Poem Fields* 1967

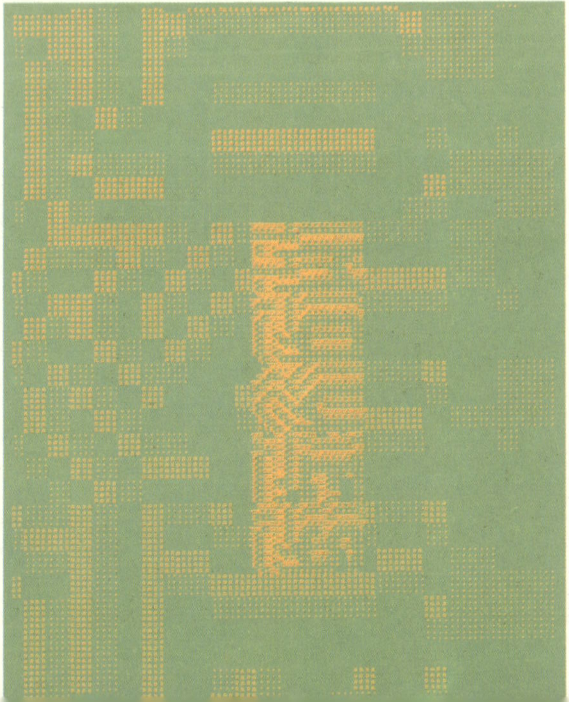

which could be used to trigger the mechanical counter. Wynn-Williams devised a circuit involving a ring of thyratrons which would trigger the mechanical counter only after several particles had been registered, thereby overcoming the mechnical limitation of the counter. This significantly improved the counting rate, but in practice the apparatus was complex, unwieldy and difficult to operate reliably, and only had limited use in the Cavendish.

In 1931, the ingenious Wynn-Williams built a new and much simpler circuit using multiple pairs of thyratrons linked in 'cascades', such that the mechanical counter registered every second, fourth, eighth or sixteenth particle, depending upon the number of thyratron pairs in the circuit. This arrangement, the scale-of-two counter, opened the possibility of a much higher counting rate than the ring circuit, and could be run off the mains electricity supply, greatly simplifying its operation. Later modified by Bennett Lewis, another Cavendish radio enthusiast, the scale-of-two counter was in constant use in the Cavendish for the rest of the 1930s where it produced many new results. Elsewhere too: by the end of the decade scale-of-two counters were in use in nuclear physics laboratories all over the world, Wynn-Williams providing circuit blueprints to anyone who asked for them. They were capable of counting tens of thousands of particles a minute. It was with these devices that modern knowledge of the nucleus began.

During World War 2, Wynn-Williams worked at Bletchley Park, where his circuits formed the basis for those used in the first code-breaking machines, leading to the 'Colossus' machines which broke the German 'Enigma' codes and which were crucial to the Allied war effort.

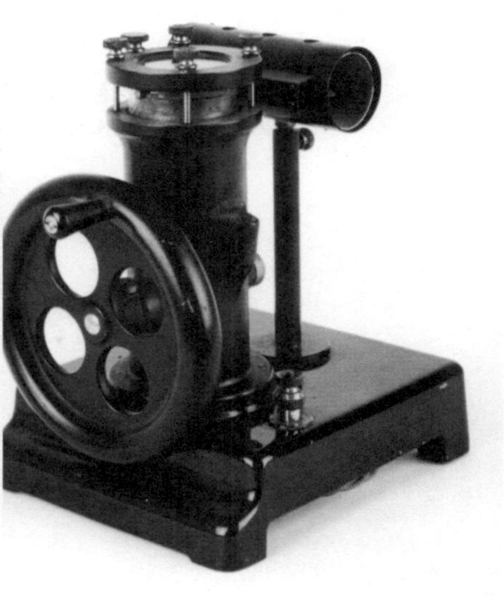

Scale-of-Two Counter
Cavendish Laboratory University of Cambridge

Dr. Jeff Hughes Lecturer in History of Science & Technology at the University of Manchester.

Charles Eryl Wynn-Williams (1903-1979) Educated at the University College of North Wales at Bangor, worked at the Cavendish Laboratory from 1925 to 1935 where he specialised in the development of electronic particle counting methods. Apart from wartime service on the design of code-breaking machines at Bletchley Park, the rest of his career was at Imperial College, London, where he devoted himself to teaching work in practical physics.

Ernest Rutherford (1871-1937) Son of a New Zealand flax farmer, he abandoned his early Cambridge work on wireless for the excitements of radioactivity in 1896; and as professor first at McGill University in Montreal, then at Manchester, established the reality and properties of radioactive disintegration and the atomic nucleus. As head of the Cavendish Laboratory from 1919 he won crucial industrial backing for atomic physics, supervised the first artificial atomic disintegrations and the discovery of the neutron, but doubted whether atomic energy would ever be exploited, and banned anyone 'talking about the Universe' in his laboratory. In a series of lantern slide lectures and widely read books, culminating in *The Newer Alchemy* (1937), he showed how counting particle emissions could unlock the atom's structure.

The Whitney Brothers
James and John Whitney collaborated on *Film Exercises* during 1941-44, and worked separately from 1945 onwards. James produced *Yantra*, an abstract animation drawn by hand on filing cards, from 1950-60. Meanwhile John worked on the construction of a hybrid optical printer similar to the one used in the Stargate sequence in 2001, but given a greater range of movement by the incorporation of a mechanical analogue computer based on an M-5 antiaircraft gun guidance system. The brothers reunited to produce an even more complex machine, used to make James's *Lapis* and John's *Catalogue*. John's sons John Jr. and Michael refined the machine's electronics, and also made a series of films. John's *Permutations* was made on an IBM 360 in collaboration with Dr. Jack Citron using Citron's Fortran based GRAF language.

Stan Vanderbeek
Stan Vanderbeek worked during the sixties and seventies in a dizzyingly wide range of kinetic media to realise his proposal in his 1965 *Manifesto* for an 'image library, newsreel of dreams, culture intercom'.

Talk Softly a photograph taken in the Cavendish Laboratory, Cambridge, by Charles Wynn-Williams in 1932.
Ernest Rutherford, with the cigarette, is hectoring the physicist J A Ratcliffe in front of an electrical particle counter used that year in the discovery of the neutron. Wynn-Williams deliberately switched the warning sign on before taking the picture.

How do you track a Cosmic Ray?

Material Tracks

PETER GALISON

Ever since **Marietta Blau** began using dental x-ray film to track cosmic rays in 1930s Vienna, the making of nuclear emulsions was a delicate, even black art somewhere between physics and chemistry. Sensitivity and instability went hand in hand as physicists signed a remarkable concord with the industrial chemists. Just after World War II, flush with the successful production of emulsions for the atomic bomb project, Kodak and Ilford made an offer that the physicists could hardly refuse. Roughly: "If you physicists agree, we will produce for you an emulsion so extraordinarily sensitive that it will register every possible charged particle. You will have a nuclear physics instrument more powerful than anything anywhere. Nonetheless — and you must pay this heed — emulsion manufacture is a highly secretive and proprietary business. Neither now nor in the future will you ever know precisely what is in these emulsions nor how we prepare them." The physicists signed.

Spectacular triumphs and immense anxiety followed. As **Cecil Powell** rhapsodized, it was as if "we had broken into a walled orchard, where [ripened] all kinds of exotic fruits" — pions, kaons, the anti-lambda-zero, the sigma plus, a myriad of new decay patterns. These "fruits" helped seed the new field of elementary particle physics, and because film was cheap and transportable, it offered the Europeans a chance to use mountaintop cosmic rays to compete with American accelerators. At the same time, both in the United States and in Europe, emulsion physicists stood on precarious ground. "The other day I was talking to [Ilford]," one American physicist

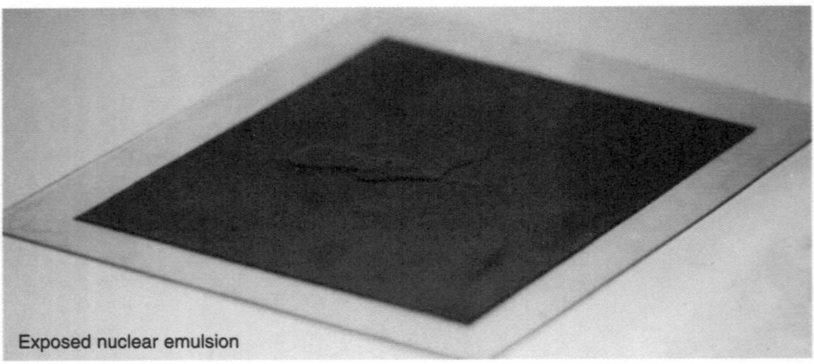

Exposed nuclear emulsion

confided, "and I told him that we take great care to keep the emulsion packages well sealed, so that we can be sure that the water content is always that which corresponds to the relative humidity of 50% at which the emulsions are dried and packed at Ilford's". "Oh," responded the Ilford chemist, "but we don't have the time to let the emulsions reach equilibrium." Suddenly the physicist's interpretations were thrown into doubt: the emulsions might vary from batch to batch, package to package, or even pellicle to pellicle. Measuring Nature's consistency would depend on that of the Manufacturer.

New particles burst on the scene. Some, like the pion, dramatically altered physicists' notions not only about what kind of entities populated the world, but also about underlying conceptions of the forces that bind matter together — though some of these new stars of the submicroscopic stage exited just as quickly. For the clumps of darkened silver were rife with instabilities, immersed in visual noise. Tracks faded over time, while new, spurious tracks could conflate with "genuine" ones at any time during the film's lifetime. During development and drying, emulsion and paper backings bent, distorting tracks and making one kind of event look like another. Physicists fretted in their notebooks, letters and meetings that scanners might only see what was expected in the events. And all this became even more complex as physicists joined in ever larger collaborations where conclusions had to be negotiated at far-flung distances.

Staring at these images we see a frozen instant of microphysical collision, halting signals against a background of noise, imprints of a moment in the 1950s when the very categories of experiment and experimenters were in flux.

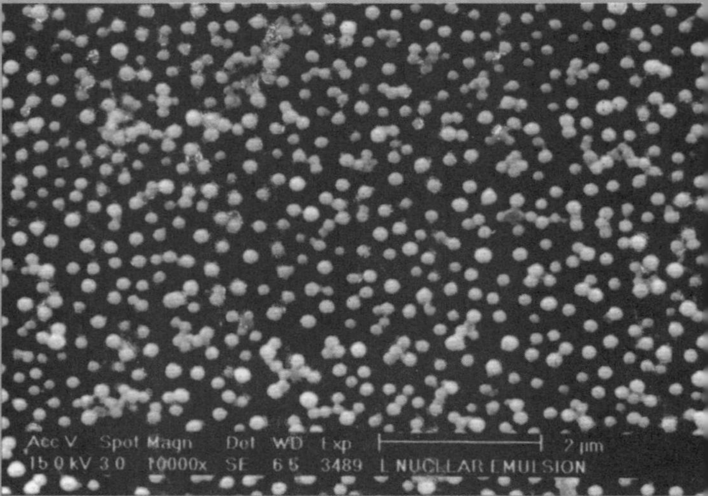

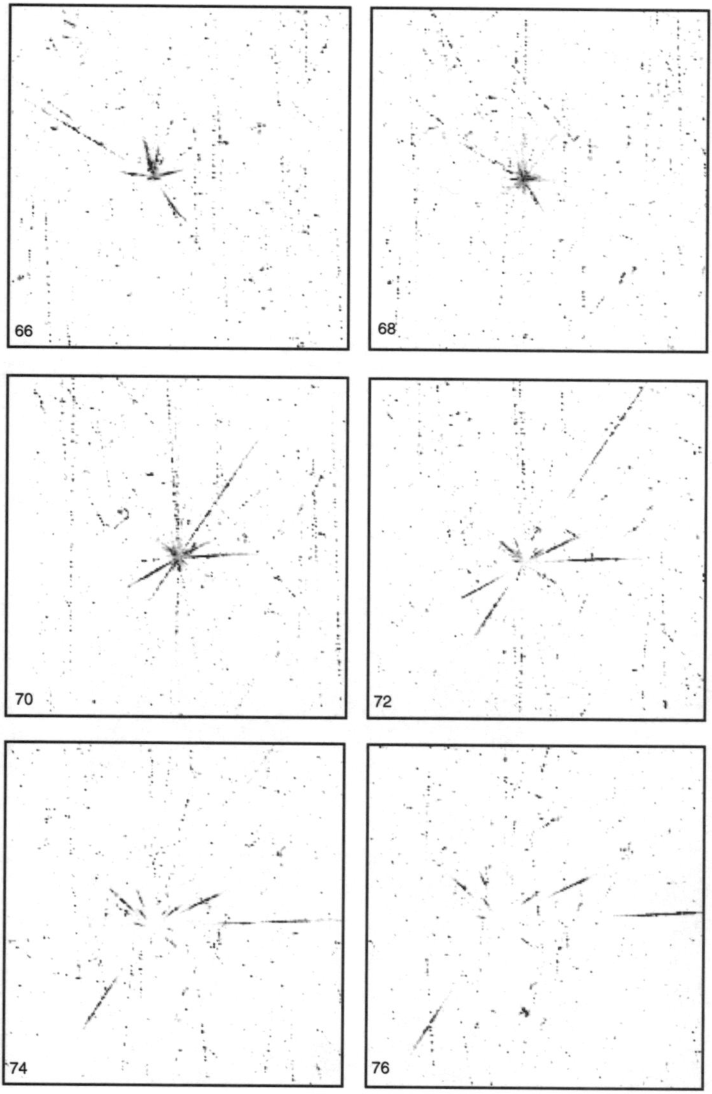

Particle tracks recorded by Adam Lowe and Dave Tovee at UCL (with the help of David Becker at the Confocal Unit). This sequence represents slices through the gelatine just before and after an event.

Peter Galison The Mallinckrodt Professor of the History of Science and of Physics at Harvard University.

Cecil Powell (1903-1969), a doctoral student of C T R Wilson at the Cavendish in 1927, then for the rest of his life a physics teacher and researcher in Bristol. He won the Nobel prize in 1950 for his photographic detection in cosmic rays of the pi mesons responsible for holding neutrons and protons together. He carried his specially designed photographic emulsions up mountains and in balloons to capture these rays' tracks. Powell was a committed anti-nuclear campaigner and led the World Federation of Scientific Workers for some years.

Marietta Blau (1894-1969), Viennese physicist. After working for an X-ray company in Berlin, Blau taught radiology, then at the Radium Research Institute in Vienna designed new kinds of emulsion on Ilford half-tone plates with which the tracks of charged particles could be followed. Always short of resources, in 1937 she performed crucial photographic detections in the Austrian alps of cosmic rays. The Nazi seizure of power in Austria the following year forced her to flee; her papers were confiscated by the Gestapo as she left Hamburg by zeppelin, and may have been used by Nazi physicists who claimed credit for her work. She pursued her career in Mexico and the USA before returning to Austria in 1960, her eyesight failing and her nominations for the Nobel prize rejected.

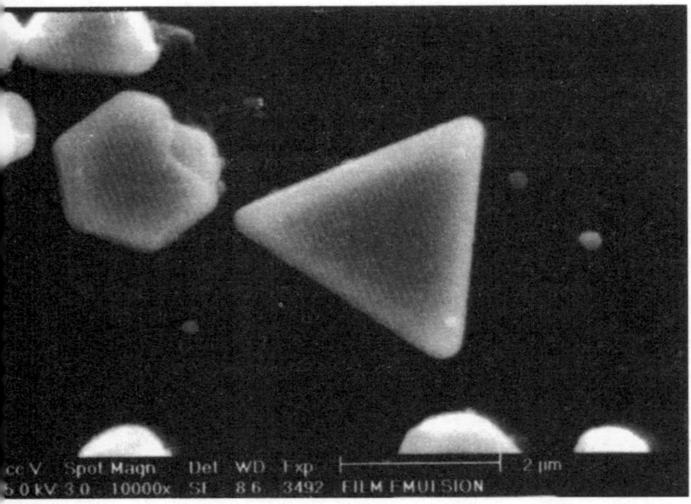

'In all our work we rely on the Principle of Uniformity of Nature; that is, we believe that if the same experiment is performed several times in exactly the same way, then the results will be the same. However I do not believe that there is also a Principle of Uniformity of Nuclear Emulsion, except by the grace of the manufacturers.'
—Cecil Powell

Is meaning behind the marks?

Dots in the Desert

ANITA HERLE AND SU DALGLEISH

In recent decades, Aboriginal artists from the central desert region of Australia have been creating vibrant works of art, many of which use "dots" as part of their vocabulary. These works in acrylic paint on canvas are connected to a western fine-art tradition, yet manifest an iconography grounded in the knowledge of local peoples, their country and its stories. The Aboriginal vision of Dreaming, which defines who people are and from where they came, is the main source of inspiration.

Dot paintings commonly refer to the topography of the land as it would appear from above. Aboriginal artists imagine this visual effect and depict it in their work. From the air much of the desert terrain has the appearance of a vast dot painting — the small bushes and round clumps of spinifex grass growing sparsely in the red sand appear as dots, often intersected by the curving lines of the dry river beds.

Dots, lines and nested circles are used as signs. The formal simplicity of the style encodes complex social and spiritual meanings within a unique space-time order. The subjects of the paintings typically refer to specific Dreamings or landscape-based stories, often accounts of ancestors' activities as they travel from site to site — hunting and foraging for food, meeting other characters, engaging in ceremonies, and fighting enemies. The movements of the ancestors created the landscape, plants, animals and people as well as the Law, the knowledge and regulations which underpin social life. By adulthood every Aboriginal knows the stories and associated responsibilities that relate to their part of the desert. A Dreaming both refers to the past and is the generative principle of the present and future.

How does one interpret these complex stories from these ordered dot-like forms? One recognises certain conventions — a nested circle commonly refers to a water hole or a fire camp, tracks across the canvas record the movements of people and animals. For the painters and members of their community, these images refer to very specific characters, places and events. Aboriginal artists have deliberately exploited the multi-vocality and ambiguity of dots to inscribe layered connections between people and places, the past and present, as well as to conceal deeper meanings from non-initiates. Knowledge of particular stories, owned by families and often specific to gender, is passed to descendants at appropriate periods in their development as part of a system of revelation. Sacred marks are revealed in ritual contexts, typically via body- or sand-painting, whose very transience emphasises the process of creation over the finished work. Works by senior Aboriginal artists are therefore steeped in meanings. Accounts given to outsiders often refer to the narrative of the stories, but not their deeper multi-layered readings.

Aboriginal artists thus use dots to both convey and conceal knowledge, depending upon whose eyes contemplate their work. Dots may highlight design elements and create dazzling visual effects, as well as obscure meanings. Painters may even give their work 'power' by using sacred — and to the uninitiated, dangerous — marks, dissembled but not diminished behind a veil of dots.

Bessie Nakamarra Sims painted the Ngarlajiyi section: diagonal right on the canvas. The central motif depicts the vine and leaves of the *Ngarlajiyi* (bush carrot). Small concentric circles represent special sites in the Waputarli area. Napurrurla and Nakamarra women (smaller "U"-shaped figures at the centre top and lower right), custodians of the land and the Dreaming, dig for Ngarlajiyi. At Kalijuta they cook and share the food they have collected. The sites, Waputarii, Yilkirdi and Kalijuta, are concentric circles on the right-hand side. Waputarli (Mt Singleton), associated with the Dreaming, lies west of Yuendumu.

Paddy Japaljarri Sims painted the lower left diagonal section: The country depicted is Kunnajarrayi. The custodians for this Dreaming are Napaljarri and Nungarrayi women. The women gather bush tomatoes or *Ngalyipi* (large circles on the left), which they cut open, discard the contents and thread them onto a long stick to cook over a fire. Long wavy lines symbolise snake vine, which the women make into rope.

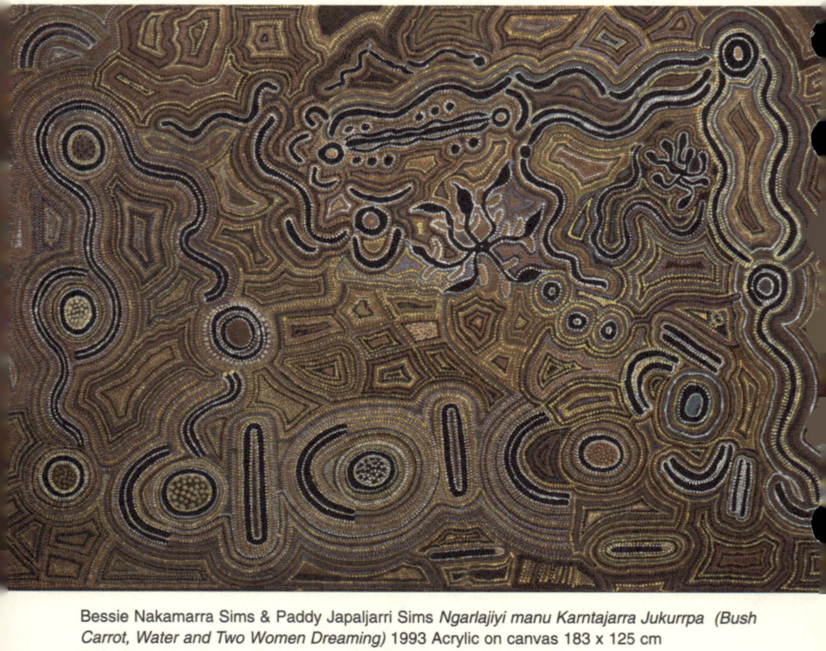

Bessie Nakamarra Sims & Paddy Japaljarri Sims *Ngarlajiyi manu Karntajarra Jukurrpa (Bush Carrot, Water and Two Women Dreaming)* 1993 Acrylic on canvas 183 x 125 cm
Coll. Cambridge University Museum of Archaeology and Anthropology
Purchased with the assistance of the MGC/V &A Purchase Grant Fund. CUMAA 1994.296.

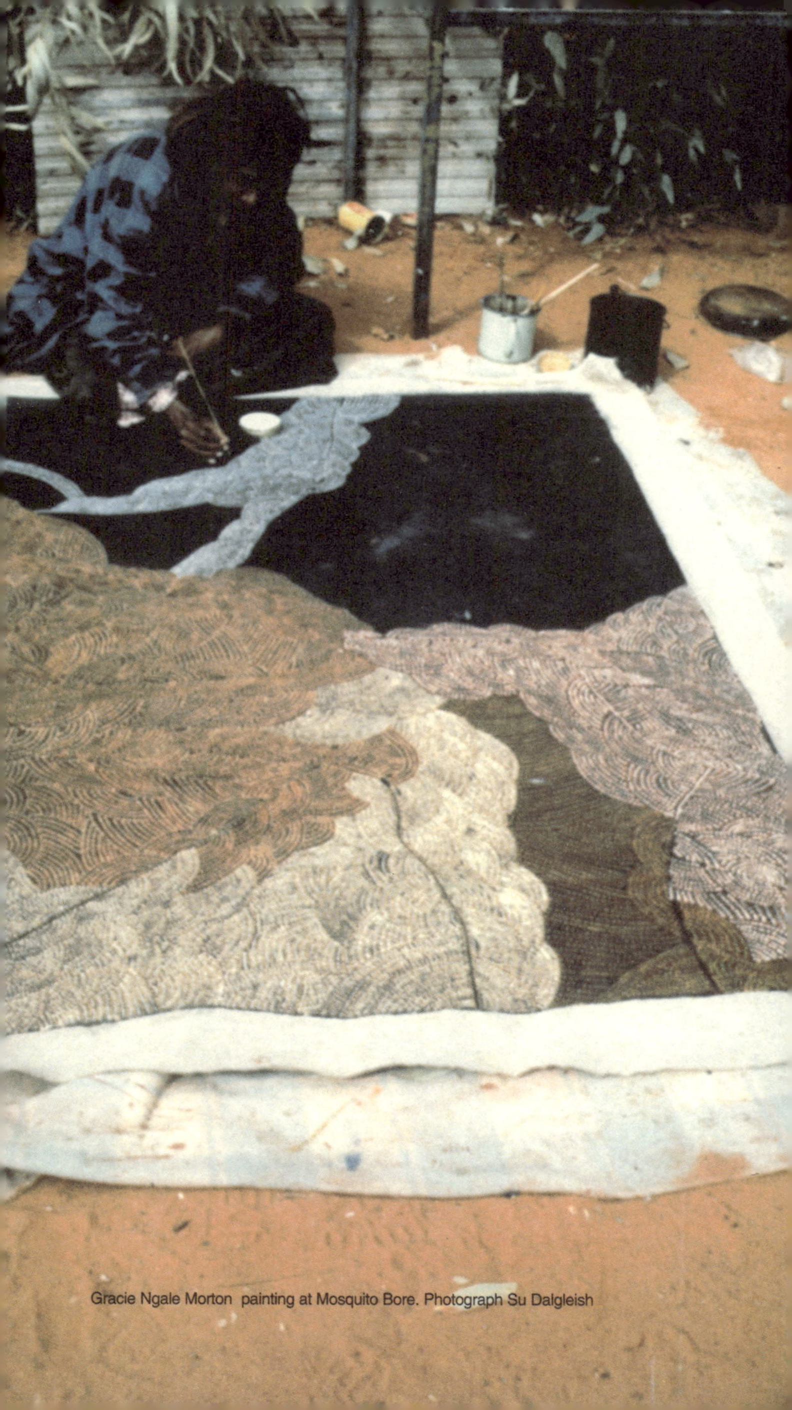

Gracie Ngale Morton painting at Mosquito Bore. Photograph Su Dalgleish

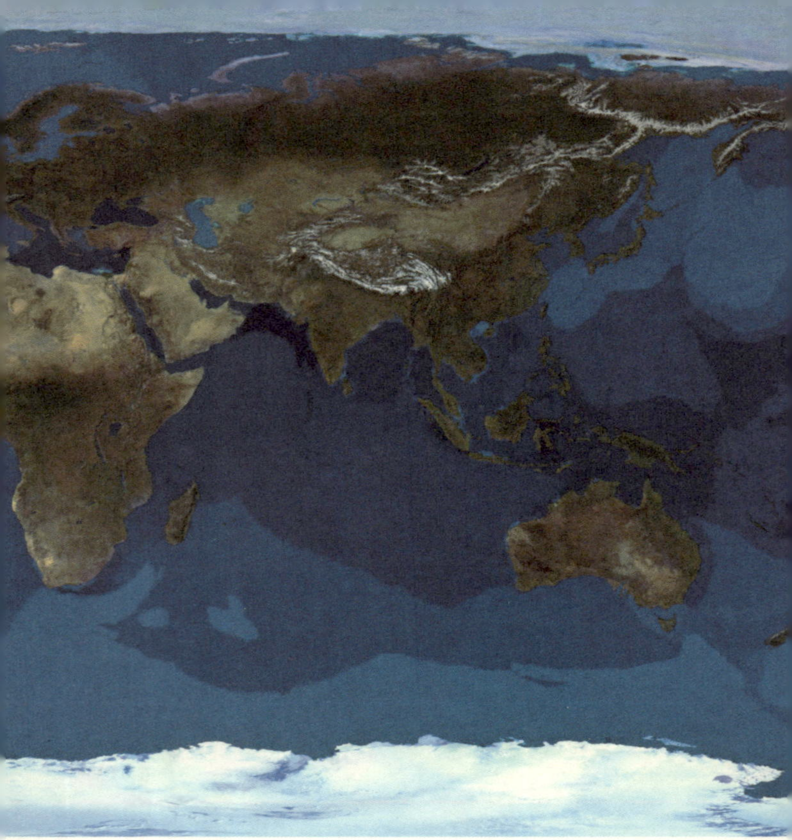

". . . Endless codes slither between the object and its image. The light reflected from the earth is broken up . . . transformed into an electrical signal . . . recorded . . . played back . . . transmitted . . . received . . . recorded again . . . calibrated . . .annotated and recorded yet a third time . . . Each of these steps reflects a code that says *this* means *that*. Take the prism in the scanner. Essentially this *filters* light over detectors tuned to different wavelengths . . . These wavelengths were not chosen at random but because alone or in combination they correspond to . . . particular things on earth:"
Denis Wood *The Power of Maps* p.54 (The Guildford Press: London 1992)

The data that Van Sant receives at The GeoSphere Project is messy, fragmented and covered with clouds — opaque matter concealing the globe, 'noise' to be removed in the production of his satellite image. He had to select, edit, paste, blend, sharpen, stretch, squeeze, colour and manipulate the data to create this seamless map, which has since entered the canon of popular cartography and now provides a noise-free backround for mapping on other layers of data — such as the movement of clouds.

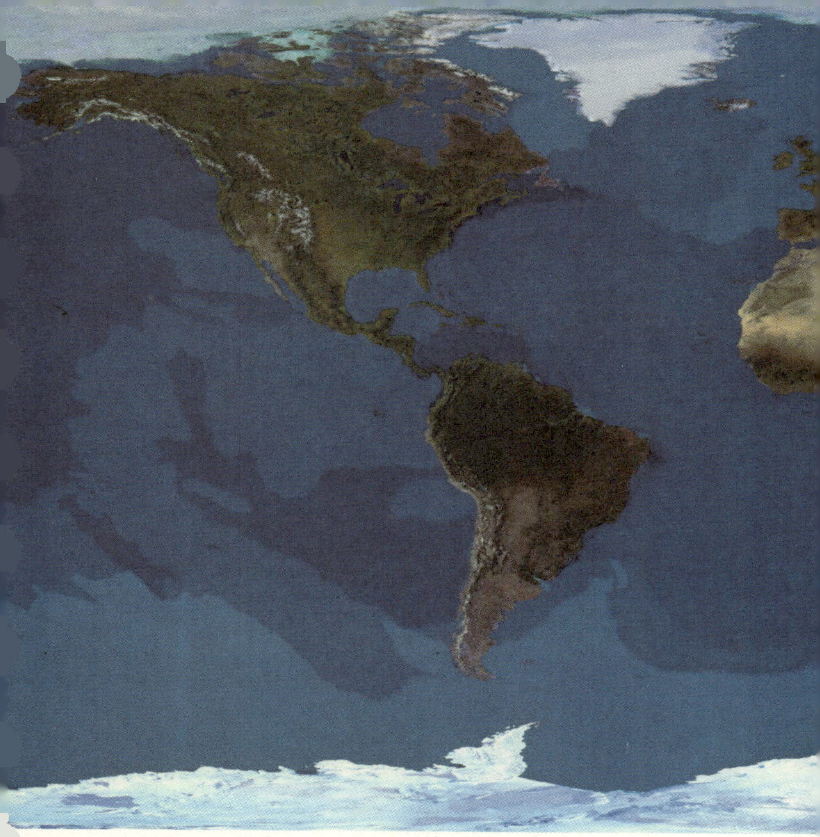

A composite photoelectric image 1997 (courtesy The GeoSphere Project, Santa Monica CA)

The World Without Clouds

Tom Van Sant

The first satellite map of the earth was created in 1990 by Tom Van Sant, Director of The GeoSphere Project, Lloyd Van Warren, Leo Blume and James Knighton, with assistance from NASA and USGS. It was assembled from both visible and infra-red data recorded between 1986 and 1989 by the National Oceanic and Atmospheric Administration TIROS 'Television and Infrared Observation Satellites' — the word 'television' here is misleading, as no photography is involved; a system of mirrors directs light bounced up from the earth into an array of photoelectric sensors, which generate electrical signals transmitted as digital data and translated into an image in photographic register. Each pixel represents an area 4 km wide at the equator; 35 million of these 4km sq sections were used to construct the map.

A second 1 km sq resolution map was completed in 1997. It measures 43,200 pixels x 21,600 pixels for a total of 933.12 million 'true colour' pixels.

Anita Herle and Su Dalgleish Anita Herle is senior assistant curator at the Cambridge University Museum of Archaeology and Anthropology. Su Dalgleish studied Anthropology at Cambridge and spent several years living at Mosquito Bore.

Bessie Nakamarra Sims & Paddy Japaljarri Sims Members of the Warlukurlangu Aboriginal Artists Association, a community-based organisation incorporated 1985 in Yuendumu, 300 km northwest of Alice Springs. Well over 100 Warlpiri artists from Yuendumu and its outstations make up the broad membership of the association.

Gracie Ngale Morton Aboriginal artist. Born 1956 into a closely related Aboriginal group living at Mosquito Bore (Lylyntja), one of the outstations of the Utopia community, 260 km northeast of Alice Springs, all the women in her family paint. Gracie is gaining recognition outside her desert home, and is presently being exhibited in the urban areas of Australia. Her canvases allude to various duties in both her daily and spiritual/religious life as keeper of bush plums, tiny black fruits, sweet and nutritious with one central seed, that grow on small trees in the desert about 50 km from Mosquito Bore. When the fruit is ripe, the women go to this spot and harvest the tiny fruits all through the long hot day.

Tom Van Sant Artist and director of the Geosphere Project.

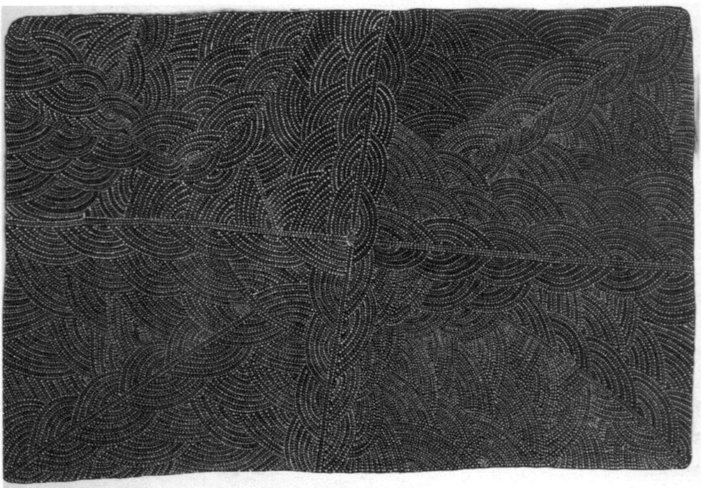

Gracie Ngale Morton *Bush Plum Dreaming* 1999
135 cm X 87 cm
Coll. Cambridge University Museum of Archaeology and Anthropology
Purchased with the assistance of the Crowther-Beynon Fund. CUMAA 1999.143.

This painting represents the cycle of the bush plum: the seeds drop from the ripe fruit, are scattered by birds, and grow into new bushes, thus maintaining their supply and the continuity of desert life. The dots refer to a special ceremony performed by the women of her family to keep the Bush Plum Dreaming 'strong'.

What follows a sphere and a cross?

Bagel Go

ADRIAN CUSSINS

Y2K has become synonymous with technological meltdown, but a period of chaos may itself be an anticipation; a genesis for the new millennium. Digital cultures are, despite their digitality, very messy: the www is an elaborate collage of information and misinformation with lost distinctions between news and commercials, editorial and advertising, working draft and authorised product. We have good reason to be anxious. Is meaning to be measured by search-engine hits? Significance is an irrelevance: ordering on Altavista or Yahoo or Infoseek, which become arbiters of popularity, themselves compete for the eye of the desktop in a popularity contest. We think of digital technologies as media for better expressing human intelligence, but what if our digital 'servants' are transforming human thought into alien echoes of n01se? The zeroes and ones move across the face of the deep.

What purity, what sacred space of meaning, could emerge from the messy noise of digital transmission? It's not for us to know (we see only the beginning), but we do need symbols to guide our search. The symbol of perfected sanctity in the millennium before the last was the sphere, the pure Form for the ancient Greeks. In the last millennium it was.... the cross?; a symbol of death? of the Will as power to remove life or to transfer it out of the mundane human world?

In 1997 – skipping out for a day from a conference on science and technology studies – I went for a trip through the Arizona desert. Being in the desert is delightful terror before its vast void, and the majesty of apparent simplicity and recreation of life. But in the symbols of Christ's millennium, the desert represents death, and human preservation requires sharp boundaries insulating life from the destructive desert.

From Tucson I went first to a Jesuit mission - St Xavier - a sanctuary for life, with death symbolised as eviction from the Spanish architectural forms of the chapel to merge in the graveyard with the formless desert. A short drive to one of the Atlas missile silos (or was it Titan?), where cold war ICBMs might have emerged from the concealing desert to wreak mega-death. A subterranean architecture devoted to insulating occupants from the threat of the desert outside: the 1960s control room is literally hung on springs to allow it to withstand the shaking of the earth outside. Air-flow is controlled, entrances reinforced, and the communications system protected by built-in redundancy of its components. Too bad if the only message that could flow

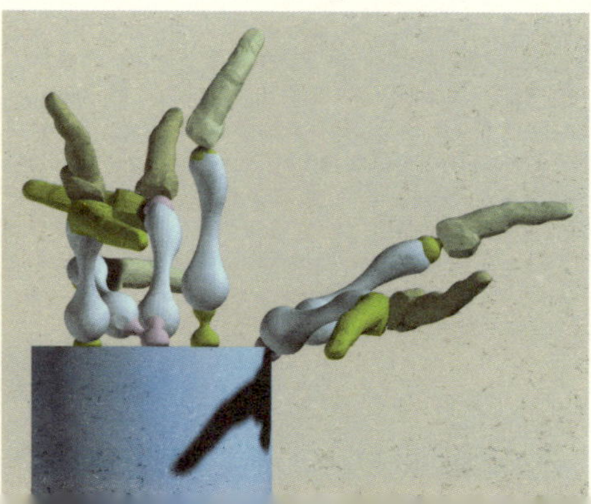

Michael Rees: 3D computer modelling

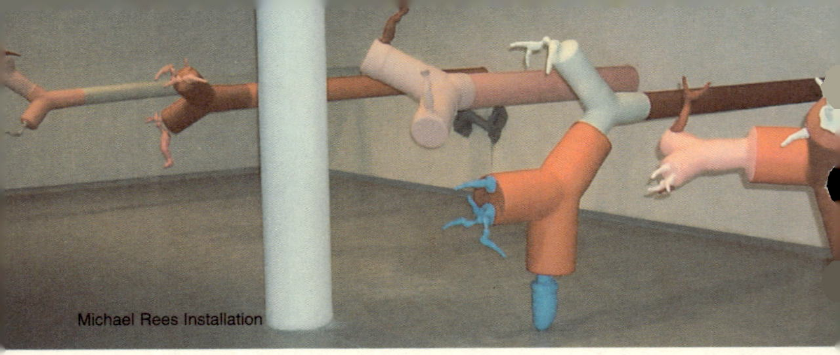

Michael Rees Installation

down its superbly insulated channel was the go-code for missile release. The 0's and 1's function by careful separation from the desert's void; the conditions for their being carriers of meaning require isolation within the information channel. The magnificent technological purification of signal-out-of-noise yields a digital icon, moving across the depths of the desert: a worthy neighbour for the Jesuits. From mega-death to mega-life: a couple of hours drive to Biosphere 2. Equally beautiful as the Mission and the Silo, its glass and concrete become NASA's Ark, insulating the 'biospherians' with a not-quite self-sustaining nature inside the huge bubble (London's was not the first 'millennium dome'). No material exchange is permitted across the boundaries of the Biosphere; although culture —the latest movies — flows uninhibited to the modernist world within.

In all three of these last-millennial places, massive structures work hard to separate society and its significances from the void-of-nature and its noise. The necessary conditions for the possibility of last-millennial meaning are the physically instituted regulations that separate meaning from void, life from death. The world as bounded. It yields meanings as hermetically-sealed: syntactically structured, formal and carried by digital messages (the ten commandments, ICBM go-codes, LED read-outs of carbon dioxide levels).

When I return to the Arizona desert, I want to leave behind a different millennial icon; one that points forward. I know what it should be. You can see its prototype here in *Noise*.

The power of the digital world rests on computers, and the power of computers lies in the explorations into intelligent activity that they make possible. There is a model of intelligent activity that is built around the idea of meanings as digital entities, which can be manipulated by rules or regulated practices. The game of chess and its artificial intelligence simulations provide good examples. When you look at a chess board you are looking at the world-of-chess: the sources of meaning and value in chess. That black bishop on the white square at the edge of the board is an object in the chess-world; it has a certain value, and it contributes this value to the determination of a total value for the Black side. In this way a chess computer can calculate how well Black is doing and how well White is doing for every legal board configuration. The key point is this: what it is to do well at chess — to be more likely to win — and the objects with which one attempts to do well in playing chess are all pre-determined by the rules of the game and the instituted structures (the topography of the board and the number and types of pieces). The space of all possible meanings is fixed by

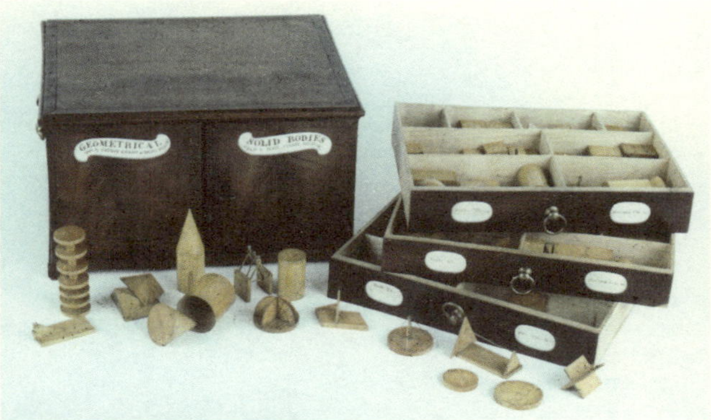

George Adams *Euclidian Solid Bodies*
105 wooden models designed to illustrate books XI and XII of Euclid's *Elements*.
In the collection of the Whipple Museum of the History of Science.

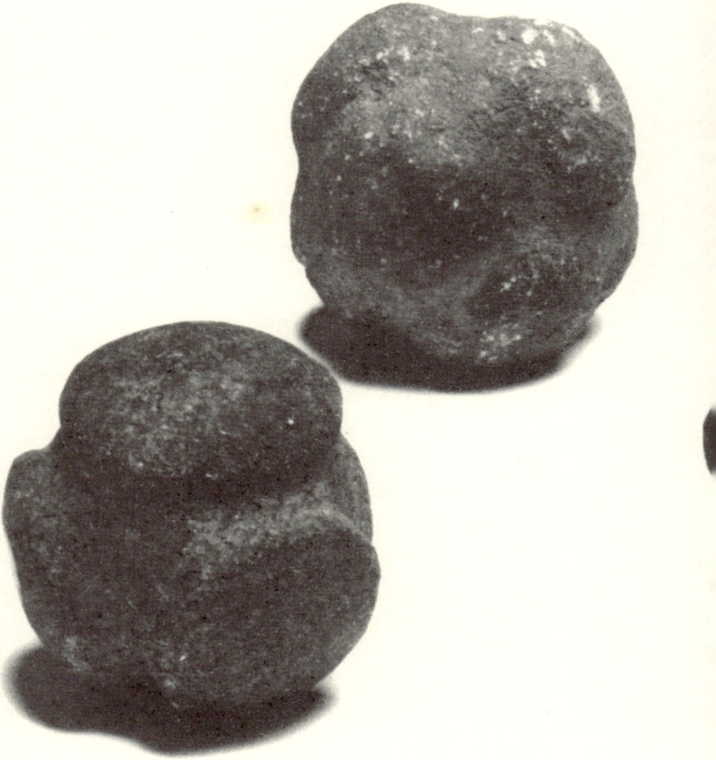

at the space in which the players negotiate the meanings of board positions amongst themselves. It is not until the end of the game that the rules of the game can apply to determine the value of a board configuration for the players. Each placing of a stone carries with it indefinitely many possible meanings; players' open exploration in the desert-space that Go provides allows meanings slowly to emerge. Meaning resides in the interactive explorations within the chaos and noise and indeterminacy of the board, some of which end in disaster, some in stable 'living' structures.

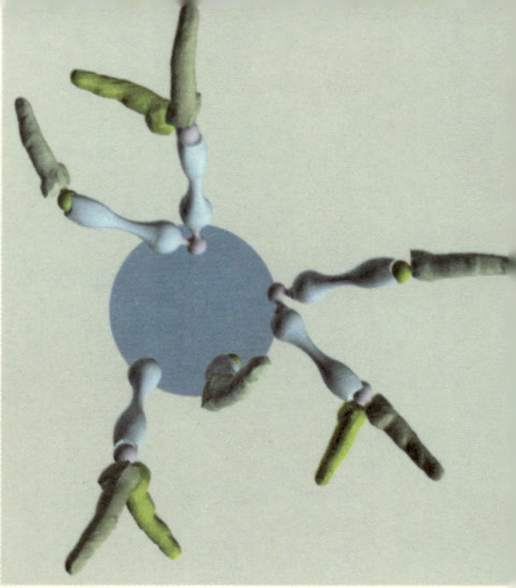

Michael Rees: 3D computer modelling

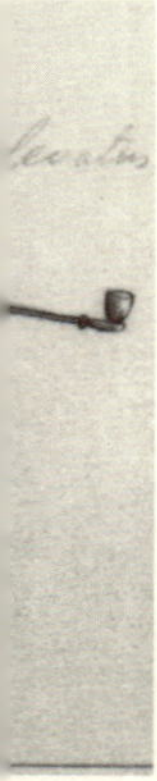

It is almost like this: when Black places the first stone on the board, it could go *anywhere*, because any placing of the first stone is as good as any other. Meaning is determined by the activity of placing of stones, and none has been placed, so no meaning yet resides in the board. The first move is, then, entirely contingent. By the end of the game it is determinate who has won. So we can think of Go-playing as the local construction of necessity out of contingency.

I say *almost* because in Go, as it is currently played, the corners and edges of the board do determine, within a small range, where the initial stone should be placed. A small distance out from the corners makes maximum use of the *natural* boundaries of the edges of the board. So to that extent the board is the world of Go, itself fixing the value of configurations of stones rather than affording a space in which the players negotiate value. Let us, then, re-make Go for the new millennium by the simple device of getting rid of the edges of the board. Each edge is folded over to meet its opposite edge, forming a torus. In Bagel-Go there are no edges, so that the first move is completely contingent. Neither the board nor the pieces fix value; they are not objects in the world of Bagel-Go, but tokens in the activity of *trading spaces* from which meaning and value emerge. Meaning is not a formal entity in Bagel-Go, but an ongoing achievement of the participants in the activity of playing. It is not alien—a competitor for control of the planet—but as human or as non-human as the participants themselves.

Bagel-Go is the pure form of intelligence. We know that chess is not such that outstanding performance at it requires intelligence: Deep Blue performs outstandingly at chess but has no intelligence whatever. It is an hypothesis for Y2K that Bagel-Go lies just above a boundary that chess lies beneath; a boundary that can be used to distinguish the intelligent creatures from the mere illusion of intelligence. A Turing Test for the new millennium. A symbolic space for meaning, both sacred *and* digital.

the rules of the game. Meaning, and not just the medium, has become digital: the boundaries of the board are the boundaries of the world; inside lies meaning, outside lies chaos. A fate celebrated so beautifully by the icons of the Arizona desert: *this* is the world of meaning, *that* is void-noise. We protect meaning by building boundaries against the 'desert'.

Since the 1950s chess has been the fruit-fly of artificial intelligence (AI). For its experimental investigations, science needs systems that are as simple as possible, easily reproducible and transportable, and yet which exhibit the phenomenon under study. What is the simplest, reproducible and transportable system of activity which is such that outstanding performance at that activity requires and exhibits intelligence? AI's answer for more than 40 years has been chess. That is why HAL in Kubrick's 2001 is shown beating Poole at chess. It's also why Kasparov's loss to Deep Blue in May 1997 has released so many *Matrix* type fears of humanity's being overcome by an alien intelligence.

Around the time of Abraham people started playing what is perhaps the most perfect board game. It was played for a long time in China, and was adopted in Japan and Korea. In the last ten years or so it has begun to have an impact in the Western world. Computers can play it, but they are no better than weak amateur players. It is much simpler in its structure than chess: there is no distinction between types of pieces, but only black and white stones. There are very few rules, just eight in the Tromp-Taylor description. It is played on a 19x19 square grid. Two players play alternately by placing a stone of their colour on any unoccupied point on the board. Stones remain where they are placed unless they are captured by being surrounded. The aim of the game is not to capture but to control *territory*, where a point of, say, White's territory is an unoccupied point on the board which is, or will become, so strongly influenced by White's stones that Black would be unable to survive there for long.

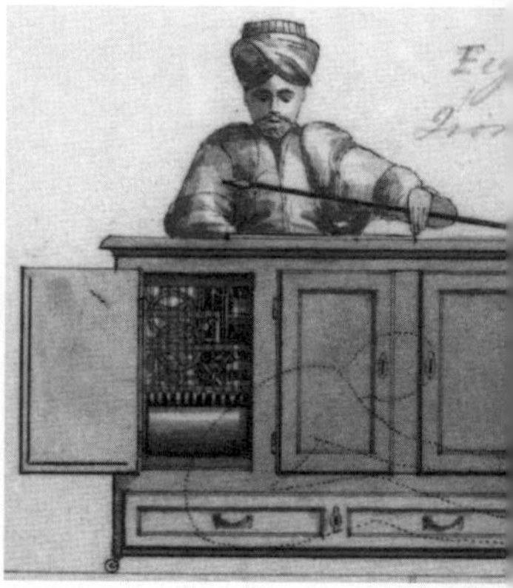

Wolfgang Von Kempelen *Chess Player*
Chess has been the fruit fly of artificial intelligence. Kempelen's Mechanical Chess Player (1769) concealed a skilful human and showed an automatic Turk. The gear system made enough noise to hide the sounds of the chess player himself.
From R. Willis, *An Attempt to Analyse the Automaton Chess Player* (London 1821)

Go, like chess, is played with a digital medium. Like chess it can serve as a fruit-fly for our investigations into mind, meaning and intelligence. Like chess it is bounded and finite and reliably achieves a state in which there is no disagreement between the players as to who has won. Go can stand as close to chess as the year 2000 stands to 1999. And it stands a millennium apart: Go does not belong to Christ's millennium. This is why: when you look at a game of Go — a configuration of black and white stones on the board — you are not looking at the world of Go, the space of possible meanings. The stones are not 'objects' as the fianchettoed bishop is an object in chess. The boundaries of the board are not the boundaries of the world of Go. You are looking

Adrian Cussins Professor of Philosophy at the University of Illinois.

Michael Rees Artist and researcher working with stereo lithographic output.

George Adams (1709-1772) Instrument maker to King George III.

Wolfgang Von Kempelen (1734-1804) Hungarian civil servant, playwright and mining engineer. He designed a printing press for blind musicians, a recycling system for royal fountains, and an automatic chess player. After touring Europe it was bought by the inventor of the metronome, Johann Maelzel, and described by Edgar Allen Poe. In 1819 it was revealed that it had in fact contained a man.

Five pictic balls from the Ashmolean Museum, University of Oxford.
Reproduced by courtesy of the Visitors of the Ashmolean Museum, Oxford.
These granite forms, carved in 3000BC without iron tools have puzzled archaeologists for many years. Keith Critchlow, (architect and professor of Visual and Traditional Arts at the School of Architecture and the Building Arts) has discussed their importance in his book *Time Stands Still.* He has identified them as geometrical representations of the Platonic solids made in Scotland 2500 years before Plato was born.

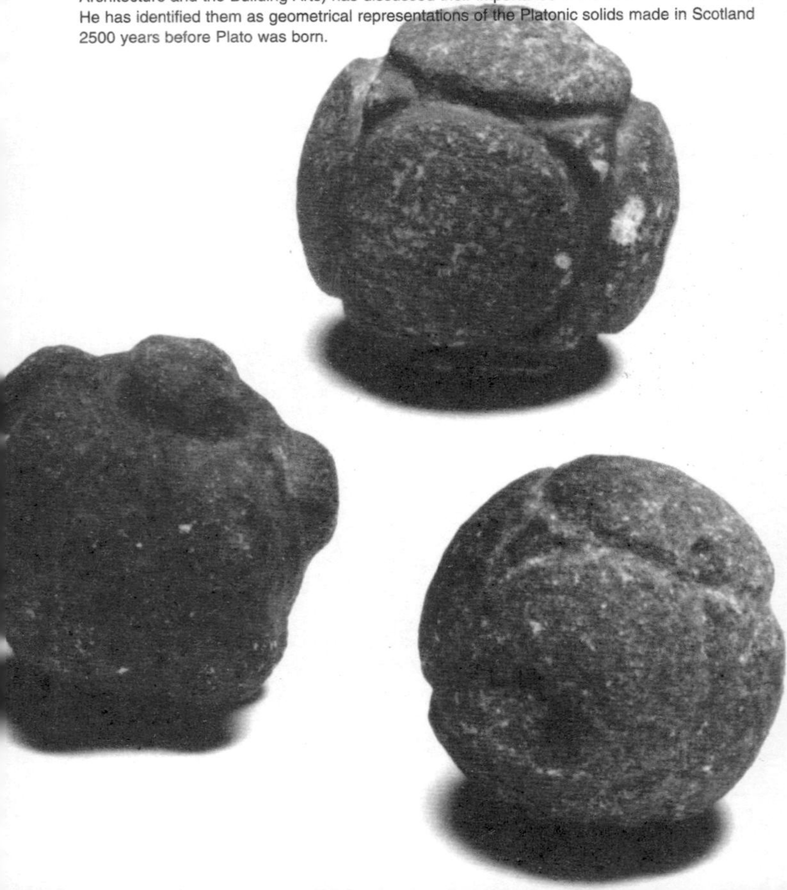

Is there room at the bottom?

Divers Minutiae

LISA JARDINE

When **Galileo** adapted his telescope to magnify tiny objects close at hand, rather than distant stars, he began by observing the houseflies buzzing around his study. Sir Christopher Wren, too, found fleas and lice diverting material under the lens of the microscope, and delighted Charles II with exquisitely executed drawings of them. His Royal Society colleague **Robert Hooke** gave engravings of household insects pride of place in his sumptuous coffee table book of much-magnified images *Micrographia* (1665).

The microscope lens revealed unimagined natural beauty, invisible to the naked eye, in these minute bodies. It also fuelled scientific speculation about the intricacy of internal anatomies, jarring the anatomist's imagination with images of the actual moving intestines and pulsating heart within the transparent flea or louse. Microscopists rapidly became anatomists — Hooke graduated from thinly slicing vegetable matter to slicing open the abdomens of flies in search of vessels found in larger animals. When he discovered them in abundance he concluded that there was no less "curious contrivance" here than in the larger animals.

The crucial novelty here for the anatomist was that the living insect under the microscope moved. The heart pumped, the digestive tract propelled its contents round the intestines under the gaze of the observing microscopist. That animation could not, of course, be captured on paper even by the most talented of draughtsmen; it was, however, vital to understanding the mechanics of bodies.

Hooke's treatment of the much-magnified natural world in *Micrographia* began, however, at a more fundamental level — with the microscopical scrutiny of the 'point of a sharp small Needle'. As in Geometry, the most natural way to begin being from a Mathematical point — he explained — so the same method proved the most genuine, simple and instructive in natural history:

We will begin these our Inquiries therefore with the Observations of Bodies of the most simple nature first, and so gradually proceed to those of a more compounded one. In prosecution of which method, we shall begin with a Physical point; of which kind the Point of a Needle is commonly reckon'd for one; and is indeed, for the most part, made so sharp, that the naked eye cannot distinguish any parts of it.

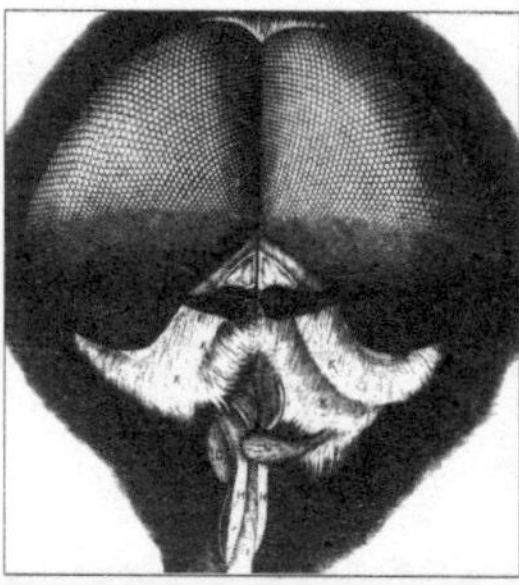

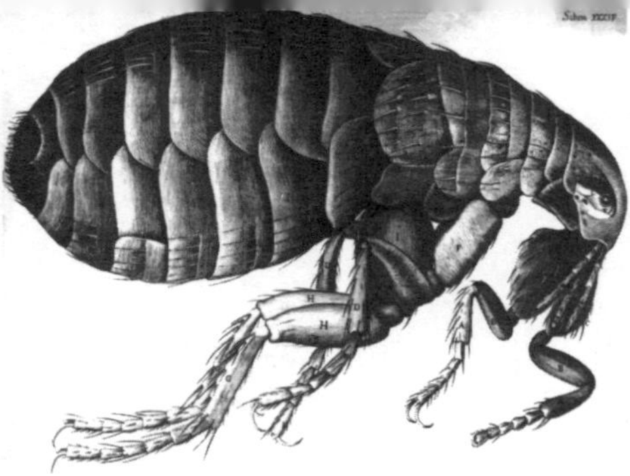

Robert Hooke *Micrografpha* 1665
Point of a Needle
The Whipple Library, University of Cambridge

When viewed *with a very good Microscope*, this apparently singular point was revealed to resemble a ragged-topped mountain range. Here, for Hooke, is a simple yet compelling lesson: beneath the smooth surface of the visible world lies a hidden world of yet greater complexity, whose secrets must be unravelled as a premise to any clear scientific understanding.

Recording what the microscopist saw with an early two-lens microscope was itself no simple matter (the diarist Samuel Pepys complained he saw absolutely nothing when he looked through the one he had enthusiastically purchased on Hooke's recommendation). Hooke describes the series of steps required:

In divers of the delineated Subjects the Gravers have pretty well follow'd my directions and draughts; and in making of them, I indeavoured (as far as I was able) first to discover the true appearance, and next to make a plain representation of it. This I mention the rather, because of these kind of Objects there is much more difficulty to discover the true shape, then of those visible to the naked eye. And therefore I never began to make any draught before by many examinations in several lights, and in several positions to those lights, I had discover'd the true form.

Occasionally, the graphic record itself, once painstakingly made, solved a natural mystery. When Hooke looked at a thin slice of cork under the microscope, it became clear why cork had such useful properties of lightness and buoyancy. Under the microscope it was revealed that cork consisted of a structural filigree of organic mesh around myriad internal air pockets. Hooke named these pockets 'cells' — a name which is still used for the minute structure of organic bodies.

In general, however, the worlds within worlds, and inner structural complexity beneath the visible outer layer, discovered by the microscope, presented the aspiring natural philosopher with a daunting task in scientific explanation.

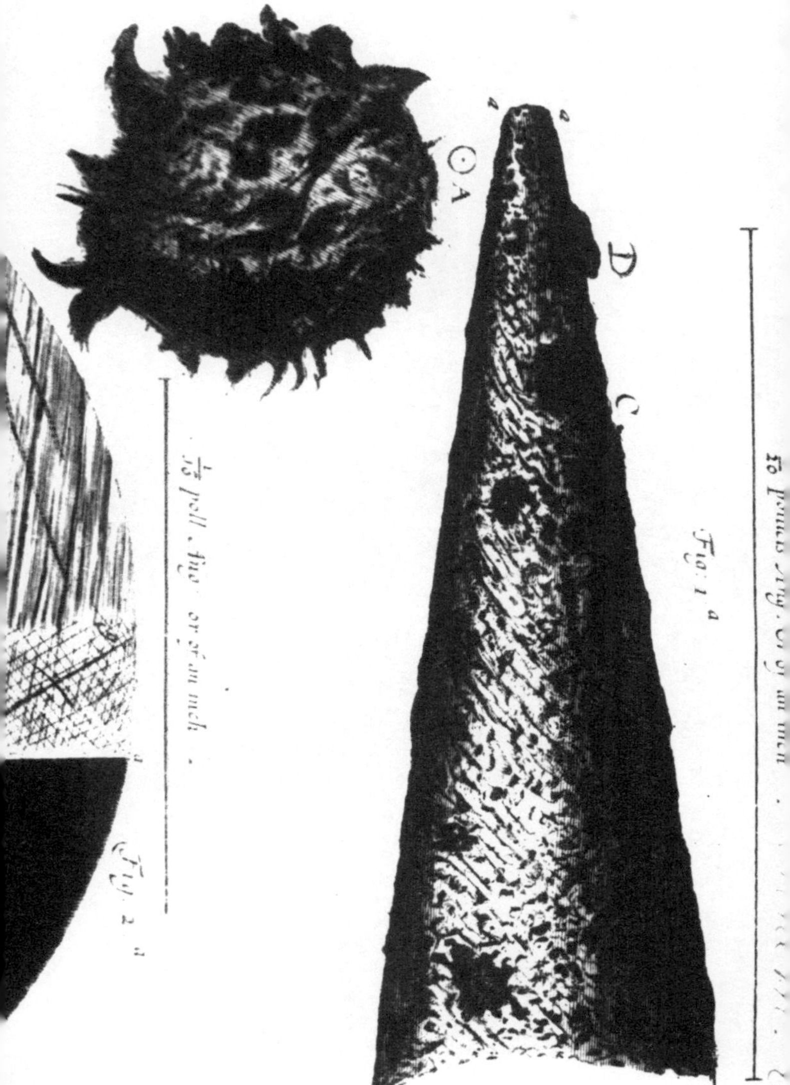

Robert Hooke *Micrographia* 1665 The point of a needle
The Whipple Library, University of Cambridge

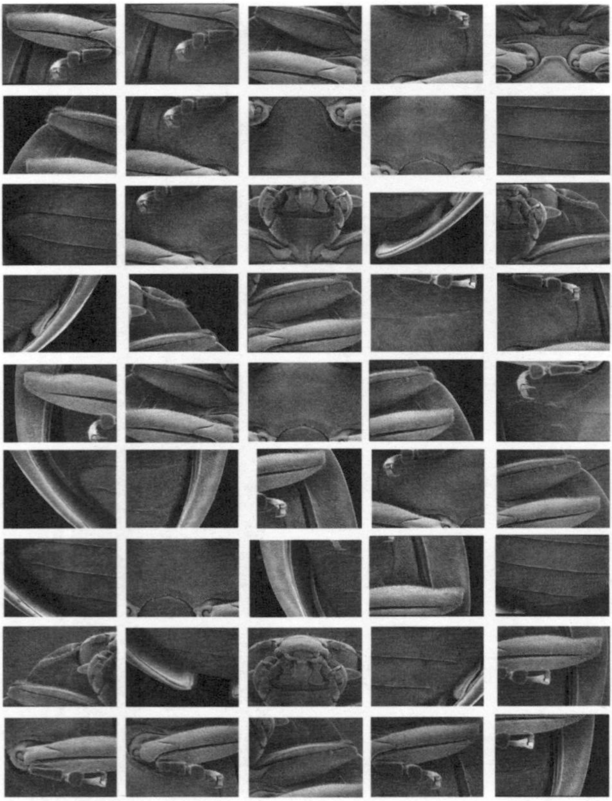

This image of a Ladybird, produced by **Giles Revell**, has been collaged from a mass of images photographed using an electron Microscope. The process begins when Revell, who trained as a geologist, gathers the specimen, transports it without damaging any of its fragile limbs to Royal Holloway, London University, where it is gold plated and arranged carefully into the correct position prior to inspection under an electron microscope. Under the microscope photographs are taken of each section at various depths of focus to provide the raw data to produce the complete, seamless collaged image. The photographs are then carefully tiled together and rescaled. The contrast is adjusted, distortions corrected, and artifact (unwanted noise resulting from the process) removed. Revell is currently working on a family of diverse insects at the same resolution and scale.

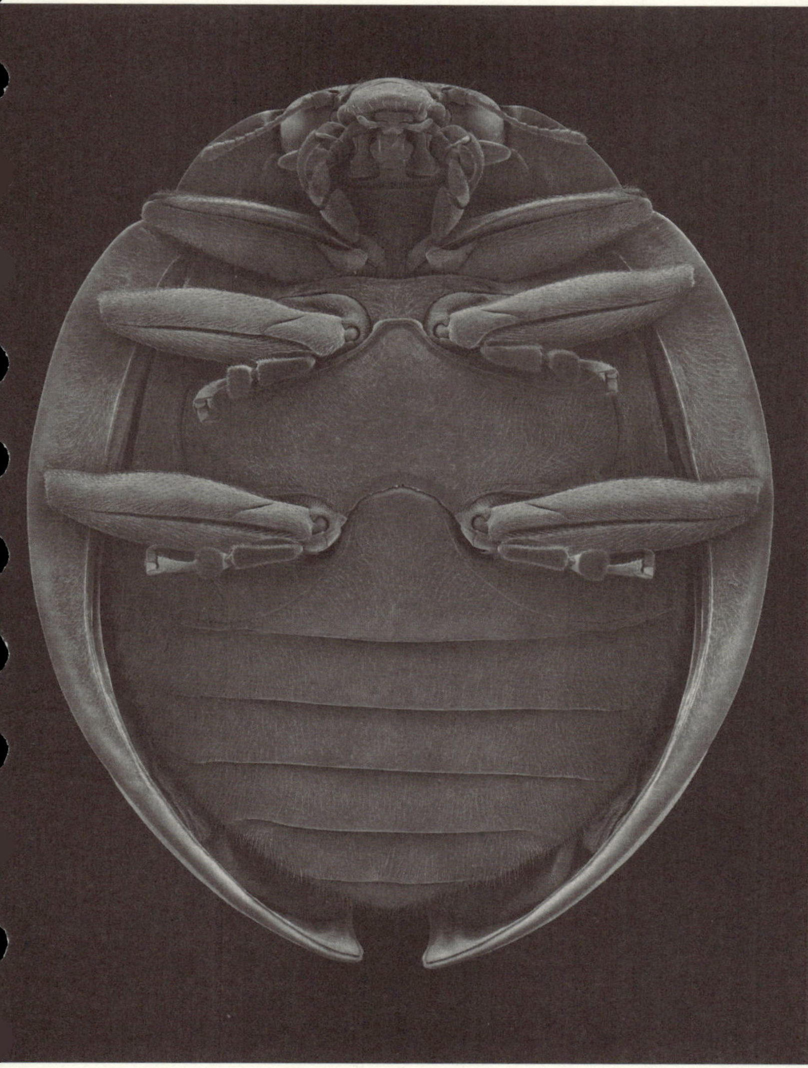

Lisa Jardine Professor of Renaissance Studies at Queen Mary and Westfield College, University of London and Honorary Fellow of King's College Cambridge.

Robert Hooke (1635-1702) A melancholy hunchback and Oxford chorister, he became the outstanding experimenter and instrument-designer of Restoration London. He produced air pumps, spring clocks, barometers and telescopic sights. His *Micrographia* (1665) was a supreme work on the use of the microscope and a host of themes in natural philosophy. In the wake of the Great Fire of London, Hooke designed Bedlam and the Monument. He had fierce disputes with Isaac Newton, lectured on the organic origin of fossils and the motion of comets, and proposed the freezing point of water as the zero for thermometers. In 1687 Newton published *Principia mathematica* and Hooke's neice and lover Grace died; after this, Hooke became increasingly morose and cynical.

Galileo Galilei (1564-1642). Mathematician and courtier. The son of a celebrated musician, then successively mathematics professor at the universities of Pisa and Padua. In summer 1609 he heard from the Netherlands of the invention of the spy-glass, and built his own instrument to observe the heavens and magnify insects. By dedicating his discovery of the moons of Jupiter to the Grand Duke of Tuscany, he was able to convince the prince to employ him as court philosopher. In 1614 both his daughters entered a convent, and attacks on Galileo's natural philosophy and astronomy began. He wrote and published brilliant and witty defences of his theories of mechanics, astronomy and hydrostatics, and perfected the compound microscope, with which Romans produced the first microscopic studies of the bee, an insect on the Pope's coat of arms. In 1632 Galileo was ordered to stand trial in Rome, sentenced to permanent house arrest, went blind and spent the rest of his life at his house at Arcetri near Florence.

Giles Revell Photographer and recepient of a NESTA (National endowment for Science Technology and the Arts) award.

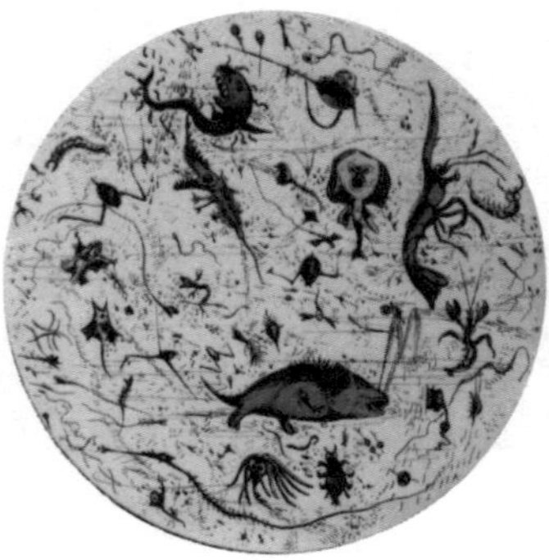

William Heath (c.1795-1840) *Monster Soup* (detail)
Coloured engraving
Wellcome Institute Library, London

Are we shocked?

First Impressions

DAVID PHILLIPS

Some crop circles may not be faked: the plant matter simply has the right properties to take impressions of minor whirlwinds whose traces on any other surface would have been erased.

This principle used to be commonly applied to recording images from nature. Again and again, often quite by chance, certain conditions — in workshop, laboratory or in nature — have made it possible to record patterns from processes going on invisibly around or over surfaces. Thus, late in the eighteenth century, **Lichtenberg** recognised a new way to visualise electrical action in the tiny stars and rings formed by the dust that settled from the resin insulation of his electrical apparatus. Later, whilst trying to repeat Lichtenberg's work, **Chladni** discovered his graphic visualisations of sound in vibrational effects on the same powder.

There are dozens of such surface traces: some familiar, like the patterns that appear in iron filings when passed through a magnetic field; others, like the exquisite ringed and scallop-edged blots in filter papers that were the signatures of chemical reactions for **F.F. Runge**, should be better known.

The most common term in the nineteenth century for these visual records was "figures" — *Lichtenberg figures, Chladni figures, Lissajous figures*. Traces of the invisible forces of nature, rendered via the patient enhancement of effects only casually observed earlier, or never seen at all. What we might now call "force figures" and think of as rough maps of force distribution, steps on the way to equations. Not that they look like *maps*, but like *pictures* — of electricity or sound or magnetism. They fascinated those other nineteenth century researchers into the invisible, the spiritualists. By the end of the century, a Lissajous figure had even been reproduced by **Annie Besant** as the visualisation of a spirit aura.

One remarkable researcher, **Margaret Watts Hughes**, stood between the scientists and spiritualists, as a musician. We don't know much about her, apart from her two books, *Voice Figures* (1891), and a slightly expanded and newly illustrated new edition, the *Eidophone Voice Figures* (1904). A short *Times* obituary (20 Nov 1907) tells us a little. She came to London from Wales in about the 1860s as a singer, married, and expanded a

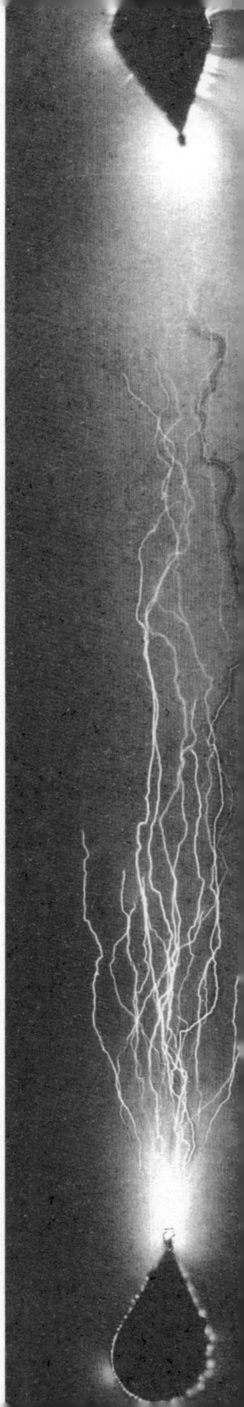

Lord Armstrong, *Electric Movement in Air and Water with Theoretical Inferences* 1897 (coll. Birmingham City Library)

programe of singing lessons for homeless boys into a full scale boys' home in Barnsbury Square, which she ran for twenty years. She was a devout Congregationalist.

In her books she explains how she herself discovered Chladni effects by accident in 1885. Seeking a way to measure the intensity of the singing voice, she devised something like a speaking trumpet, but with a horizontal, rubber membrane over the trumpet end. She sprinkled sand on the membrane, planning to measure how high it jumped when she sang into the tube. Instead she noticed regular patterns in the sand with some notes and intensities. She developed two sets of figures, intending to visualise voice properties: one set from observations of varieties of powder and liquid patterns on the membranes; the other, her impression figures, including banded spiral and cloudlike forms, made using a version of the apparatus that faced downwards, the vibrating membrane passed across a glass plate coated with one of a number of coloured liquids.

The Hand Eidophone.

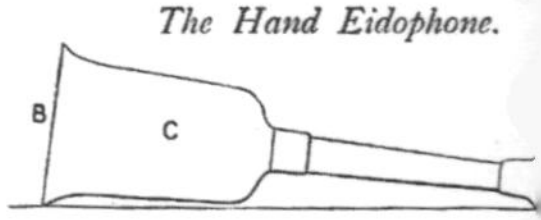

Her 1891 book has a foreword by **Walter Besant**, which implies that the figures should be taken in some way as manifestations of the spirit, but Watts Hughes's own emphasis is on the scientific and musical properties of the figures. The foreword has gone by 1904, leaving only a hint of mystery in the plant-like forms of some of her figures and a pious suggestion in her introduction that her figures may help with interpretation of certain rather challengingly unspecified passages in the Bible. Otherwise she emphasises the various properties of the singing voice, expressed in the figures.

Expressed, not plotted out, is the word. She described a feeling of extraordinary release from resistance at the point where the apparatus suddenly began to respond to the singer with patterns. As in music, her images gain interest as they take on overtones, not pure tones. They are, in many ways, a unique discovery of meaning in noise.

Spirited Vibrations?

The images made by **Margaret Watts Hughes** in the late 1800s depend on interference and adhesion patterns caused when a vibrating elastic membrane is pulled away from a glass plate covered with watercolour paint. The viscosity of the paint affects the adhesion patterns, producing a variety of marks either geometric and regular or unpredictable and organic, resembling plants. These images prefigure the decalcomania works of Max Ernst and Oscar Dominguez. But whereas the latter sought to exploit chance, Mrs Hughes pursued means of visualising sound in all its subtle nuances of sensory information.

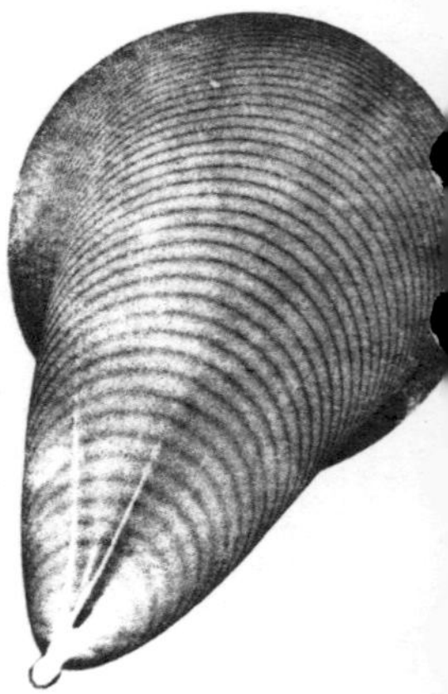

This represents the note

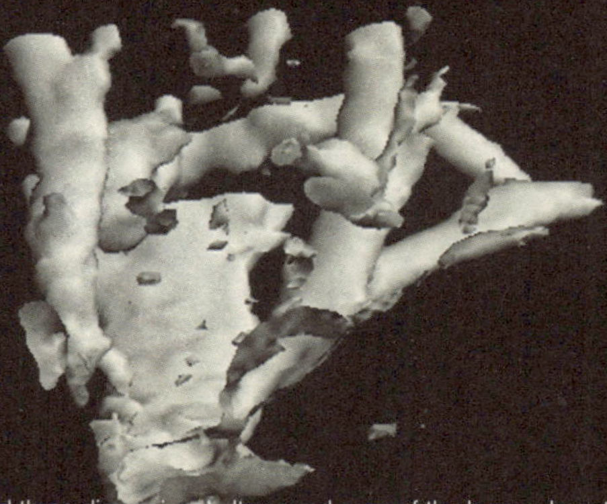

An uncleaned three dimensional ultrasound scan of the human hepatic system produced by Andrew Gee and Richard Prager.
By attaching an electromagnetic position sensing device to the ultrasound probe, 2D ultrasound images can be positioned in a 3D space. The colour signals are visual representations of the Doppler shift in the acoustic signal, highlighting moving material, in this case the hepatic blood vessels inside the liver.
Unwanted data, artifact, (a result of the ultrasound process caused by too much movement, pressure, incorrect settings or other physical considerations) is usually cleaned to foreground the intended subject more clearly.

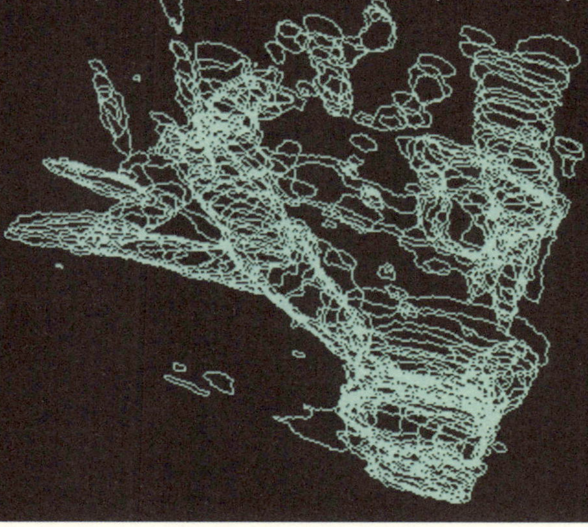

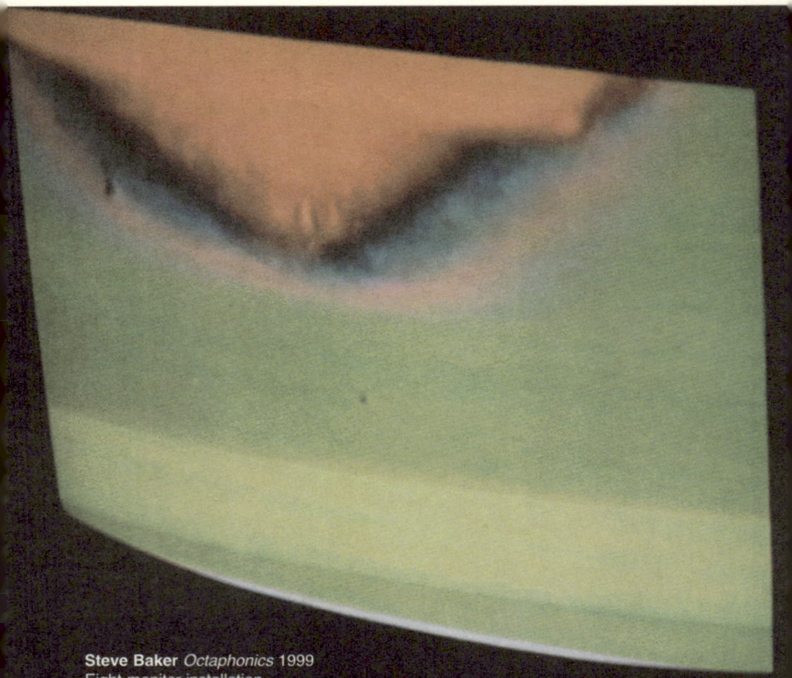

Steve Baker *Octaphonics* 1999
Eight-monitor installation
Octaphonics is based on the translation between audio and visual counterparts.

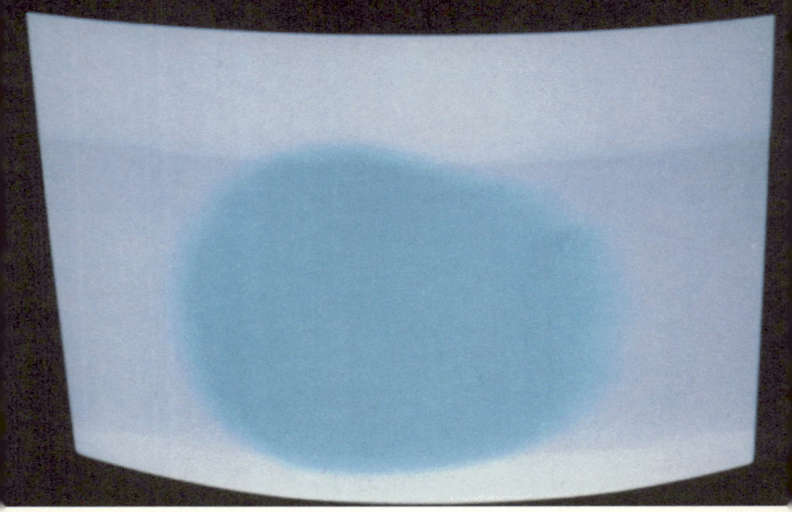

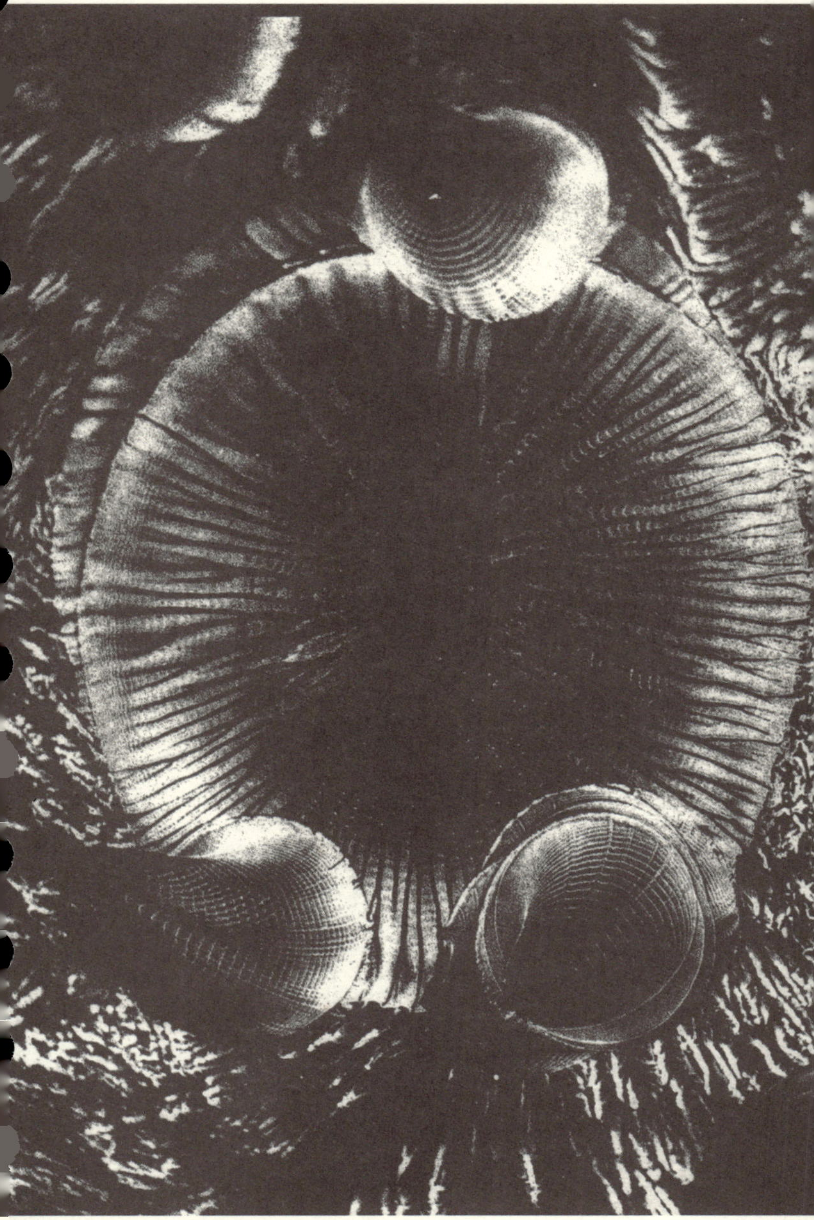

Margaret Watts Hughes Voice Figures 1891
from *Impression Figures & Linear Curves, Group EX*
and "Linear Curves, Group F" (left)

David Phillips Art historian. Former lecturer in Museum Studies,University of Manchester, and Curator at the Castle Museum, Nottingham. His work into the origins of abstraction in the 19th century has led to a comparative study of scientific imaging and spiritualist visualisations.

William George Armstrong (1810 -1900) Hydraulic engineer and co-founder of Armstrong Vickers munitions manufactory. From the 1860s, Lord Armstrong lived at Cragside, a great Northumberland palace outfitted with a full laboratory. In 1897, in collaboration with local cameraman John Worsnop, he published a remarkable study of patterns made by discharging electricity across photographic plates.

Margaret Watts Hughes (died 1907) An independent researcher into the visualisation of sound, whose reputation depends almost solely on two books published in 1891 and 1904.

Georg Christoph Lichtenberg (1742 -1799) Satirist, theatre critic and professor of experimental philosophy at Göttingen University. His 1777 experiments with patterns made by electric discharge through glass have been cited as the origins of photo-copying.

Ernst Florenz Friedrich Chladni (1756 -1827) German lawyer and amateur musician. After experimenting with improvements to the glass harmonica, in 1787 he published a collection of sand figures produed by drawing a violin bow across glass plates, later shown to Napoleon in Paris in 1808. His experiments are fundamental to our present understanding of sound.

Friedlieb Ferdinand Runge (1794 -1867) Berlin chemist who first studied the effects of deadly nightshade, then from 1831 became an industrial specialist in synthesizing brightly coloured dyes from coal tar. In 1850, Runge published the first systematic study of chromatography: concentric circles of different coloured substances diffused through paper.

Annie Besant (1847 -1933) Fabian socialist and atheist converted to Theosophy in 1893. She went to India, campaigned for Indian independence, 'discovered' Krishnamurti, and announced her adopted son was the Messiah.

Walter Besant (1836-1901) Annie's brother-in-law, a Cambridge-trained mathematician who taught in Mauritius. Later, a Hampstead Freemason, novelist and brilliant antiquarian.

Steve Baker Contemporary American musician. Recent graduate of the University of Michigan with studies in printmaking and sound, he performs in the ambient / atmospheric band *Tomorrowland*.

Andrew Gee and Richard Prager Department of Engineering, Cambridge University researching 3D ultrasound imaging.

Does DNA have a pulse?

DNA and Music

MERRILL GARNETT (in conversation with Ben Neill and Bill Jones about his own research and its relation to their installation *Pulse 4,6,7,8*)

In 1997 Ben Neill and Bill Jones began their collaboration on light/sound installations that resonate like pulsed biological systems. During that same period Jones began working with Dr. Merrill Garnett on a book about Garnett's cancer research in biochemical energetics. Garnett's electro-analytic measurements reveal the presence of a second genetic code by which DNA segments and cell membranes, exchange ultra-low frequency sinusoidal currents. His theory is that these pulsed currents are the basis of all physiologic pulses and determine the polarization, charge, and folding of enzymes, nucleic acids, and membrane phospholipids. The restoration of these charge transfer pathways forms the basis of new methods of medical management (hot-wiring) of diseases of failure of cell differentiation such as cancer or psoriasis. Investigators at the State University of New York at Stony Brook, the University of Utah, and Columbia University have collaborated on his first hot-wire: palladium DNA reductase. This is the first non-toxic chemotherapy, a liquid crystal polymer complex of palladium and lipoic acid. In 1998 Jones' separate collaborations with Garnett and Neill found common ground in terms of the numerical ratios used in the sound light compositions and in Garnett's research.

"In working to develop a safe chemotherapy, I assumed that gene behaviors existed beyond those for replicating code and synthesizing RNA and proteins; that living gene material must programmatically energise the organism. I looked for substances that contributed electrons to DNA or took them away.

The discovery was that palladium lipoic acid polymers contribute a charge to DNA, and proved to be non-toxic cancer chemotherapy agents. We went on from there to the idea that the charge must make a circuit - a current going into the cell and a current returning. My concern being that electrons released from the DNA would be oxidants and would imperil the integrity of DNA at the "G" base, as many mutagens and carcinogens do.

We couldn't just remove electrons from DNA. Adding them tends to be healing and repairing; removing them is fraught with side-effects. I conjectured that the part of the DNA to release current might be coiled around a protein to stabilize its structure, which would also place its charge density in a resonant state, so that after discharging it would quickly be replenished.

In the chromosome, structures called nucleosomes which are DNA coiled around histone proteins exist by the billions. They are found all through the chromosomes. This is exciting because the nucleosome is characteristically a stabilising presence. As a coil, it has electronic inductance, and since we have a series of coils, we have a series inductance circuit. DNA current passes initially through the helix in a state

Bouquet Pattern resulting from the destruction of palladium lipoic acid fern pattern by an electromagnet.

where it can discharge its field energy. Hence we have a pulse within the DNA interacting with other biomolecules like the membrane. The pulse can go in and come out, and the DNA is not imperiled. This proves an interesting model for the biological pulse.

We now have found two additional drugs that remove electrical charge from DNA, apparently from the nucleosome.

I've shown that isolated molecules not only discharge into one another as a part of this circuit, but that they have a variety of frequencies. They cross distances greater than 30 angstroms. We call this long range electron transfer. Energy catalysts in liquid crystal form can transfer charges further than 30 angstroms, their dendrameric or branching structures explain their electronic continuum in the cell. It's hard to believe until you see the fern pattern of the palladium liquid crystal polymer.

When we were doing preliminary electrochemical tests on the palladium complex and calf thymus DNA, we found charges being transferred at certain frequencies. The ratio of the first frequencies was 6 :7 : 8. I had just completed my book *First Pulse* with Bill Jones and was excited to see Bill Jones and Ben Neill's installation *Pulse 48*, which musically explored the harmonics of the numbers 4, 6, 7 and 8. These numeric relations have efficiency in an equational relationship. The installation not only coincided numerically, the computer-generated sound and light created an aesthetic.

I would expect there to be formula relationships in music. Forms that are efficient. If there are harmonics in the organism, its physiology will recognize certain signals. This would create the possibility of aesthetic relation. I look at music as one of those biological functions by which we recognize something within us and outside of us to be the same. I'm hoping everyone will be able to appreciate the music in the installation performance and in my experiments.

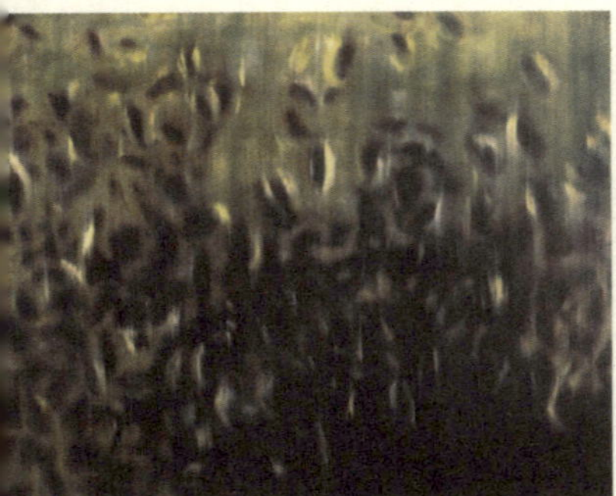

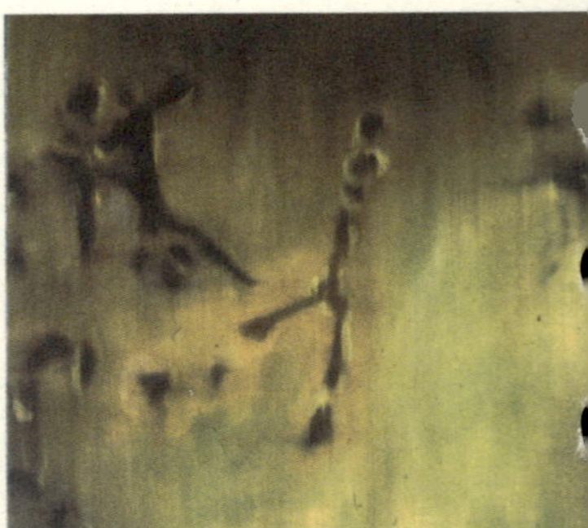

Two paintings by Joy Garnett based on photographs of Monkey Kidney Carcinomas before and after treatment with the Palladium Complex. Oil on Canvas 1998

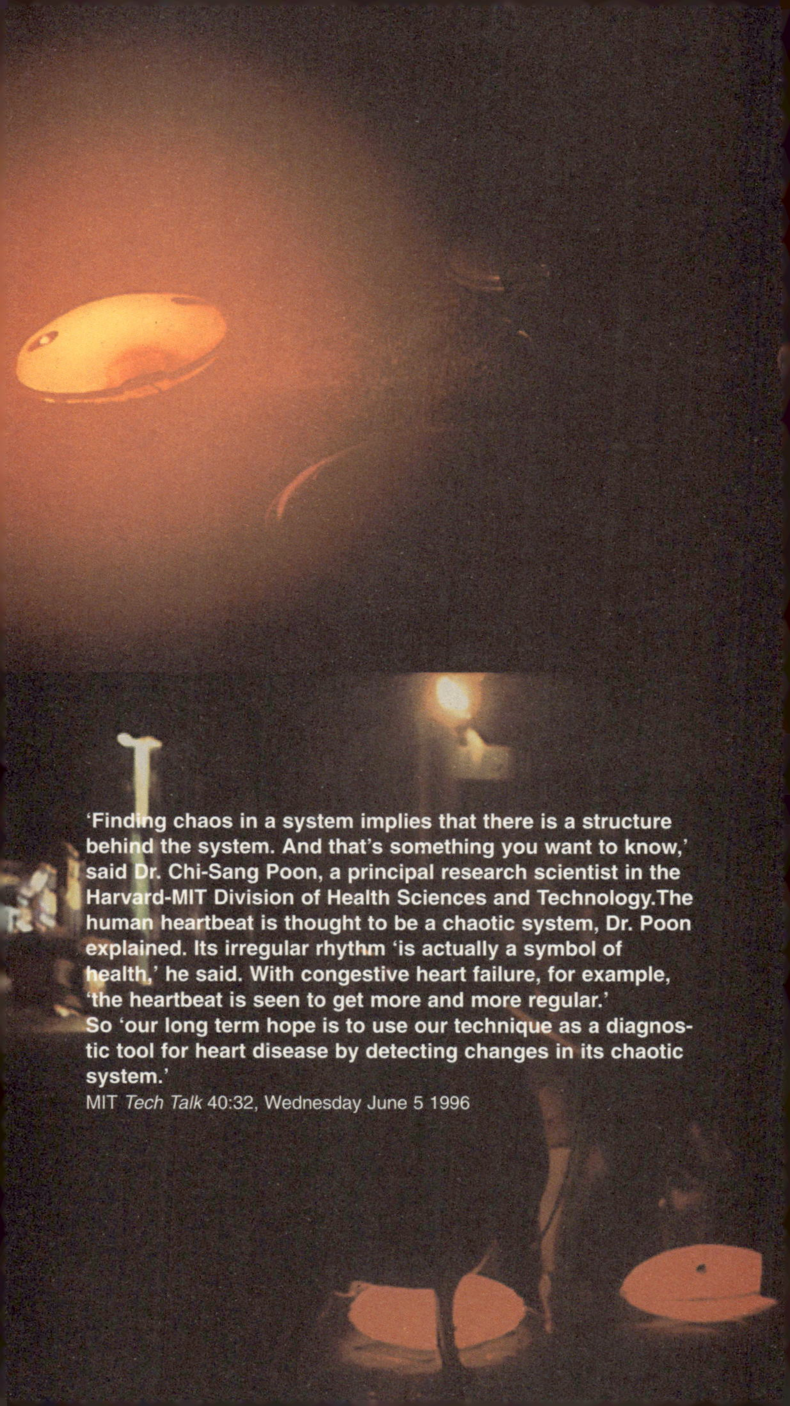

'Finding chaos in a system implies that there is a structure behind the system. And that's something you want to know,' said Dr. Chi-Sang Poon, a principal research scientist in the Harvard-MIT Division of Health Sciences and Technology. The human heartbeat is thought to be a chaotic system, Dr. Poon explained. Its irregular rhythm 'is actually a symbol of health,' he said. With congestive heart failure, for example, 'the heartbeat is seen to get more and more regular.'
So 'our long term hope is to use our technique as a diagnostic tool for heart disease by detecting changes in its chaotic system.'

MIT *Tech Talk* 40:32, Wednesday June 5 1996

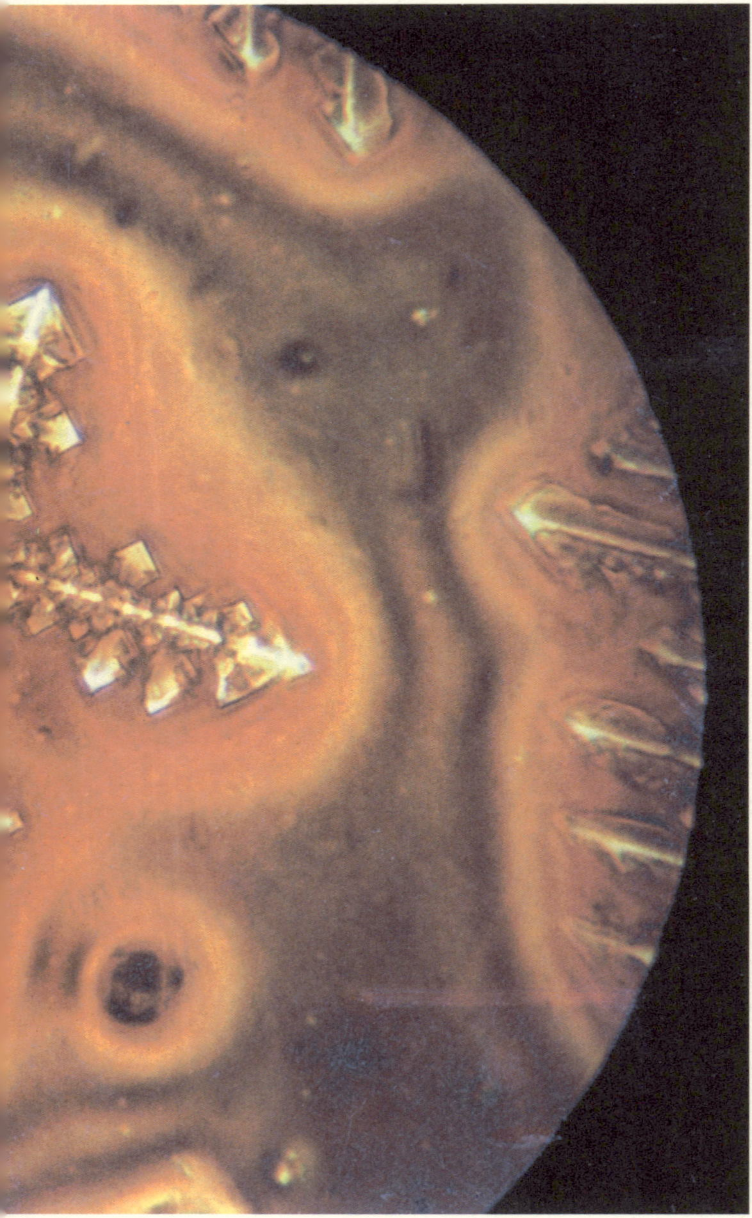

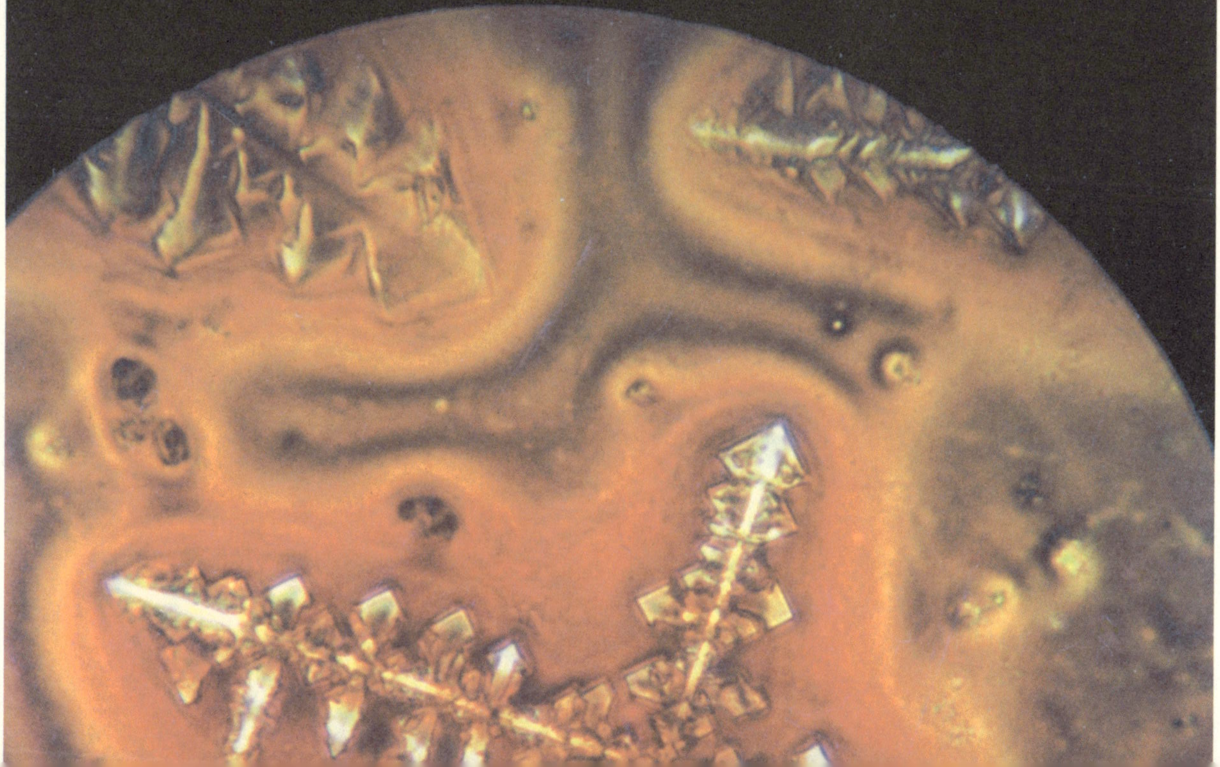

Cross Pattern. The destruction of palladium lipoic acid fern pattern by tobacco smoke,.DNA and Music

Dr Merrill Garnett A research Scientist at the Department of Biochemistry and Cell Biology, State University of New York, Stony Brook. After almost 40 years of independent research into non-toxic chemotherapy, his approach to energy transfer is gaining acceptance. His work on the effects of palladium-lipoic acid on cancer continues in a drug development program.

Bill Jones Editor of ArtByte (the Magazine of Digital Culture). He currently collaborates with Ben Neill and is represented by the Sandra Gering Gallery in New York. Neill and Jones' most recent exhibition was for the millennial opening of Rose Center (formerly the Hayden Planetarium) at the Natural History Museum in New York.

Ben Neill Musician, sound and light artist, protegé of minimalist composer LaMonte Young, also worked with John Cage. Has carried many of his mathematical concepts and ideas on resonance from the world of art into the world of contemporary pop music, and it was in this sphere that he began to work with Bill Jones on computer-controlled interactive slide pieces.

Joy Garnett Painter whose works derive from scientific imagery, and the intersections between science, art, and popular culture. She received training in environmental biology at McGill University and studied painting at the Ecole des Beaux Arts in Paris.

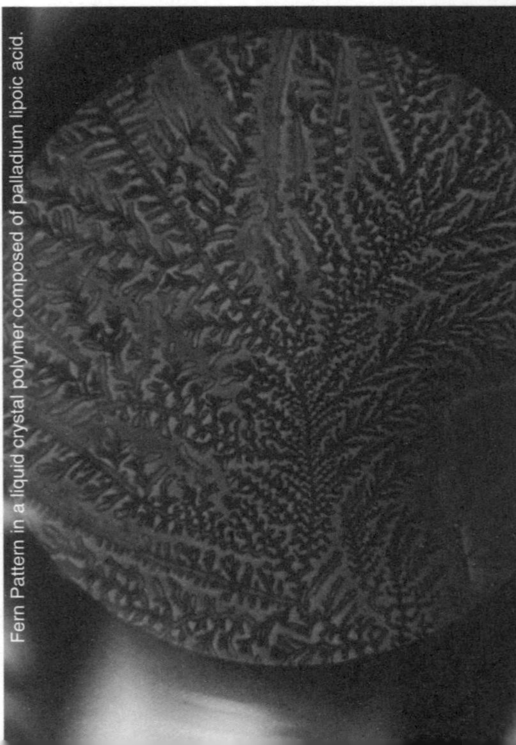

Fern Pattern in a liquid crystal polymer composed of palladium lipoic acid.

How do supermodels get a life?

The DNA Model

SORAYA DE CHADAREVIAN

The double helix, representing the structure of DNA that carries the genetic information of all organisms, has become a cultural icon. It is available as a DIY kit, it decorates T shirts and mugs, it appears in the form of a perfume bottle. Salvador Dali and other artists have appropriated it. It appears on the millenium stamp. The twenty-first century, we are told, will be the era of DNA. Specialised laboratories around the globe are now engaged in a costly effort to establish the full base sequence of the human genome, as well as that of a series of model organisms — including yeast, a nematode worm, a fruitfly and mouse. (The next challenge is to "translate" the genetic information stored in a universal four letter code and assign a function to the almost endless string of DNA bases.) Experts predict that in a few years time we will all carry in our pocket compact discs with the full text of our genome, which we can pull out and exclaim: "Ecce homo — behold the human — me !"

The first double helical model of DNA was presented by James Watson and Francis Crick at the Cavendish Laboratory in Cambridge in spring 1953. The two researchers, one American, the other English, are credited with having started the information revolution in biology. But should we attempt to make a pilgrimage to the original model, as the faithful are supposed to do, we will be sorely disappointed. Something described as "the nearest there is to the original model" is kept in the Health Matters Gallery of the Science Museum in London, which preserves scientific relics — an appropriate enough home for a scientific cult object. Inquiry reveals, however, that the exhibit contains only a few original bits; most of the metal plates, skeletal model-building parts and clamps used for the structure are replicas. The Science Museum model was rebuilt on the basis of the only surviving record of the original structure, a photograph taken by Cambridge photographer Anthony Barrington Brown on the occasion of an open day at the Cavendish in summer 1953, when the Watson-Crick model was on display. Intended for a report for TIME magazine, the photograph, now an all-pervasive image, was apparently not considered significant enough to be published at the time. While the model in the photo, once object of intense discussion, but soon superceded by more refined models built at King's College London, slowly fell to pieces and was finally disassembled. Possibly it was not even the one actually used by Watson and Crick for deducing the structure – they themselves differ in their recollections.

What, then, was the impact of the Watson-Crick model at the time? Its most striking and novel feature lay in the pairing of the four bases, already known to be part of the building blocks of nucleic acids, hence also in the resultant complementary structure of the two strands of the molecule. This feature suggested a copying mechanism for the genetic material, which related the structure of the molecule to what some proclaimed as the fundamental secret of life itself: the replication of living matter. Yet the helical structure of the molecule, in particular, posed serious theoretical problems for the actual mechanism by which replication could occur. For this reason, Crick himself, reflecting on the historical importance of the DNA model, reckoned that the helical structure of DNA represented a "nuisance".

The notion of genetic information was not itself original to Watson and Crick's work. As historian Lily Kay has shown, the language of "information" and the very notion of a "genetic code" entered genetics even before DNA displaced proteins as a candidate for the hereditary material. These terms were imported into biology – as well as many other social sciences – from cybernetics, information theory and computer sciences, whose development was deeply rooted in World War II and the Cold War. John von Neumann and Norbert Wiener were themselves keenly interested in extending the use of their new tools to biological systems. While the application of the technical notion of information to genetics failed, the language of information remained.

In their second paper on the genetical implications of the DNA structure, Watson and Crick concluded that the sequence of bases most likely represented "the code which carries the genetical information". They used this notion without much ceremony. Which confirms that by 1953 the concept of a genetic *code* was by no means new, and the notion of information, in its metaphoric or commonplace sense, was widely used. Apparently, the picture Crick had in mind was the telegraphing of information in Morse code. Only later did he realise that the term genetic *cipher* would have been more appropriate. The astrophysicist, military advisor and children's writer George Gamow proposed the first genetic code, following the publication of Watson and Crick's model, Gamow was also a member of the scientific-military network to which von Neumann and Wiener belonged. The actual four letter code of genetic information, however, was not to be established by crypto-analysis, but instead by biochemical experiments of in vitro synthesis.

It seems, then, that the double helix model of DNA acquired the key role in the biological information revolution it is granted today only in retrospect. Rather than being the cause, it is instead a symbol of our current obsession with information and with the reduction of complex phenomena to sets of encoded instructions.

Opposite top:The Representation of the Genetic Code. This chart shows how genetic information is translated into amino acids, the building blocks of proteins.
Opposite bottom: The internal structure of neon, meta-neon, argon and metargon, as described by Charles Leadbeater through the facility of astral vision or theosophical clairvoyancy. Leadbeater and Annie Besant systematically explored the elements of the periodic table in this way in their book *Occult Chemistry* (1908); their findings in some ways prefigured the discovery of the 'isotopes' of neon, argon and the other elements.

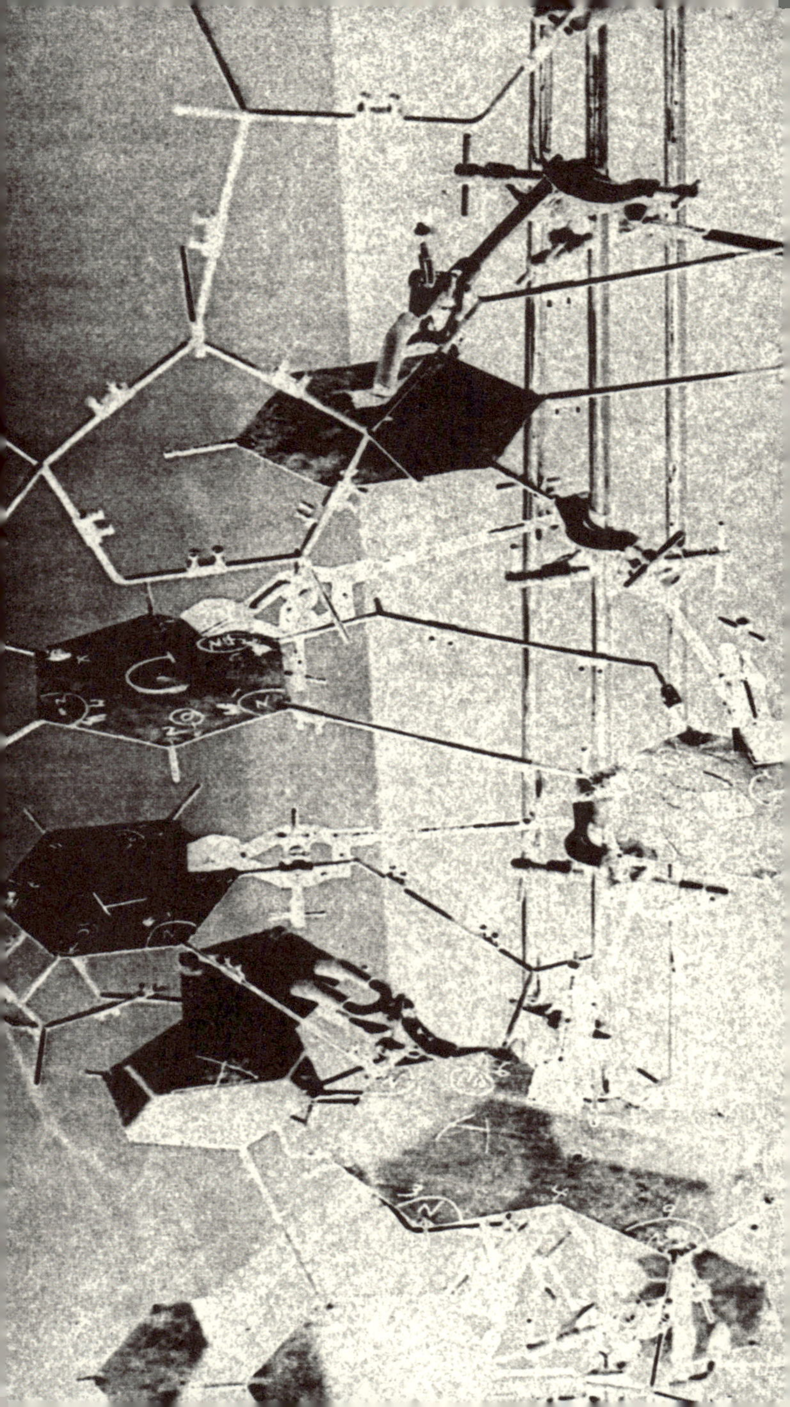

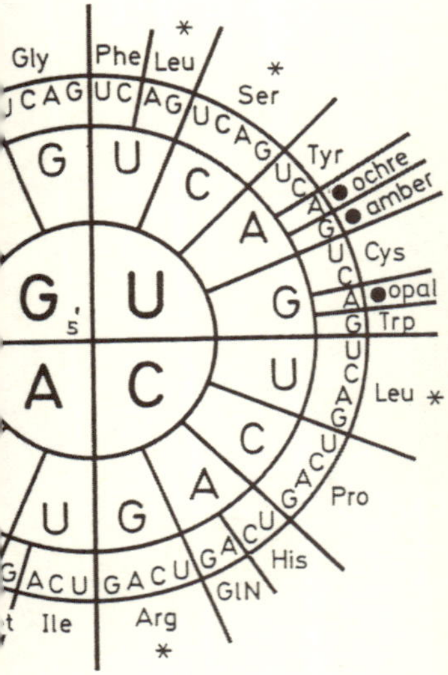

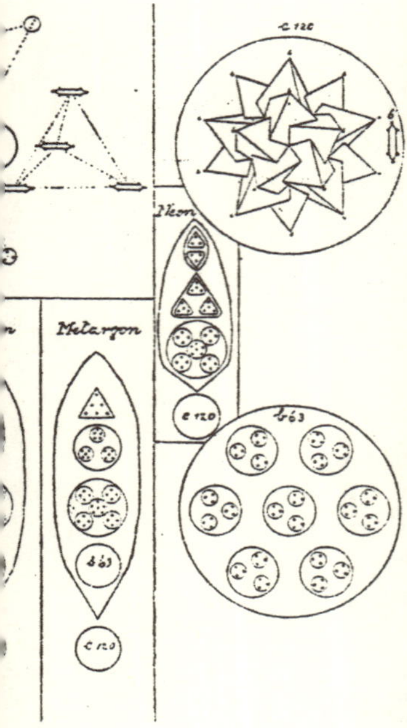

6
2
7

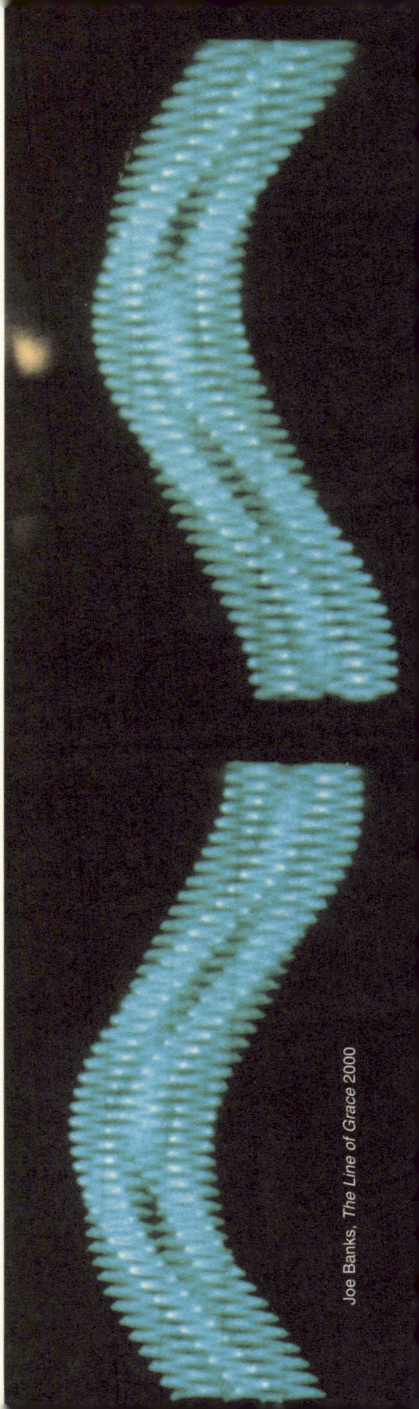

Joe Banks, *The Line of Grace* 2000

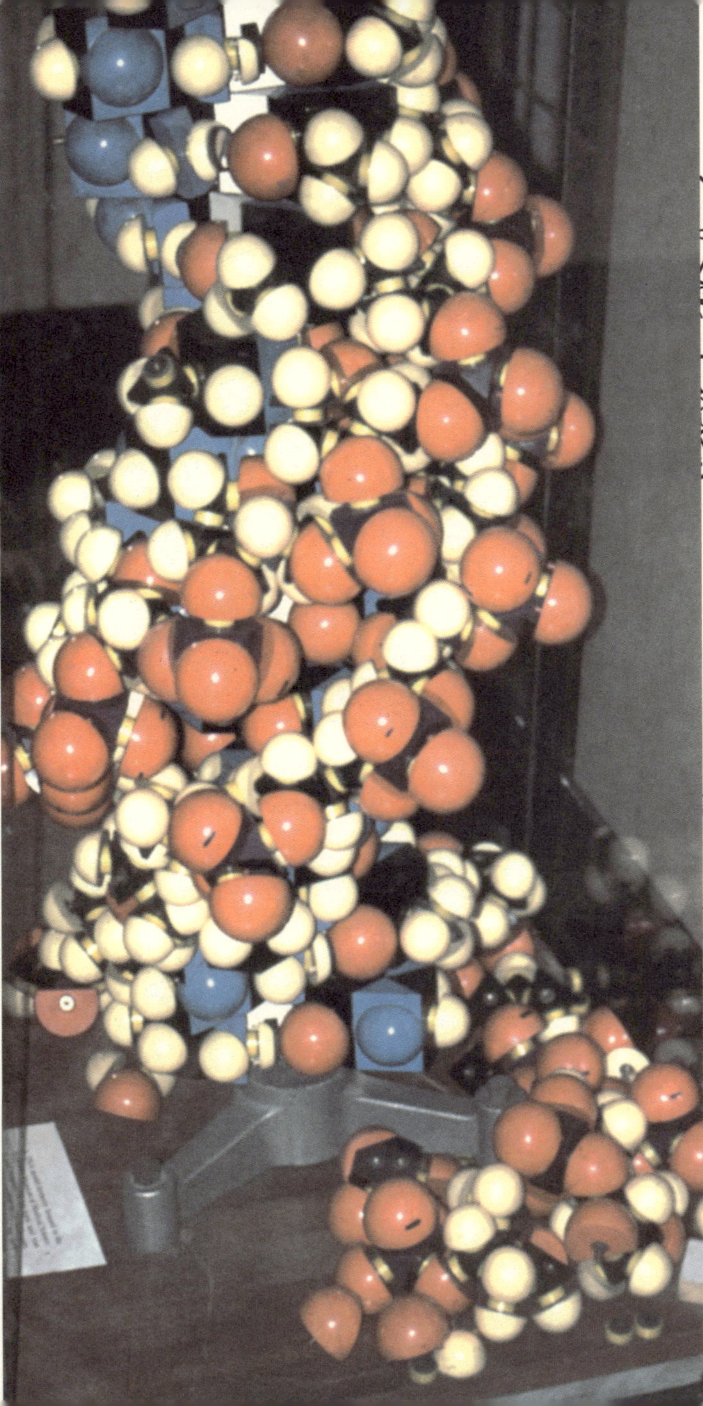

A damaged DNA model

Soraya de Chadarevian Senior research associate and affiliated lecturer at the Department of History and Philosophy of Science, Cambridge.

The MP Group At the Cavendish Laboratory, University of Cambridge. The group consists of: Ian Smith, Andrew Bleloch, Mick Brown, Archie Howie, Stephen Bond, Nadia Stelmashenko and Yasuo Ito.

Joe Banks Sound artist whose *Analysis of Beauty* is a tribute to William Hogarth's work of the same name.

The texture of the surface of Atoms?

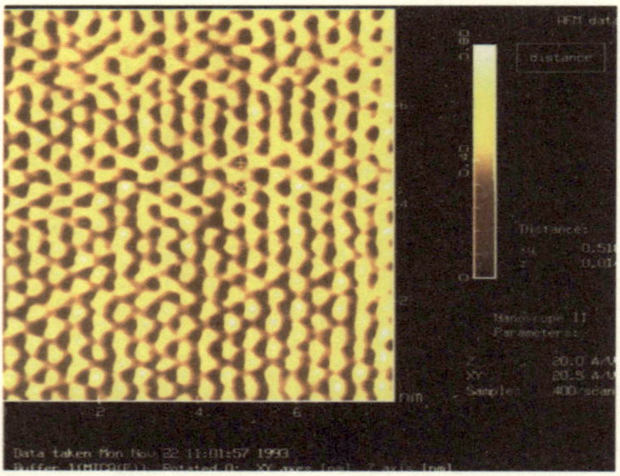

Atomic Force Microscope (AFM) is a variation on the Scanning Tunneling Microscope (STM) capable of a resolution of less than a nanometer. The image above is an Atomic resolution AFM image of Mica. Mica (consisting of linked silicon-oxygen tetrahedral groups) cleaves along flat planes of atoms that are revealed by the AFM. Note that the ring of atoms surrounding each dark spot form a hexagonal array, characteristic of cleaved mica.

The conducting polymers were examined on a molecular scale in the STM.The subject of investigation was how the polymers arranged themselves on various substrates. This provided important information on the degree of ordering of the material, something that can significantly alter the electronic properties of the molecules.

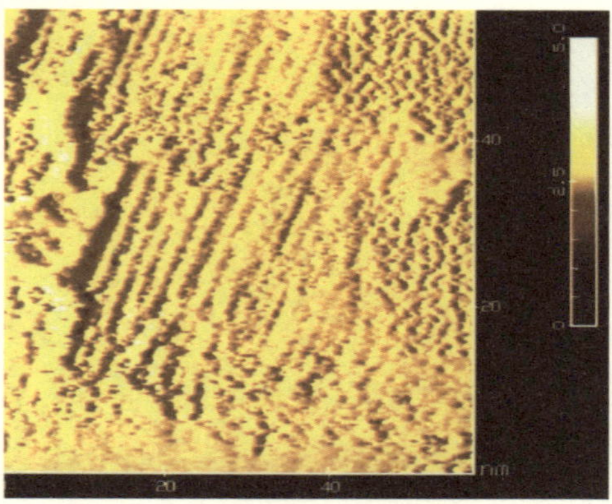

Does DNA mirror life?

The Imagination of Matter

KATHLEEN ROGERS

Maize mythology is full of anthropomorphic and biological imagery and the metaphorical explanations often reveal empirically verifiable facts. Myths surrounding its genesis (its DNA) are an example – the ultimate ancient high technology and the basis of an entire culture. Through DNA profiling it may be possible to find in the residue of maize matter an informational field with structural resonances that echo its origins in pre-history.

The scientific investigative procedure for extracting DNA from pre-historic maize involves irreversible destructive analysis. Several ideal specimens were identified in the Museum of Archaeology in Cambridge and with the help of Robin Boast and Martin Jones at the museum it was arranged that the analysis of a sample of pre-historic maize from El Reigo caves in Puebla Mexico could be carried out at the department of Biomolecular Sciences, University of Manchester under the supervision of Fabio de Oliverira Freitas (A microbiologist making DNA comparisons between ancient and modern maize in Brazil).The process of separating and identifing the DNA is slow, precise technologically demanding, volitile and not guarenteed success. Working on microscopic level the process is painstaking and involves many stages, each of which effects the isolation of the DNA.

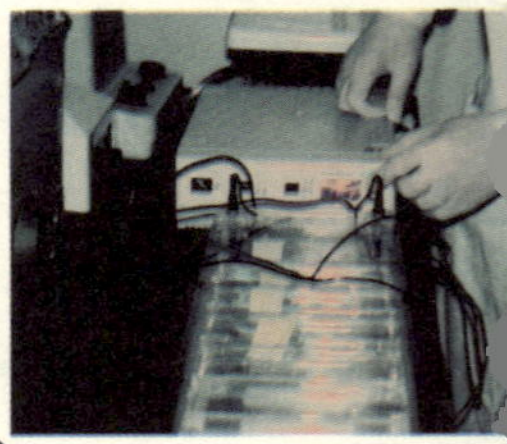

In sterile laboratory conditions the sample of maize is ground to dust in a pestle and mortar. A liquid buffer is added and the resulting mix separated using centrifugal force. The resulting substance is incubated, spun again made into a pellet, re-suspended and turned into a gel. The aim of the skilled technician is to optimise the reactions through control of the time, temperature and molecular chemistry in order to separate the DNA from the specimen. Using Enzymes of different concentrations the nucleotides are tagged and again exposed to heat, cold, drying and centrifuge. Finally using electrolysis the ions ore driven from one side of the gel to the other and visualised using ultra-violet light. This repeated spinning, pressure, dilution, compression, erosion, absorption and rejection results in a separation of an identifiable DNA sequence of 300 base pairs....or not. It is never exactly predictable.

The methodologies of art offer a similar potential and emotive synthesis while making visible a different level of information that is more difficult to quantify or analyse.The video that was shot during the extraction of the DNA, edited down from 4 hours to just a few minutes, is a meditation upon the complex mediation that was taking place on a 3000 year old sample of Maize from Mexico. It failed to reveal any DNA but contributed some new narratives to this already heavily mythologised food.

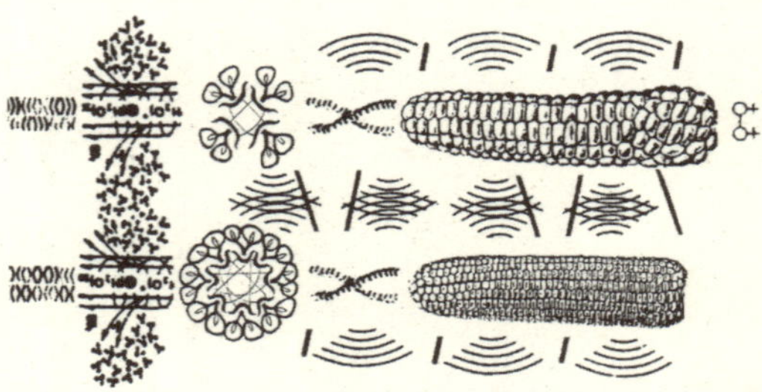

Quantum field conscoiusness of maize DNA based on Penrose and Hameroff

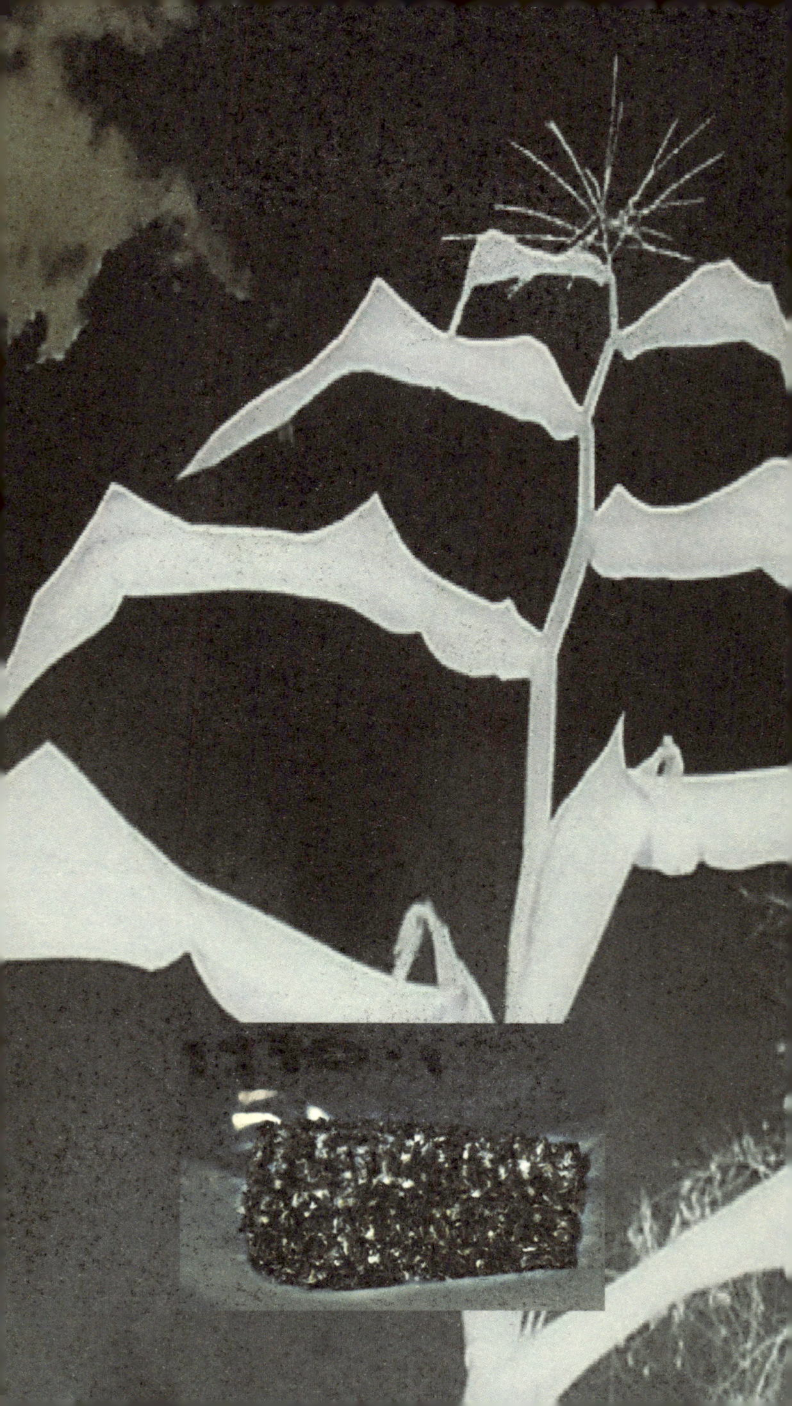

What's the Point?

MIKE LYNCH

What is this small featureless *thing*?
Is it a point, a digit, a speck, a tiny black square, a punctiation mark, elephant dung from 1000 feet? Does it have dimension or shape, or does it symbolise a number or a dimensionless point in space?
Standing alone it represents nothing other than itself, and it is not even clear what it is. For convenience we'll call it a *dot.*

Here are two of them (whatever they are). Two of them equal a pair (2=1)
A pair is not just one and another one; its a unified *thing*. Taken together, the members of the pair frame an empty space between them.
The juxtaposition of the two dots furnishes a context for seeing each dot as a member of the pair and the space between them as an interval.

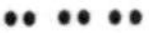

A row of pairs makes a line(2x2x2=1).
Each dot is now a passage point for the line. The spaces between the dots are differentiated into longer and shorter intervals. Both the dots and the emptyness around them have taken on a new contexture.

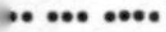

Now we have a series followed by ... an ellipsis.
No longer just dots and intervals, this mixture of symbolism and punctuation enables us to extend our imaginations into numerical and grammatical infinities.

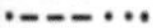

Dots and dashes - a code,
Our dots now dwell in time, together with dashes and silent intervals, making up and elemental encryption device: a translation carrying a voice pleading for help from one distant node to another.

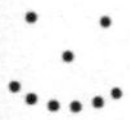

A pictorial icon.
Pebbles on the face of a snowman. Each dot makes up a picture element - a pixel. No longer mere points in space, punctuation marks or symbols, they now outline features on a visible object.

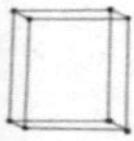

Connect the dots together and add another illusory dimension.
The dots are now pivotal points in a virtual lattice that extends beyond the surface on which they are printed.

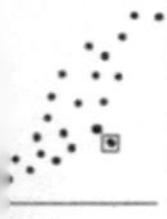

This dot works for science.
It is a data point: a point on a plot thick with other points.
What it does and what it represents depends on what surrounds it. It is an elementary cultural object - in turns an objective signal, noise, part of a picture, a numerical sign or a combination of all these. What any element *says* depends on the work thet composes the space in which it dwells. The space, with its mathematics, graphic frame and hints of resemblance is a gallery of innovation attended by a noisy assemblage of scientific characters.

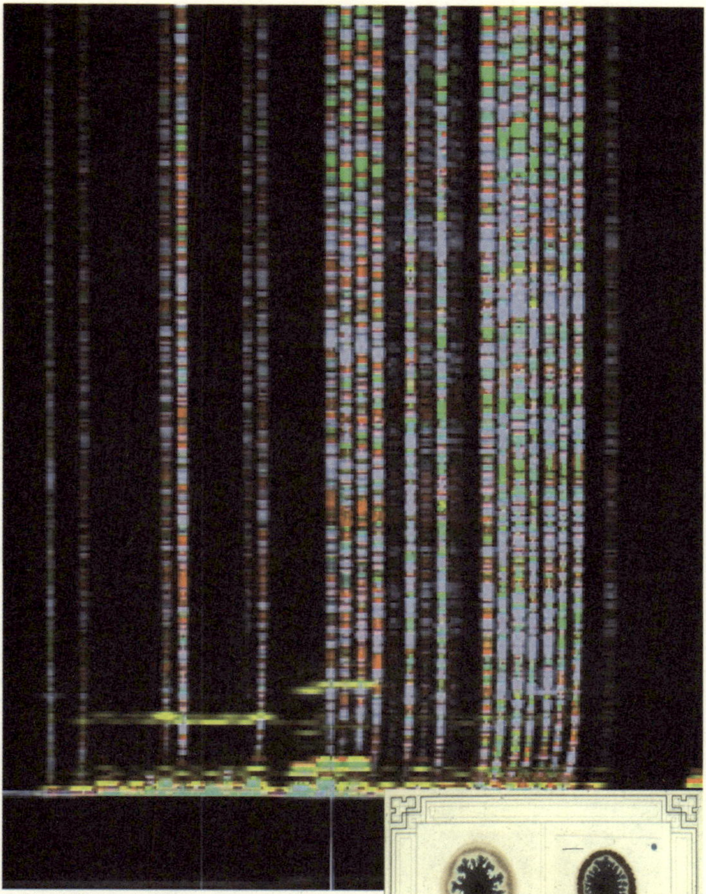

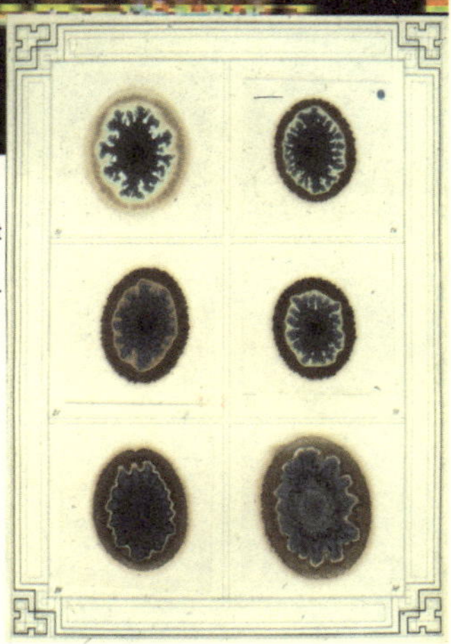

Fabio de Oliverira Freitas
This image is the result of DNA sequencing of ancient and contemporary maize from the Americas. The target genes are transformed into four colours using laser spectroscopy. Each colour represents a different molecular length of the nucleic acid base and is alternately identified by a letter of the DNA alphabet ACGT.

Friedlieb Ferdinand Runge *Chromatogram* 1850
The principles of Runge's Chromatography have led indirectly to todays developments in DNA profiling.

Kathleen Rogers is a research fellow for Imaging and Digital Culture at the West Surrey College of Art and Design Farnham. She has collaborated with a number of artists and scientists including John Latham, James Turrell and Jack Corney. This project has resulted from many years work with Maize in both Mexico and the UK

Michael Lynch An Ethnomethodologist based at Cornell University. He has written on a variety of subjects including birdwatching, satellite imaging and the use of DNA profiling in the OJ Simpson case.

Roger Guillemin Neurobiologist awarded the Nobel Prize for his work on enzymes of the thyroid. He was the subject of a book by Bruno Latour, *Laboratory Life*. He has been working as an artist for many years and his work was exhibited at the last Venice Biennale.

Friedlieb Ferdinand Runge (1794 -1867) Berlin chemist who first studied the effects of deadly nightshade, then from 1831 became an industrial specialist in synthesising brightly coloured dyes from coal tar. In 1850, Runge published the first systematic study of chromatography: concentric circles of different coloured substances diffused through paper.

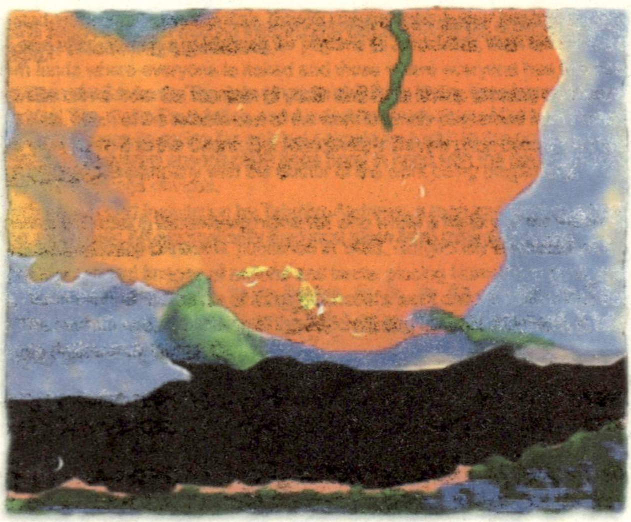

Roger Guillemin
Matter Mythology 72x90 cms 1997 Iris print on paper

Matter Mythology was inspired by a series of conversations during a gathering of Nobel Laureates with the physicist Murray Gell-Mann, the originator of the concept of quarks as the elementary particles of matter.
Guillemin's images are rooted in an American Abstract Expressionist tradition dependent on gesture and colour relationships. The images are computer originated and printed using the technologically advanced Iris Printer - a continuous stream ink jet printer originally designed for the textile industry but popular with artists due to its high resolution and relative longevity.

Who's Minding the Garden?

SIMON SCHAFFER

"The relation and likeness between two brothers is an expression of the same phenomenon as the relation and likeness beteen two leaves on the same tree"
William Bateson, 1901

So we're all related, but we're all different. Genetics is the twentieth-century science which relates the way we are to individual, specific, discrete units; and then to one kind of uniform stuff, the ingenious molecules of DNA. Go back to 1900, and look how then and now careful experiments on peas in a pod carried difficult messages about the discrete and the continuous building-blocks of life.

No-one is more aware of the enormous work needed to keep things going on in the same pleasing pattern of inheritance and variation than are keen gardeners. In May 1900, London's Royal Horticultural Society invited a distinguished Cambridge biologist, William Bateson, to give them a talk on questions of plant breeding. Bateson knew all about breeding. His father had been the Master of his own college, St John's; his sister was a distinguished historian and energetic feminist at nearby Newnham. One day, his son would help invent cybernetics. Bateson made himself an expert on plant hybridization, then invented genetics. Every reader of Charles Darwin, a man well at home with the plant breeders, knew that the raw material for evolution was the way offspring differed from their parents. Darwin thought there were two kinds of variation. He reckoned natural selection worked on one kind, the continuous small differences between siblings. He denied natural selection could ever work on the other kind, discontinuous monstrosities which happen rarely and are scarcely ever fertile.

But there were obvious (and possibly fatal) problems with Darwin's story. Most naturalists reckoned parents' traits were blended in their offspring. Any unusual character generated by small-scale continuous variation would soon be swamped by breeding with the much larger number of normal individuals. Hugo de Vries, a famous Dutch expert on plant breeding, instead supposed that an organism's traits were dependent on individual particulate entities in every cell nucleus of each organism. When these entities suddenly mutated, de Vries argued, a dramatic discontinuous set of new traits would appear. This could generate a new species.

Bateson himself already judged that the "problem of species" was just this: "by what integral steps did the new form come into being?" "What we first require," he thought, "is to know what happens when a variety is crossed with its nearest allies. It must be recorded how many of the offspring resembled each parent, and how many showed characters intermediate between those of the parents".

On the train down from Cambridge on 8 May 1900, Bateson leafed through the pages of a new paper by de Vries about experiments on breeding fertile offspring from two different plant varieties. Inheritance did not blend, but could be subjected to the statistics of discrete numbers. So once he got to London, Bateson told the Horticultural Society to keep their own numerical records to check how often the character of one or other parent variety predominated in the offspring made by breeding crosses. Then back in Cambridge, Bateson went to the university library. In de Vries' original paper, there was an intriguing reference to an essay by a Moravian monk, **Gregor Mendel**, published back in 1865. Bateson found Mendel's paper on a library shelf, and saw at once how to use the monk's fascinating experiments with hybridizing peas for his own ambitious purposes.

Try separating two different varieties of garden peas into tall and dwarf characters. If you cross the tall and short pea varieties, the next generation of peas would all be tall. Then cross these tall offspring with each other, and in the next generation a quarter of them would be dwarf. Then, for example, cross this dwarf population with other dwarf plants, and all their offspring would be short. In hybrid peas, it seemed, there was a discrete factor for tallness got from one parent, another factor for shortness from the other parent, and the tall factor predominated over the short one. Bateson soon checked these results with pea varieties, and extended them to chickens and mice, moths and guinea pigs. By 1906, he coined the word 'genetics' to describe the science of inheritance and variation, and by 1909 he was Cambridge's first professor of genetics.

These pea hybrid experiments suggested a new story about inheritance, especially if you assumed that any visible characteristic, like tallness in peas, depends on a pair of factors within the germ cells of the parents. When germ cells are made, these factors are separated and end up in different eggs or sperm. What's in each germ cell would be a random collection of these factors. Bateson thought this kind of Mendelism could be used to base the true theory of evolution, unlike that he read in Darwin, on the sudden and discontinuous emergence of character from the observed patterns of these inherited factors.

But there was also a clever way of giving these factors a home - the dark staining strands inside cell nuclei which cell biologists could see through their microscopes, and which they called chromosomes. Humans have twenty-three pairs of chromosomes; peas have three pairs. By trying to track how these pairs might divide between the cell nuclei of offspring, American biologists soon identified the material of heredity with the stuff inside these chromosomes. They seemed to obey the same sort of laws as those Mendelians constructed for inheritance. By 1909, the word 'gene' had been coined, and the Americans supposed these factors, or genes, must be arranged in very long lines in every chromosome.

This was not the route Bateson wanted to follow. He admired the obvious discontinuities he saw in hybrid offspring; he loathed the speculative attempt to explain these discontinuities by the action of blind matter. Look at chromosomes. They were supposed to be the source of all those vital factors determining the visible characters of living beings. But "the appearance of chromosomes is not suggestive of strings of beads of extreme heterogeneity, but rather with that seen for example in drying mud". A dried mud look-alike was not a plausible nor appropriate basis for life.

Bateson moved down to a London suburb to run the high-powered John Innes Institute for plant breeding. He set out to show how "a living thing is not matter", but a "system vortex through which matter is passing". Instead of the muddy chromosomes and their unobservable strings of genes, which would make life's development into nothing but the sorting of lumps of silent chemicals, he compared the activity inside the cell nuclei with transient eddies, spinning whirlpools and the gorgeous patterns made by sound in sand.

These beautifully resonant biological patterns matched Bateson's own fine taste, his collections of Chinese porcelain and Japanese prints, or the etchings of William Blake in which he saw inspiration for his ideas about the fate of civilisation. Bateson reckoned there was an "essential difference between the ideals of democracy and those of biology". The leaders of society should not "abolish class, but provide that each individual shall so far as possible get into the right class and stay there, and usually his children after him". Bateson's hybrid peas certainly showed that inheritance and variation were not dependent on continuous change and blending qualities, but were the direct results of specific, individual, discrete factors which determined the expression of character and directed progressive evolution. They proved inheritance was digitized. But they also helped him use his biology against the noise of modernity, in which true values were being destroyed and "chaos is acclaimed as art".

For Bateson a dried mud look-alike was not a plausible nor appropriate basis for life.

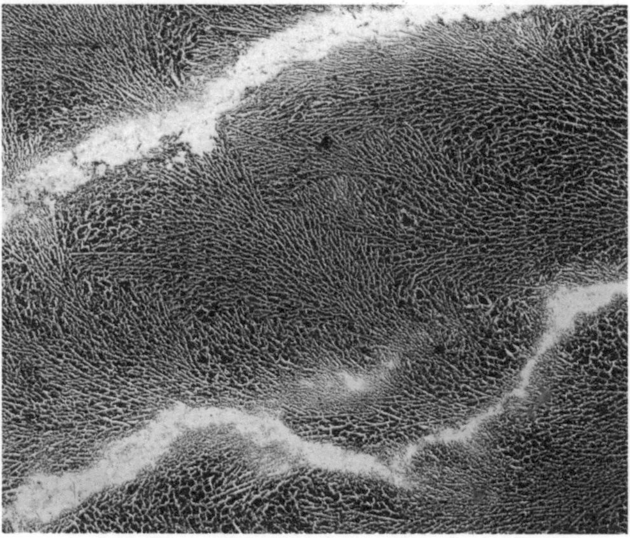

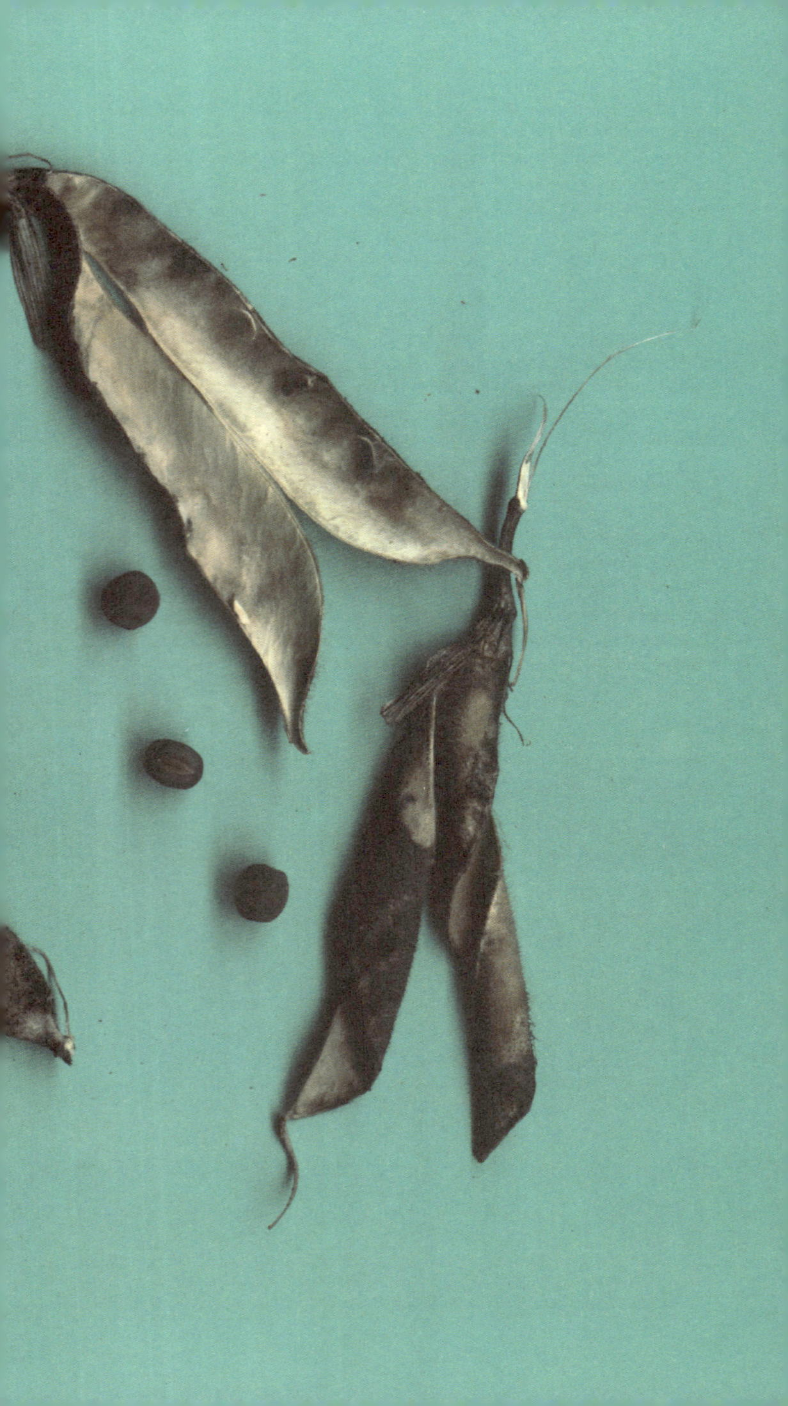

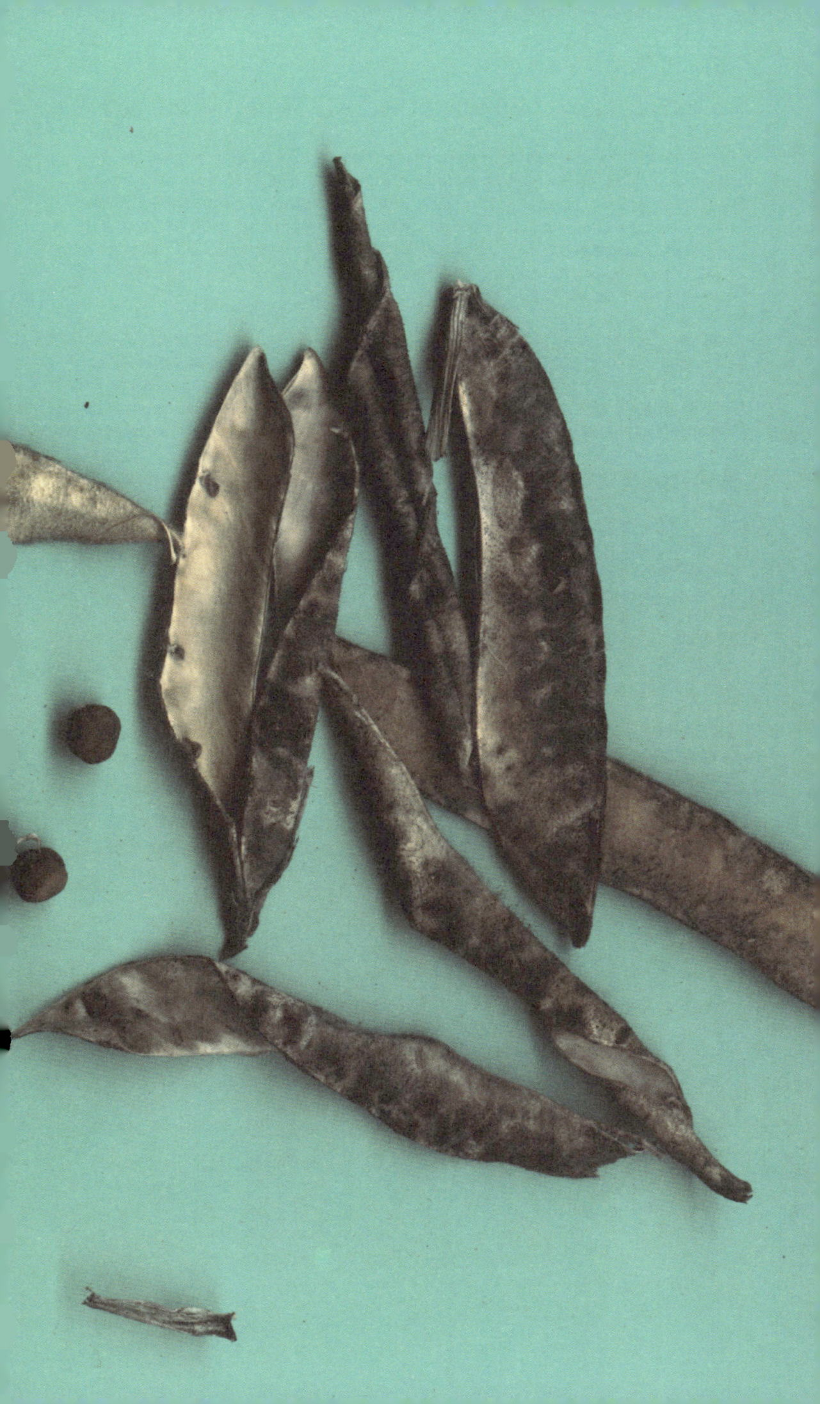

William Bateson (1861-1926) Aesthetic Cambridge natural scientist eminent for his work in Chesapeake Bay and the Russian steppes on embryological development, then on experimental hybridization and arguments for evolution without natural selection. His reading and reinterpretation in 1900 of Mendel's work on breeding peas changed his career and that of genetics, a word Bateson invented in 1905. He loathed the newfangled statistical methods of London biometricians and the ambitions of geneticists who asserted that the agent of heredity was material. From 1910 he ran the John Innes Institute, centre of British horticultural research, and served as trustee of the British Museum.

Johann Gregor Mendel (1822-1884), son of a German-Moravian peasant, joined a monastery at Brno in 1843. Its garden was run by a Hegelian philosopher later forced to migrate to America, but who encouraged Mendel's work on experimental natural history. After successful studies at Vienna University, Mendel started teaching science himself and worked in meteorology. At the monastery, he launched an eight year programme of trials on pea hybrids, about 28,000 plants in total, yielding surprisingly strong evidence for fixed laws of heritability. Mendel became abbot, extended his hybridisation work to bees, and was offered a bank directorship by the government in an unsuccessful attempt to gain his support for their party.

Louis Thomas Jerome Auzoux (1797-1880), the inventor of *plastic* anatomy, a Paris student impressed by the papier maché used to make street puppets, started in 1816 building anatomical models, gained his medical degree, and by 1830 had built a complete papier maché man out of 129 pieces and more than 1100 numbered details. He set up a factory to mass-produce cheaper, more robust anatomical models which soon dominated the medical market.

Wardle/Micalef Piers Wardle is the pseudonym of Lewis Draper, an artist and keyboard player who performs with poet Steve Micalef. Both founder members of the Brixton poets, they have branched out to produce collaborative images.

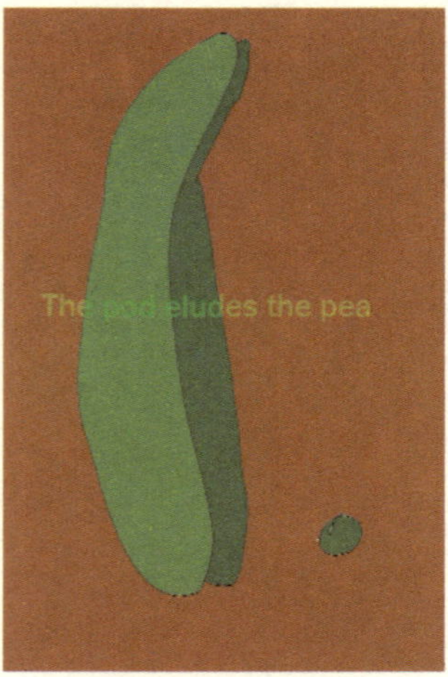

Steve Micalef/Piers Wardle 1999
The Pod Eludes the Pea.

What shape does a chicken taste?

Synaesthesia

ROY PORTER

Synaesthesia denotes the rare capacity to hear colours, taste shapes or experience other unusual sensory blendings. A synaesthete might describe the flavour of a voice or music whose sounds looks like 'shards of glass'. Something sweet may be experienced as bluish/purple, or, seeing the colour red, a synaesthete might detect its 'scent'. Synaesthesia, the word is derived from the Greek syn (together) + aesthesis (perception), seems to have some organic basis. Synaesthetes tend to be high in intelligence, but possessed of skewed cognitive skills: left-right confusion is common. It apparently runs in families. A famous case is of that of the Nabokovs. The Russian novelist, his mother and his son perceived letters and words in colours.

Known for almost 300 years, from the mid-nineteenth century the phenomenon attracted the attention of artistic movements interested in exploring the range or union of the senses. Multimodal concerts of music and light (son et lumiere) were tried out. Colour organs were developed, keyboards equipped with coloured lights as well as musical notes. After the invention of the 'clavecin oculaire', or optical harpsichord, by the eighteenth-century French Jesuit Castel, the nineteenth century brought many attempts to produce a device that could generate music and colour simultaneously on the basis of tone/colour correspondence schemes. Rimington patented the name 'colour-organ' in 1893, and had success in concert halls with his colour-music performances of works by Wagner, Chopin, Bach and Dvorak. But deliberate aesthetic contrivances are to be distinguished from the involuntary experiences of synaesthesia.

The artist Wassily Kandinsky, for example, discovered his synaesthesia while attending a performance of Richard Wagner's 'Lohengrin' in Moscow. 'The violins, the deep tones of the basses, and especially the wind instruments at that time embodied for me all the power of that pre-nocturnal hour', he recorded. 'I saw all my colours in my mind, they stood before my eyes. Wild, almost crazy lines were sketched in front of me'. Kandinsky had a profound sympathy for sensory fusion, both genuinely synaesthetic and as an artistic ideal. He explored the harmonies between sound and colour, and used musical terms to describe his paintings, calling them 'compositions' and 'improvisations'. His own 1912 opera, 'Der Gelbe Klang' ('The Yellow Sound') specified a compound mixture of colour, light, dance and sound, typical of the goal of the 'Gesamtkunstwerk', the complete art work envisaged by Wagner and so many of his followers.

Throughout the history of synaesthesia, attempts have been made to explain it naturalistically. As early as 1704, Isaac Newton struggled to come up with mathematical formulae to connect the vibration of sounds with a corresponding hue of light. Goethe noted colour correspondences in his 'Farbenlehre' ('Theory of Colour') (1810). From the late 19th century, synaesthesia was brought within the domain of psychological experimentation. Cases were explored by Charles Myers, the British

Instrument	A	H	Rf	Rs	L
ioloncello	Brown to pink	Indigo blue	-	-	Chestnut to carmine
orn	Brown to rose	-	Purple	-	-
larinet	Yellowish to bright blue	Yellow	-	-	Yellow
boe	Yellow	Rose red	Yellow	Blue	Chrome yell
iolin	Pink to blue	Very bright blue	-	Deep violet or glossy black	Garnet, orang yellow to whi
lute	Light blue	Dark red	Intense azure blue	Blue	Yellow, blue white
lageolet or ife	Light blue to green	Violet	Grey	Deep violet or glossy black	-
rumpet	Scarlet to bluish pink	Bright red	Scarlet	Brilliant yellow	-

psychologist, just before the First World War. On one subject (A) he tried out musical notes of various pitches and timbres. 'A' judged a note with a bell-like sound to be a light blue colour. A sound which suggested the high note of a fiddle was experienced as white or silvery grey. Myers then tabulated the colours ascribed by various subjects endowed with colour synaesthesia:

A's case was unusual in Myers' experience, on account of the complete absence of visual imagery. The colours came to him as mere thoughts. He contrasted this subject to those examined by the French experimenter Alfred Binet, who showed a marvellous wealth of imagery in describing their mental state.

Myers examined the Russian composer Alexander Scriabin while the musician was on tour. Scriabin sought to express his own synaesthesia in his 1910 symphony *Prometheus - the Poem of Fire*, for orchestra, piano, organ and choir. The composition also required a mute keyboard controlling the play of coloured light in the form of beams, clouds and other configurations, bathing the auditorium. Believing that his synaesthesia had an emotional basis which heightened his musical experiences, he sought to explore the artistic possibilities of the simultaneous playing of colours and of music. Confident of his own coloured hearing, he criticized that of his friend, the composer Rimsky Korsakov, as being 'artificial', on the grounds that they both reported different cross-modal associations. Scriabin informed Myers that whereas the key of F sharp major was in truth violet, to Rimsky Korsakov it erroneously appeared green.

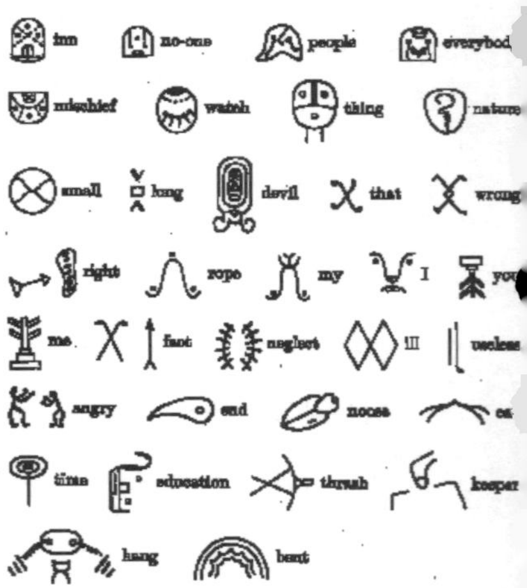

Signs used in experiments on memory
F.C.Bartlett *Remembering* 1932

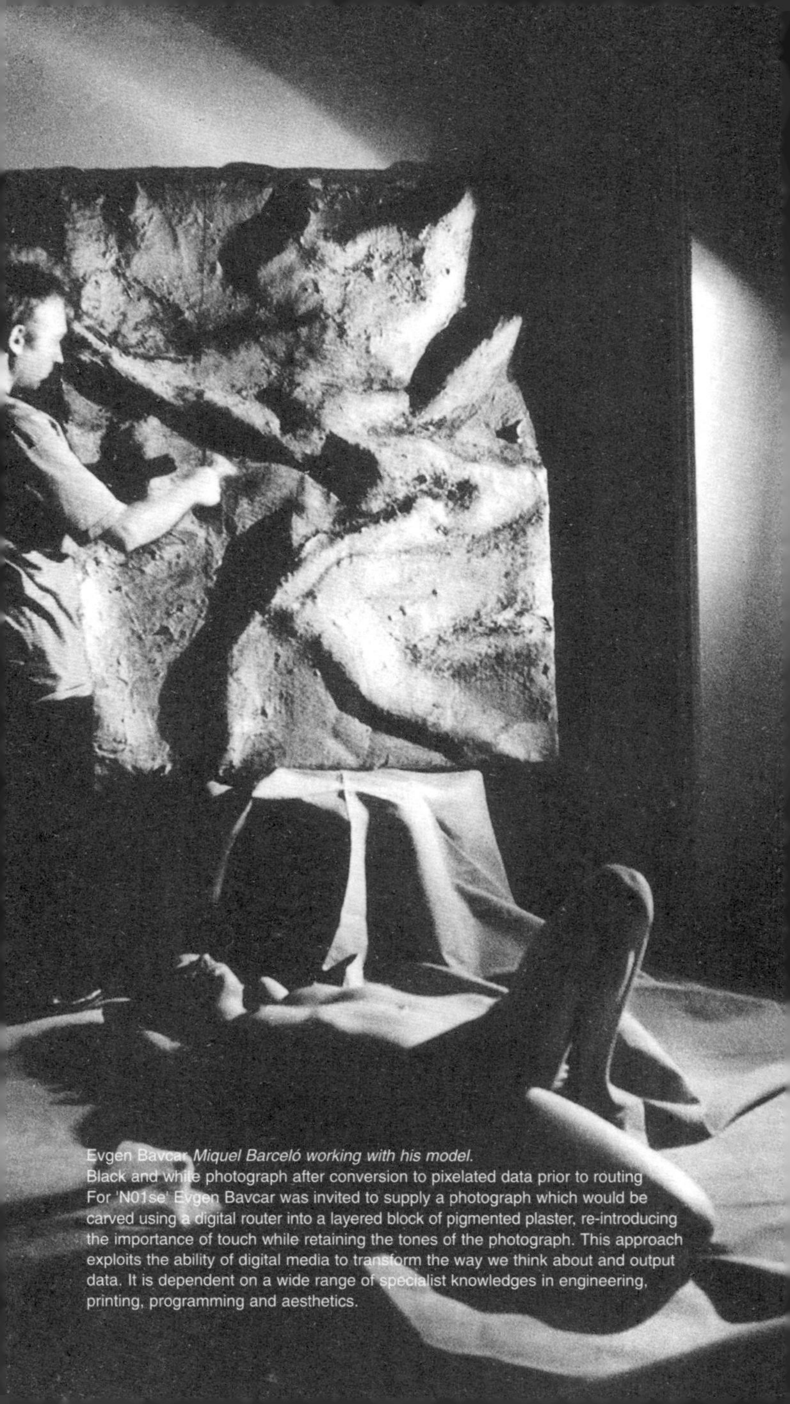

Evgen Bavcar *Miquel Barceló working with his model.*
Black and white photograph after conversion to pixelated data prior to routing
For 'N01se' Evgen Bavcar was invited to supply a photograph which would be carved using a digital router into a layered block of pigmented plaster, re-introducing the importance of touch while retaining the tones of the photograph. This approach exploits the ability of digital media to transform the way we think about and output data. It is dependent on a wide range of specialist knowledges in engineering, printing, programming and aesthetics.

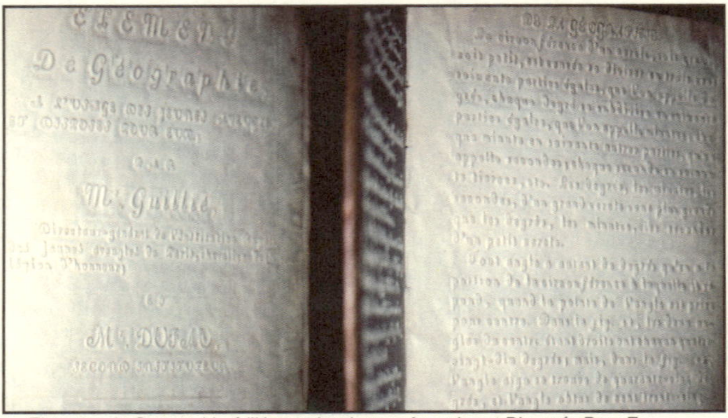

Elements de Geographie á l'Usage des Jeunes Aveugles et Disposés Pour Eux
Sébastian Guillié published in 2 volumes in 1819.
(Coll: Colin and Charlotte Franklin).

Tactile Photography

At the Workshops of Tragacanto near Madrid a digital router was constructed to produce tonal tactile photographs. Images by Evgen Bavcar and Marc Quinn were converted to digital information which was mapped as XYZ co-ordinates and routed into blocks of plaster cast in thin layers from black to white. The resulting 3D digital prints have a relief of about 30 cms, the uncut area remaining white and the tone increasing with depth to black. The possibilities of combining and transforming data offered by digital image manipulation present new possibilities for high resolution output of tone, texture and other sensory characteristics.

One of inspirations behind this work for **n01se** can be found in the history of *Tactile Typograph*. In 1821 Charles Barbier visited Sebastian Guillié to seek his help in getting his system of *Night Writing* recognised. He hoped that its use as an aid to the blind would assist his attempts to persuade the army to adopt it. His system consisted of a series of 12 raised dots on a strip of wood which could be combined to form letters. The young Braille was introduced to Barbier's system, simplified it, and produced his own version a few years later. Braille's version uses six dots like a domino. It consists of 63 symbols, 23 representing letters and 10 punctuation marks. The first book to use it was published in 1827 but Braille did not become established until 1868. Many find Braille difficult to master and prefer the simpler Moon System which uses lines and curves. Dr William Moon invented his system in 1845. It depends on only 9 symbols used in different configurations. Other *Arbitrary Systems* of Tactile Typography include; Lucas System 1838, Frére's system 1838 , and Carton. There are also a number of alphabetical systems and various musical and pictorial systems. The first embossed book for the blind was produced in 1786.

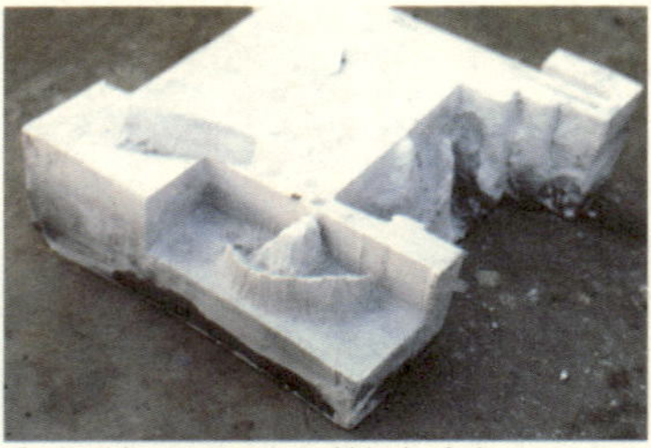

Trial cut into a pigmented block of plaster.

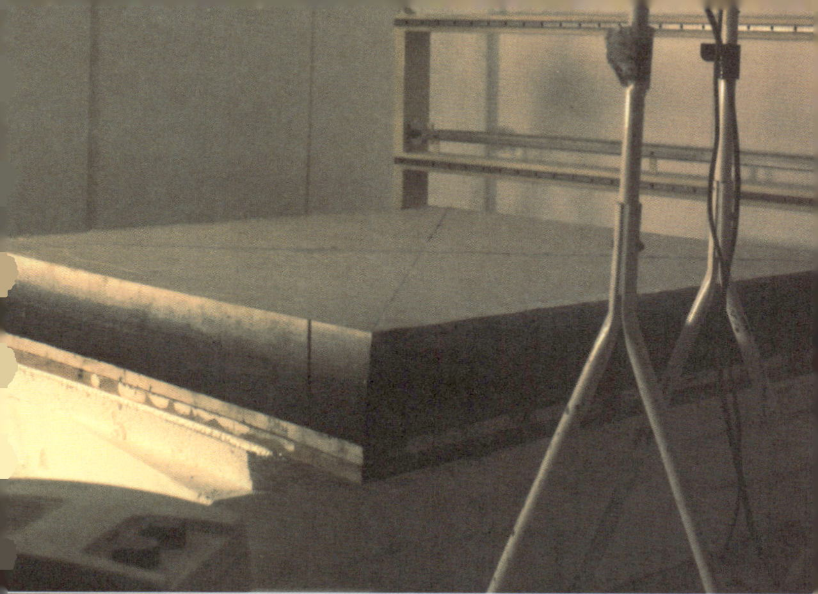

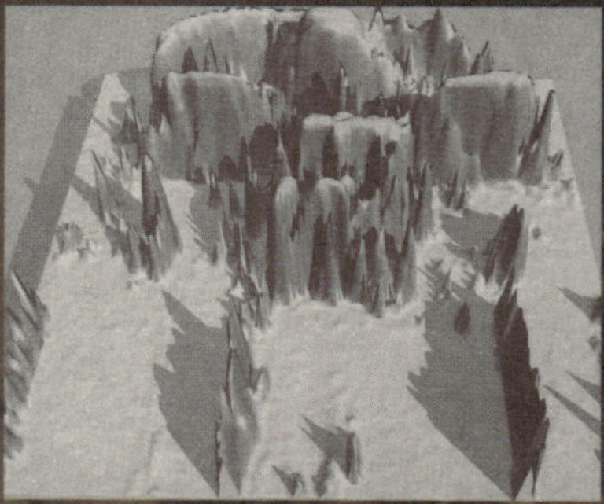

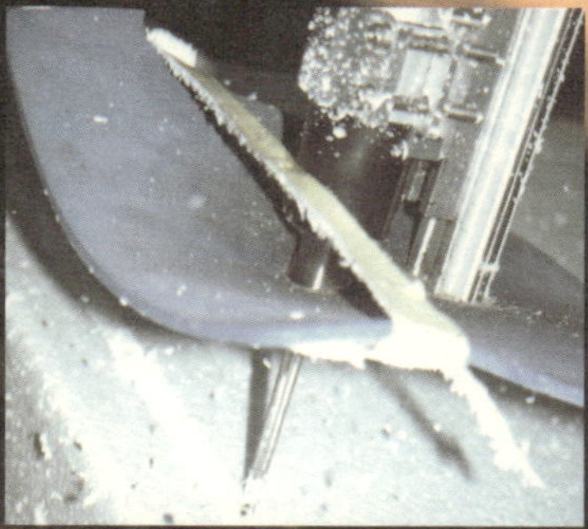

Left: A 3D image produced from a black and white photograph of a skull by Marc Quinn.
Right: The router in action cutting a block of potystyrene
Background top: The digital router and pigmented plaster block at Tragacanto, Madrid prior to the cutting of the *Tactile Photographs* by Evgen Bavcar and Marc Quinn
Background bottom: The computer made by Manuel Franquelo to drive the router.

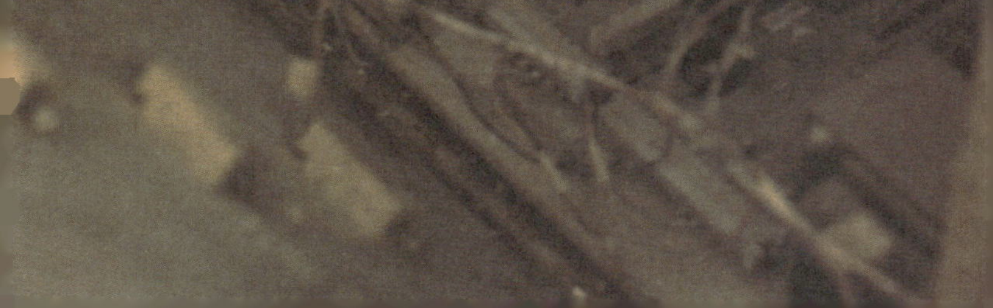

Roy Porter Professor of the History of Medicine at the Wellcome Institute for the History of Medicine, London.

Evgen Bavcar Born in Slovenia, Bavcar lost his sight at the age of eleven. He Has lived in Paris since the seventies when he studied aesthetics at the Sorbonne. He now works as a writer, photographer and film-director.

Marc Quinn Artist working in London

Tragacanto A specialist model maked in Madrid specialising in the production of facsimiles on a scale of 1:1. They adapted their specially constructed digital router to produce the tactile tonal photographs for Marc Quinn and Evgen Bavcar.

Louis Braille (1809-1852) went blind at the age of four, losing one eye in an accident with an awl (a sharp tool used to punch leather) and the other through infection. He was fortunate to be sent to the Häuy Institute, a school for blind children in Paris where the director, Guillié (director from 1814-21) taught the children to read using embossed typography printed by blind printers in Paris.

Sebastien Guillié Director of the Institut Valentine Häuy where the young Louis Braille was admitted as a student. He introduced Braille to Barbier's system of *Night Writing* and worked closely with blind printers in Paris on the production of books of tactile typography

Wassily Kandinsky (1866-1944). Russian painter, devotee of the piano and the zither, who is often credited as the founder of modern abstraction. He taught at the Bauhaus in Germany from 1922 where he nurtured an interest in Theosophy. On the Nazi seizure of power in 1933 he moved to Paris, where he died a few months after the Liberation.

Alexander Scriabin (1872-1915). Russian composer and insect-lover. Professor of musical composition at Moscow Conservatory until 1904, and much devoted to theosophy, Nietzsche and alcohol. In 1912 he was introduced to Persian Sufism, then planned an entertainment entitled *Mysterium*, in which several thousand artists would perform in front of a sound and light show projected onto the Himalayas. He died of an infected pimple on his upper lip in 1915.

Charles Myers (1873-1946). British psychologist, trained at Cambridge in natural sciences and lawn tennis. Myers was a committed freemason and a fine violinist, though his instrument rotted during his epoch-making scientific work in the Torres Strait islands in 1898. He simultaneously held the professorship in experimental psychology at King's College London and a similar post in Cambridge, where he set up the first experimental psychology lab in Britain in 1912. During World War One he initiated the first systematic work on soldiers' shellshock as consultant psychologist for the British Expeditionary Force. After the war, Myers was instrumental in promoting industrial psychology and research on occupational health.

Time for a new Icon?

An apparition, as on a screen darkly.

BRUNO LATOUR

The program was called *Claris Organizer*. A piece of project-management software, it promised to alert me to important deadlines, remind me of urgent appointments, and flash me messages about which tedious chore I needed to do before which of the other even more tedious ones. After ten minutes of devoted amusement, I found the constant reminders of pressing obligations so irritating that I permanently erased Claris from my hard drive.

And yet, every once in a while, with a celestial periodicity I have not been able to calculate reliably, a comminatory message materializes on my screen: *Finish the article about the Assumption of the Virgin Mary before x*, followed by a date that perpetually changes, without clear reason, hovering out in some near-term, apocalyptic future. The first appearance of this message filled me with the deepest mystery. I'd finished the article more than two years before. My piece on the Virgin had long since completed its academic mission: to go forth, be published, and thereafter to perish.

Why did this message continue to come back and haunt me? At first, I simply ignored the command. Then I tried to delete it, more and more enraged, at last cursing the computer screen. “You stupid idiot! I did that work, long ago. Why do you insist on harping on my past sins?” In an attempt to live conscience-clean and safely ever after, I even committed an act of radical iconoclasm. I used another software tool, Sherlock, to seek out and commit every icon with the Claris tag to the eternal flame of the Macintosh waste basket.

And yet, after a few weeks, the moving finger wrote again. The writing was on the wall, or rather, on my computer’s phosphorescent screen. How was I to interpret this sign? Then, in a flash of (electronic) light, another possibility dawned on me: It was a miracle! Of course; why hadn’t I thought of this before? The Virgin Mary, whose strange apparitions my paper on the transformations of messages had examined, had found a new, high-tech way of manifesting herself, even after the advent of the age of electronic information. Why bother continuing to appear in a blue dress to poor shepherds in some backward country’s damp grottoes? Why couldn’t she profit from the digital age, redeeming my wretched soul through the narrow conduit of buggy software? Here was the ideal way for her to test my credulity and faith, by repeating her Assumption, this time taken up into the new empyrean heaven of virtual reality, the firmament that, in this age of *globaloney*, each spirit looks to for its own salvation.

But what message was she sending me? I had to be careful in my exegesis, as one double-click could suffice to banish the revelation to a limbo where it would lie hidden again for another indefinite interval. Was her message secret and deep, like the disclosures at Fatima, hearable only by the innocent ears of poverty-stricken children?

Was it written in the inscrutable tongues of RTF, AHC, RCC, or LPC, like those attachments I receive from friends that appear, as corrupt and enigmatic as Essenian parchments, rolled up in jars in desert caves for millennia? What software could make manifest, in full clarity (in Claris), the meaning of this garbled appartion? What mortal sin had I committed, in my paper two years before, that forced the Holy Mother to insist so strenuously on my repeated, eternal contrition?

But then, perhaps *strenuously* is the wrong word. Perhaps I had misinterpreted the faint, evanescent message. The word from on high might be nothing more than a flurry of noise inside the microscopic circuits of a failing silicon chip. What would the Church Fathers had concluded, back in the 4th century after Christ, had they concurred not upon the Virgin's paradoxical substance but upon her digitality? True, the finger of God rests upon her. True, as revealed in a thousand painted Annunciations, she opens her hands to the grace of God. But all those open hands do not yet make for a digit.

I need some further gloss to account for her new embodiment. How apropos, that my fateful paper dealt with the difference between trans-formation and trans-portation. This distinction is precisely the one that our new digital incarnation ignores. Once encoded in long strings of zeroes and ones, the final import of a binary message might be anything at all, providing that message can find a binary medium in which to unfold its essence. Sound waves, pixels, odors, shapes, hues, ASCII-encoded letters: the strings might partake of any substance that the soul can imagine.

Here is the fascination of the information age: transportation is no longer threatened by transformation. Digitality invents a new relation between germ cell and its plasma: safely protected by a shell of digital encoding, data move through the world appearing one day as words, another as images, and still later as sounds, all without the threat of corruption or loss, so long as the message is constantly retransported into ever-new media, jumping like selfish genes from one organism to another, unchanged.

Does this mean that digitality has become the one, true, apostolic spirituality of our age? Is universal transportability the functional equivalent of the eternal soul? Where, in such scripture, would meaning lie? To be sure, the Assumption tells the story of a body transported intact from earth to heaven. The body of the Virgin is a prefiguration of our own salvation, when we will be at once alive in our own bodies, while nonetheless eternal. The question I asked, in that paper which I must have written so badly, was: how can you paint the Assumption of the Virgin in a space that has become indifferent to direction, where you must show a movement, not from one location to another, but from one state to another? How can you paint transformation between death and eternal life, between despair and glory, when your visual medium has already been compromised beyond the ability to depict any movement at all, except through changes in three-dimensional, Euclidean coordinates?

Is it possible to say that the Virgin has simply been transported to Heaven intact, without being transformed as well? And might Roman Catholics, those who believe in this dogma formally approved in this century, almost two millennia after the event, might they themselves be transformed, transported, converted by witnessing those images that foreshadow the movement of all flesh?

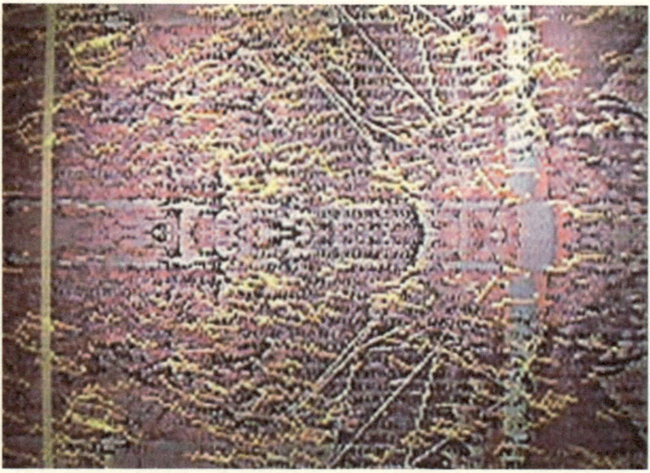

Joseph Nechvatal
Above Viral Painting. Pigment inkjet print onto canvas 1998

The Bit-Streamed Viral Body as Non-Logocentric Mental Prosthetic

Joseph Nechvatal

William Burroughs said that sexual desire is like a virus that is always on the hunt for a new host. In response to this idea, Joseph Nechvatal, while working as the Louis Pasteur artist-in-residence at Arbois, France (Louis Pasteur's home town) developed a method for creating viral computer-robotic assisted paintings which stem from a computer virus program. This computer program was written on Hypercard in Basic with the assistance of Prof. Jean-Philippe Massonie of Laboratoire MIS, Université de Franche-Comte, France. At the same time (1993-4) Nechvatal also became the first artist to utilize the new computer/technology studio at the Saline Royale at Arc-et-Senans; site of Chaux, the utopian worker's municipality designed and half-built by King Louis XIV's principal architect Claude-Nicolas Ledoux. This computer research laboratory, set up at the Claude-Nicolas Ledoux Foundation's International Center for Reflection on the Future, allowed Nechvatal to carry out an extensive type of retrospective *contamination* of his own previous artistic production. By up-loading his entire archive onto an Apple FXII computer he randomly infected it with the computer virus program for various lengths of time.

The basic premise behind the viral paintings is the rhizomatic exploration of host/parasite omnijectivity (the metaphysical concept stemming from the discoveries of quantum physics which teaches us that mind, previously considered the subjective realm and matter, previously considered as the objective realm, are inextricably linked by today's high-frequency, electronic, computerized environment).

The viewer's are free to navigate their way through the deep perceptual space which the paintings suggest.

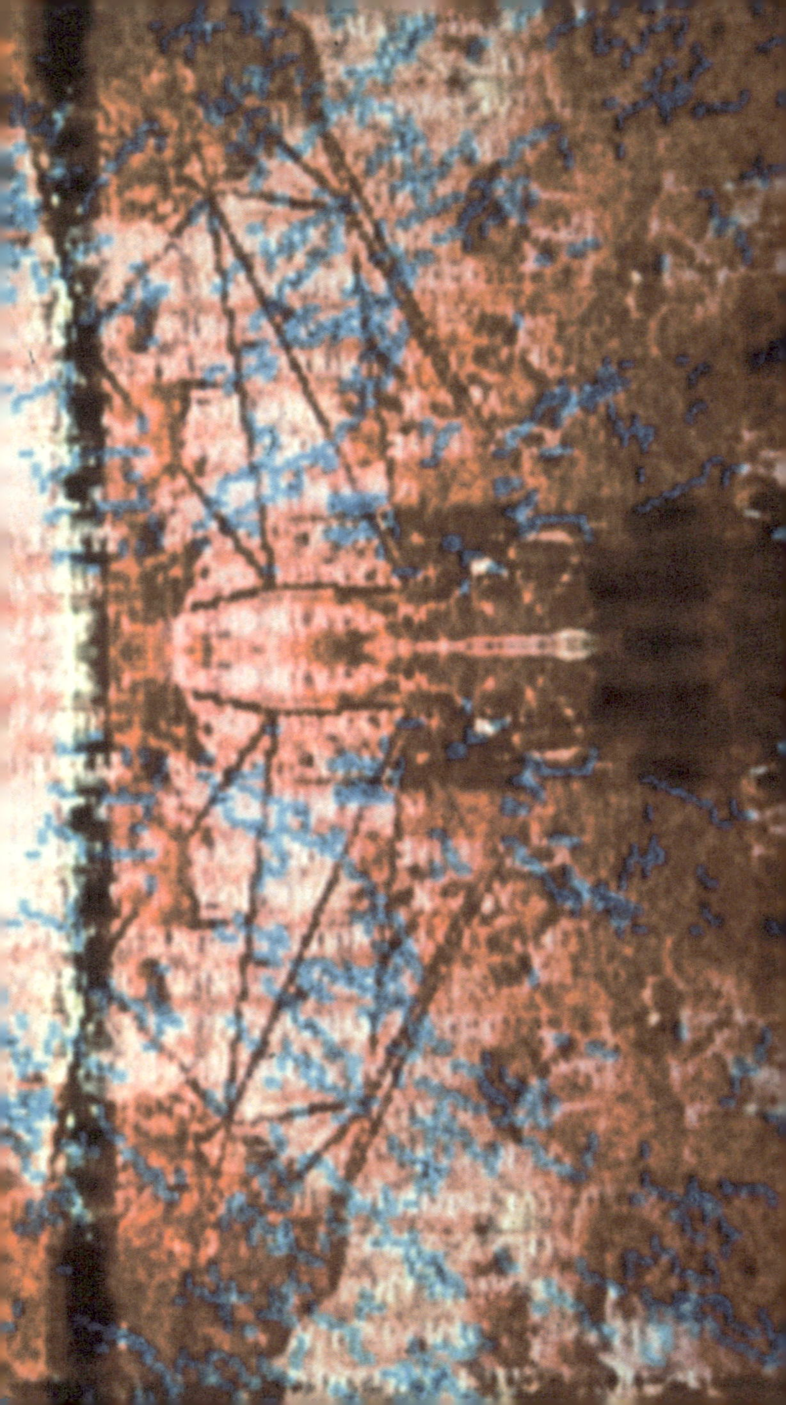

Here, at last, might be why the Virgin's message persists in flashing on my screen, in all its obscure clarity. What was already so terribly difficult in the 17th and 18th centuries has become almost inconceivable by the end of the 20th, precisely in this sacred moment designated by the Pope to be the Great Jubilee. The little gesture of the moving finger *double-click* has surpassed all other gestures, and the Mediatrix herself appears as nothing more than an instantaneous hyperlink to that web site lying somewhere in the new heaven of transfigured bodies distributed through virtual, dimensionless space.

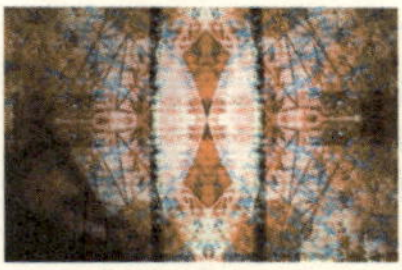

Yes, of course: this is why she has chosen this novel and improbable medium to reach me. The work of envisioning the unenvisionable must be done again, just as it was reinvented in the 17th century, through the sudden turmoil of Baroque painting. We must give life and movement, we must re-animate what it means to experience the Assumption again. This is the work of theology in the age of electronic reproduction: to re-produce anew, this time with bytes and baud, the miracle of our transformation by those messages; to escape, while still in our own flesh, the sad, mortal fate of double-click information.

A new, Baroque predication and expression: that is what she begs for. Just as God chose to incarnate himself in the fragile body of a living creature, so the Virgin takes up an equally fragile flesh, freeing me from the sad destiny of transportation without transformation. Yes, yes: the next time she appears in another fleeting message, I will light a candle by the screen and kneel by it. The time has come for a new icon.

Mediated by Richard Powers

Joseph Nechvatal
Above: Viral Painting. Pigment inkjet print onto canvas
150 x 210 cms 1998
Oppposite:Viral Painting Detail

Bruno Latour Professor at the Centre de Sociologie de l'Innovation at the Ecole Nationale Supérieure des Mines in Paris.

Richard Powers is an American author.

Joseph Nechvatal lives in Paris and New York. He has worked with electronic visual information and computer-robotics since 1986. His computer-robotic assisted paintings and computer animations are shown regularly in galleries and museums. He developed *The Computer Virus Project* while artist in-resident at the Louis Pasteur studio and in conjunction with the Ledoux Foundation's computer laboratory in Arbois, France . In 1999 he received a Ph.D. in the Philosophy of Art at the Centre for Advanced Inquiry in the Interactive Arts, University of Wales, Newport. He is the Paris editor for the internet magazine *Rhizome*.

We are surrounded by noise. And this noise is inextinguishable. It is outside - it is the world itself - and it is inside, produced by our living body. We are in the noises of the world, we cannot close our door to their reception, and we evolve, rolling in this incalculable swell. We are hot, burning with life; and the hearths of this temporary ecstasy send out a truceless tumult from their innumerable functions. If these sources are stilled, death is there in the form of flat waves. Flat for recording, flat for closed ears. In the beginning is the noise; the noise never stops. It is our apperception of chaos, our apprehension of disorder, our only link to the scattered distribution of things. Hearing is our heroic opening to trouble and diffusion; other receptors assure us of order or, if they no longer give or receive, close immediately. None assures us that we are surrounded by fluctuation and that we are full of fluctuation.

Michel Serres, *The Parasite*

Who gives form to noise?

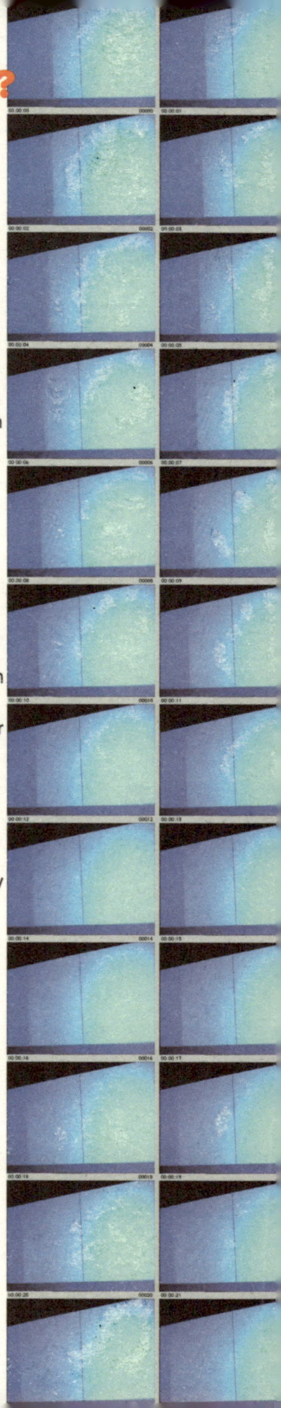

Interactive Music

ROMANDSON

Noise by Jacques Attali was first published in France in 1977 under the title *Bruits: essai sur l'économie politique de la musique*. In it, Attali imagines a form of musical practice which he calls 'Composing', a practice in which musical production and musical consumption are dissolved one into the other and become inseparable. This 'new music…on the rise', is one in which there is no exchange and no alienation - nothing but pure use value. Not music as commodity but as gift. A practice of music where there is no distinction between artist and audience and where 'playing for one's pleasure' is the only goal.

Attali's central argument is that music is not simply a code - '…the principle of giving form to noise in accordance with changing syntactic structures' - but that it is also an economy, and that moreover - 'the political economy of music is not marginal, but premonitory. The noises of a society are in advance of its images and material conflicts. Our music foretells our future'. Music - or noise - in Attali is a harbinger of new forms of political economy. He proposes that each development in the wider economy is preceded by a similar development in the economy of music. The next stage in this progression - composing - will usher in a new practice of music among the people, and presumably (although Attali is short on detail here), go on to overthrow the tyranny of commodity exchange a bit later.

It is easy to be cynical about Attali's sweeping vagueness and what appears now as unreconstructed political utopianism. His references to Jimi Hendrix or *Street Fighting Man* read like some excruciating quote from Tom Wolfe's 70s essay *Radical Chic*. The idea that where music leads the rest of the economy will follow is a curious one. And yet… is there any sector of the economy which fears the transformations brought about by home PCs and the spread of the internet quite as much as the music industry does? Is it really that far-fetched to suggest, as Attali does, that musical practice was the first to develop a political economy of the immaterial and the first to face the challenge of an economy without quantity?

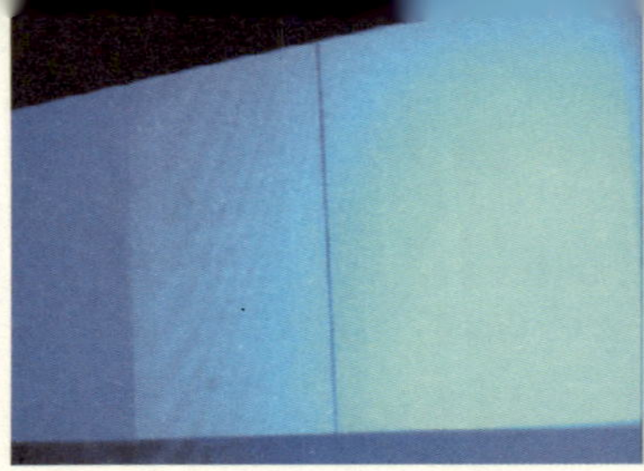

Composing for Attali involves a redrawing, or an erasing, of the line which separates the labour of production and the labour of consumption. This has a strong resonance with ideas about new technologies and the novel cultural forms which can develop out of them. One of the most exciting of these cultural forms in recent years has been that of 'interactivity'. Interactivity gives rise to a new type of representation in which doing is added to looking and listening and reading, a representation which is essentially a game (i.e. process), rather than a sign (i.e. product). Interactivity creates new kinds of relations between audiences and artefacts. Interactive music artefects for example, might encourage the user to interact with and change a piece of music, becoming composer, performer and audience all at once.

Of course, making music has always involved interactive technologies - usually known as instruments - and new developments in these technologies have always given rise to new ways of composing and performing. The piano for example, represents one of the greatest technological achievements of the 18th century, with its complex mechanism and large number of precision components. Its ability to relate the pressure with which the finger strikes the key to the volume of the sound produced, and to do so across both hands independently of each other allowed the development of new forms of music and of new constituencies of composers, performers and audiences.

Attali notes that the process of inventing new instruments, after a pause of nearly 3 centuries, is gathering speed again. Such instruments are rarely traditional, based as they are on digital recording and synthesizing technologies. In their innovation, diversity and ease of use, they hold out the promise of unprecedented new social and aesthetic formations.

It is hard not to share Attali's excitement at the opportunity for a musical practice which elides the difference between musician and non-musician, and which makes Luigi Russolo's dream of *Arte Dei Rumori* ('The Art of Noises') an everyday reality.

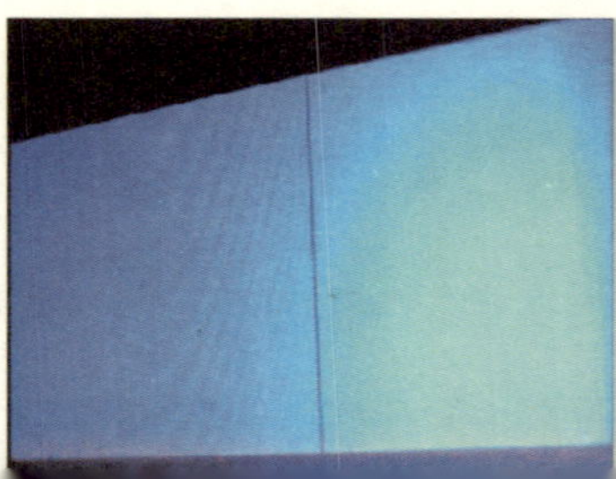

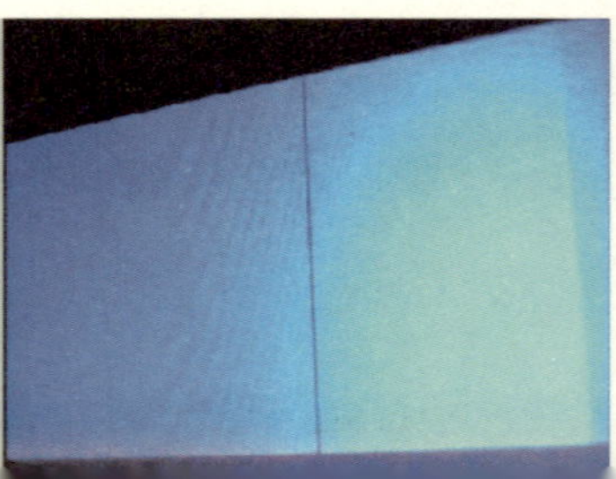

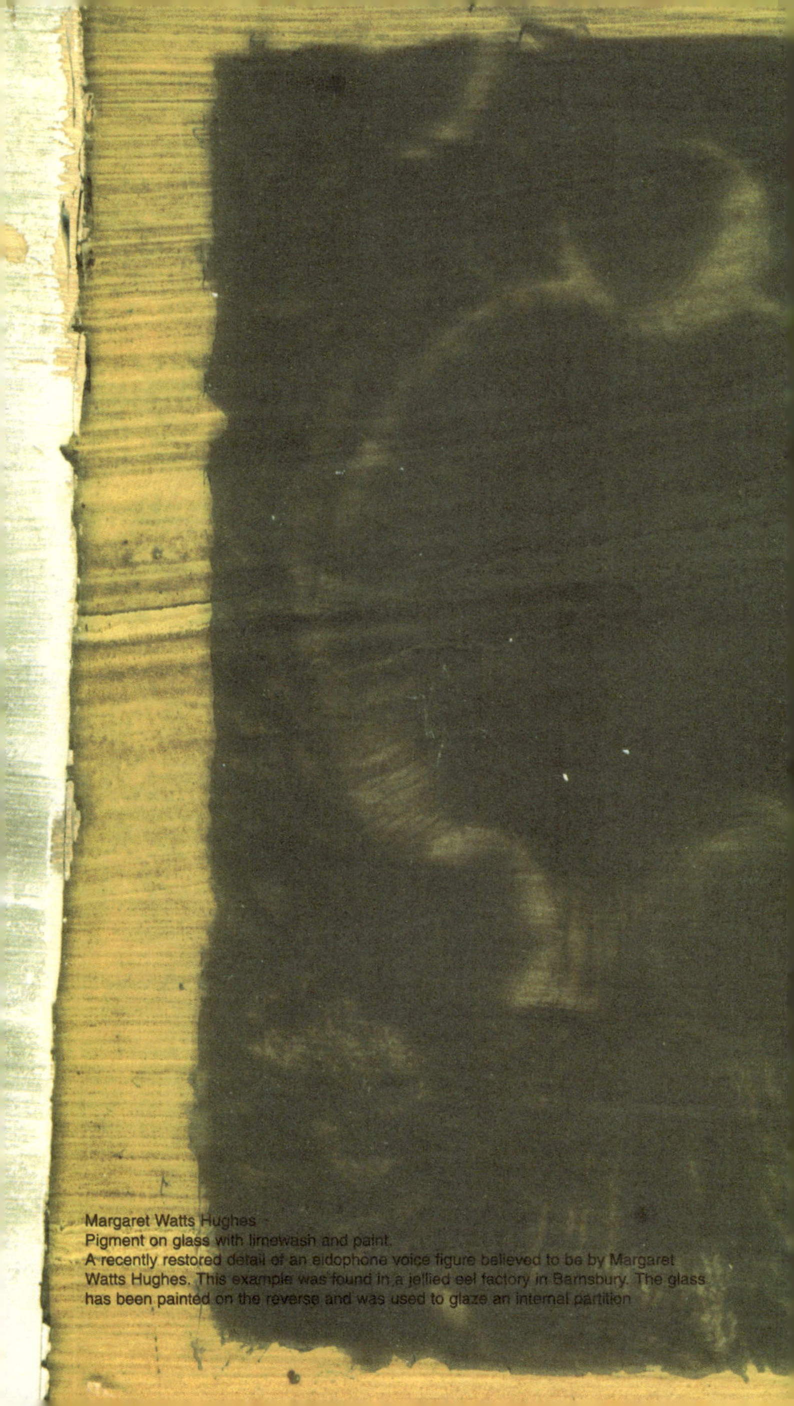

Margaret Watts Hughes
Pigment on glass with limewash and paint.
A recently restored detail of an eidophone voice figure believed to be by Margaret Watts Hughes. This example was found in a jellied eel factory in Barnsbury. The glass has been painted on the reverse and was used to glaze an internal partition

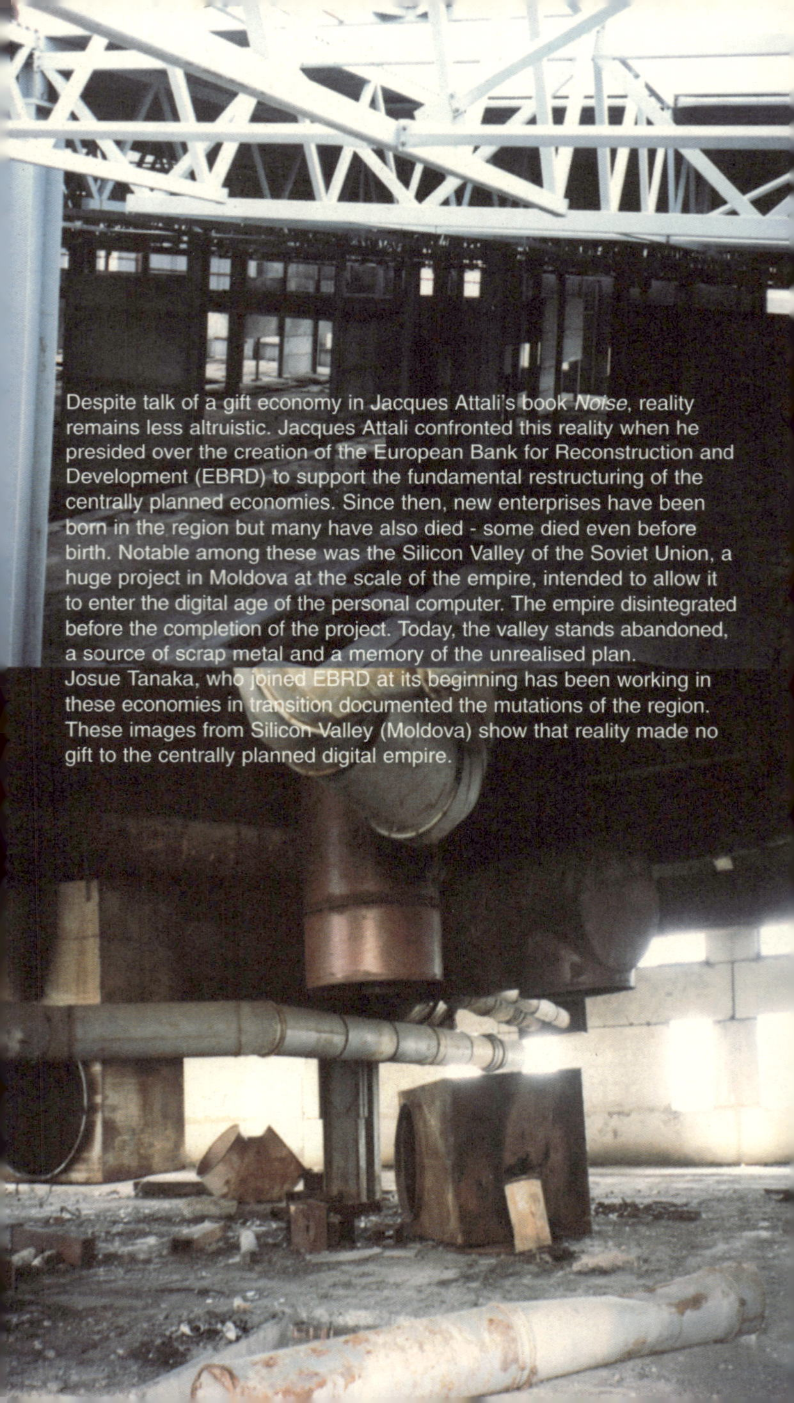

Despite talk of a gift economy in Jacques Attali's book *Noise*, reality remains less altruistic. Jacques Attali confronted this reality when he presided over the creation of the European Bank for Reconstruction and Development (EBRD) to support the fundamental restructuring of the centrally planned economies. Since then, new enterprises have been born in the region but many have also died - some died even before birth. Notable among these was the Silicon Valley of the Soviet Union, a huge project in Moldova at the scale of the empire, intended to allow it to enter the digital age of the personal computer. The empire disintegrated before the completion of the project. Today, the valley stands abandoned, a source of scrap metal and a memory of the unrealised plan.
Josue Tanaka, who joined EBRD at its beginning has been working in these economies in transition documented the mutations of the region. These images from Silicon Valley (Moldova) show that reality made no gift to the centrally planned digital empire.

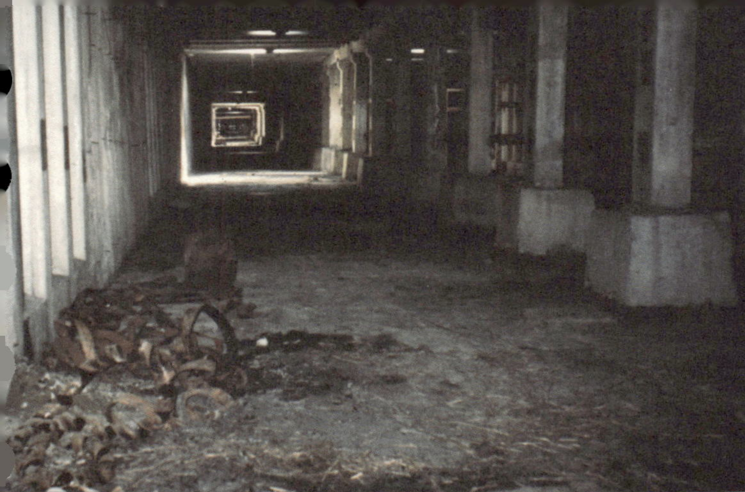
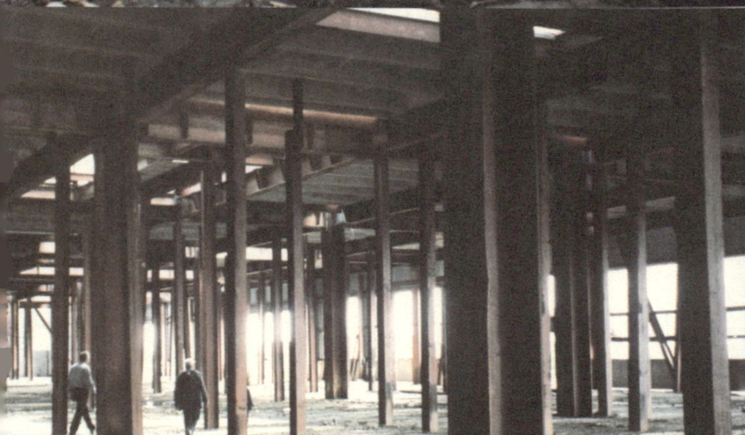
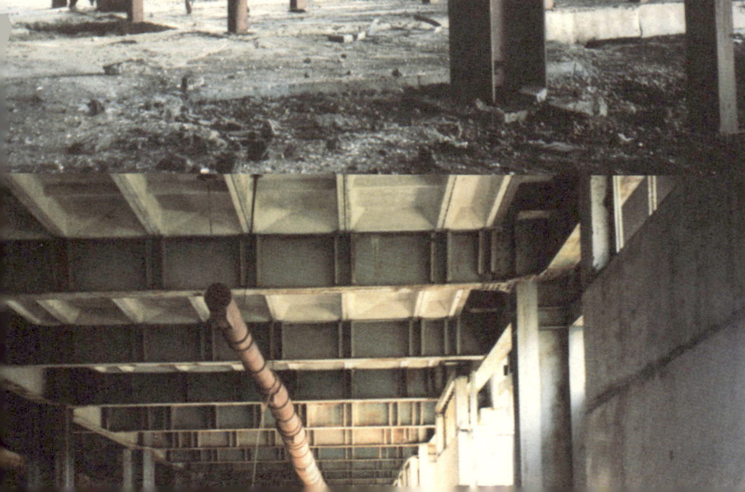
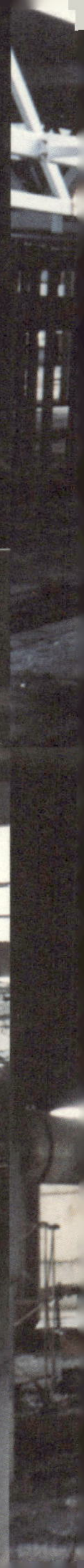

Andy Cameron, Andy Allenson and Romandson - All members of the HyperMedia Research Centre at Westminster University.

Josue Tanaka Director for Strategic and Corporate Planning at the European Bank for Reconstruction and Redevelopment. He has been involved since the fall of the Berlin Wall in the financing of projects supporting the economic transition of the former communist bloc. While working on these projects he has been photographically documenting economic landscapes in flux.

Jacques Attali Novelist, essayist, special adviser to President Mitterrand. He was the first President of the European Bank for Reconstruction and Redevelopment until hounded out of office by the British Press over his taste in interior design.

Margaret Watts Hughes (Died1907) An independent researcher into the visualisation of sound, whose reputation depends almost solely on two books published in 1891 and 1904. Her work with interactive sound, her visualisations of sound and her work running a childrens' home suggest she might be a role model for a gift economy.

Luigi Russolo Author of *Arte dei Rumori (The Art of Noises) 1913*. He wrote: "Let us cross a large modern capital with our ears more sensitive than our eyes. We will delight in distinguishing the eddying of water, or air or gas in metal pipes, the muttering of the motors that breathe and pulse with an indisputable animality"

'What's happening?' Oedipa whispered.
'That's by Stockhausen,' the hip greybeard informed her, 'the early crowd tends to dig your Radio Cologne sound. Later on we really swing. We're the only bar in the area, you know, has a strictly electronic music policy. Come on around Saturdays, starting midnight we have your Sinewave Session, that's a live get-together, fellas come in just to jam from all over the state, San Jose, Santa Barbara, San Diego...'
'Live?' Metzger said, 'electronic music, live?'
'They put it on tape, here, live, fella. We got a whole back room full of your audio oscillators, gunshot machines, contact mikes, everything man.'
Thomas Pynchon, *The Crying of Lot 49*, 1966

Restoration or replication?

Virtually a reality

ADAM LOWE

In 1997 the artist **Manuel Franquelo**, and **Sven Nebel**, director of Tragacanto, began work on a facsimile of the Altamira Cave from laser-scanned information, on a scale

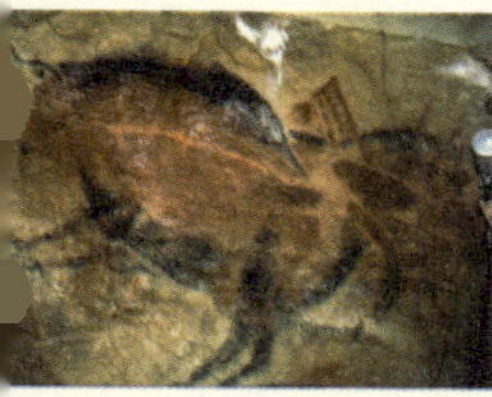

of 1:1, accurate to a resolution of 3mm. Using a composite rock made from pulverised limestone collected near the cave and painted, by Pedro Saura and Matilda Musquis, with iron oxide and charcoal, the facsimile is breathtaking in its accuracy and attention to detail.

The cave at Altamira,containing some of the finest and best preserved pre-historic paintings, was discovered by Don Marcelino Sanz de Sautuola and his daughter **Maria** in 1879. It was the first painted cave to be discovered and its authenticity was disputed until the early 1900's. Carbon dating of the charcoal gave a date of about 14,000 years old. The caves have been closed to the public since the late 70s as they were being irreparably damaged by the volume of visitors. Work is now complete and the resulting replica, indistinguishable from the original under the lighting conditions inside the cave, will be installed in a new museum at the site of the cave and will be open to the public later in the year.The accuracy of the replica, complete with all the cracks and blemishes in the rock, makes the interdependence between the rock and the paintings explicit – facilitating a new approach to the study of the caves. It will now be possible to test a variety of hypotheses, such as the relationship

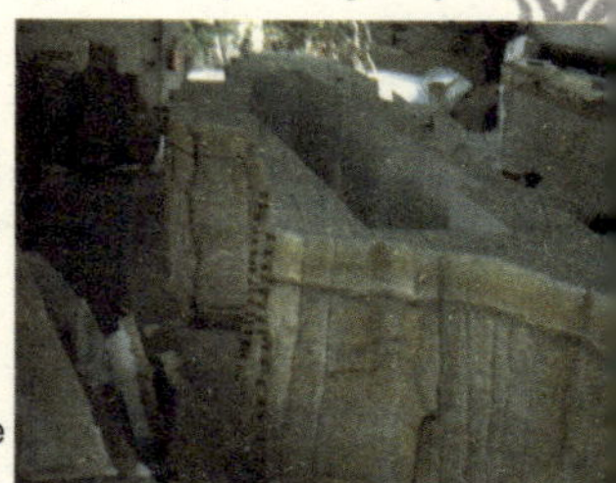

between the location of the fires and the shadows cast on the ceiling, which have remained theoretical due to the fragile nature of the original. Issues surrounding

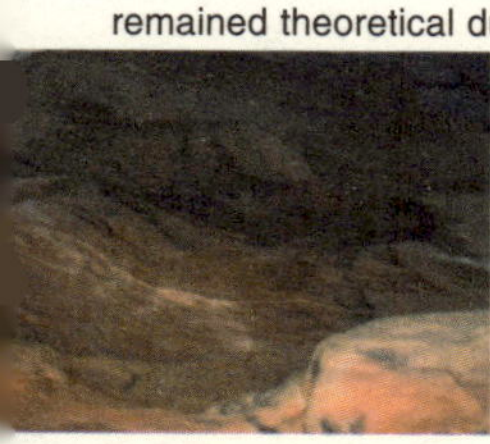

replication and simulacra pose difficult questions for museum directors and those involved in the museum industry. Public access is always balanced with issues of conservation and display. The panoramas and dioramas of the late C19th drew large crowds, and the same spirit of optimistic belief in representation led many to predict that the virtual museum would take over in this digital age.

Greek sculpture can be dated, and differentiated from the Roman copies, by looking at the anatomical detail. The restoration of paintings by the conservation departments within the museums of Europe and America reveal more about the value judgements of the restorer than the intentions of the artist – the facsimile of Lascaux, once the subject of praise, now looks decidedly dated. Electronic mediation and digital technology, tied to traditional craft skills, have made it possible to produce replicas on a natural scale that are indistinguishable from the original under museum conditions. A fact that has fundamental implications for the furure of cultural tourism.

Speculum, Exemplar, Imago

ROBIN BOAST

As a young boy I delighted in visiting the museum. We would go to the large Natural History museum in the State where I grew up several times a year. There was a continuity to the museum, it did not change much from year to year: the same Diplodocus and Stegosaurus stood where they always stood in the centre of the Fossil Hall; the half-sectioned "Eskimo" igloo greeted you as you entered the Native American Hall; in the Mineral Hall the multitude of fossils and minerals sat in their mahogany cases. As a young boy, or girl, you could prostrate yourself on the glass and count the rings on the trilobites or follow the changing shape of the braciopods.

However, our museum was known for its Dioramas. These scenes of nature were carefully crafted with a reconstructed foreground and a painted background, the two seamlessly merging into one. Like framed store windows, you could lose yourself in the scene. You could watch the still Black Bears and imagine that you were standing just there on an adjacent path in the Rocky Mountains, or sitting on the rocky ledge with the mother Puma and her cubs. The huge plate-glass windows added to the zoological effect. In the late 1970s, the museum created an African watering-hole of huge proportions without glass: the effect was lost, it was clear that it was just a display full of dead animals.

Every time I went, there were memories of details previously discovered and anticipations of newly discovered lore—the snake hidden in the grass with the White-tailed Deer or, best of all, the Tarantula hidden in the rocks below the perched Golden Eagle. As time went on, there was also the prospect of new scenes, new worlds.

When I was older, and I had moved away to places as far afield as India and had returned in the late 1960s as a young teenager, the objects in the museum had another life. It was now that those groups of incomprehensible fossils and the assemblages of Native American artifacts grabbed my interest because they all now relate to stories—stories that lived outside the museum. The artefacts were the objects that were used by the people I now knew to be "Indians." I knew of "Indians" before, you don't grow up in the western US, or anywhere for that matter, and not know about "Indians." There were plenty of Indians in my youth: on the telly, as toys, on advertisements, in movies, and, where I grew up, you went to school with Indians (but they were nothing like the other "Indians"). There were also the Indians that I went to school with in India, but they too were not like these "Indians." These "Indians" were a part of history, a history I was increasingly learning, in one form or another, in school, through books, through increasingly vocal Native Americans and through museums. The images of Indians from my youth were now "enriched" with stories told by authors, museum curators, teachers, and Native American activists. The meaning of these artifacts in the museum were never just filled with the meanings of the labels—which I never much read anyway—they were filled with a thousand stories and associations.

The objects in the museum—whether fossil, artifact, painting or diorama—are able

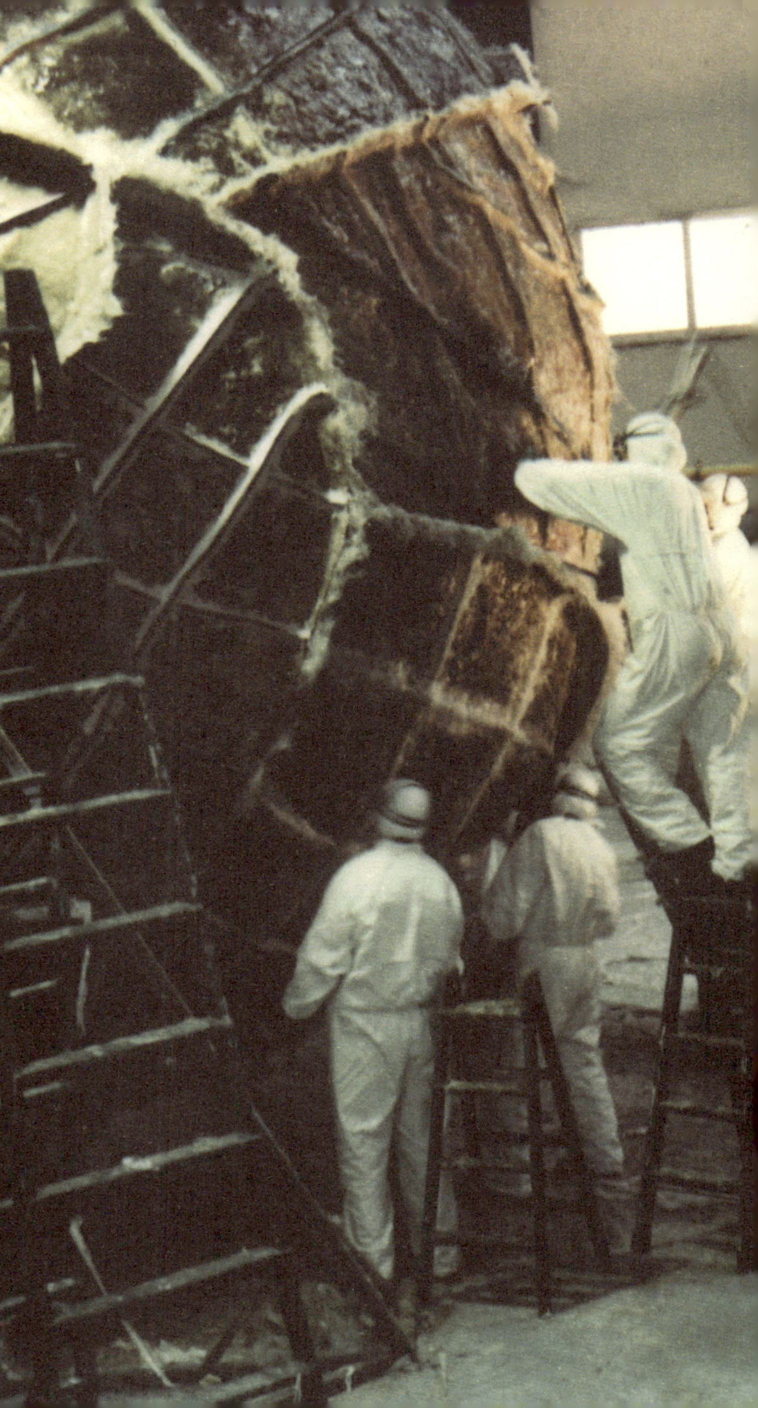

Working on the mould for the world's largest globe made from satellite data in the workshops of Tragacanto, Madrid

to carry such stories in our culture. Their detached physical presence is an emblem of place, people, event, innovation, life, prophesy or change.

In the museum of my youth, the objects were essential to the process of meaning. I went to the museums to see things and have stories evoked about those things. Or I went to evoke my own stories about these things, to remember visits, tales, knowledge that I had collected at another time. I did not go to the museum to see images of things (unless it is a photographic museum where we were there to see the objects that are photographs): images or “fake” reproductions were not good enough. The diorama’s effect is the “real” animals, “real” soil, “real” plants—only the background is painted—situated, ordered, measured on to the other. I went to the museum to become lost in the settings, in the stories that they had accumulated, in their details, in their identities. I do not go to the museum to see just images, each an icon of itself. In the museum, things are placed, measured and ordered. In the museum there is a pattern, a pattern I can recognize, that goes beyond the object’s covenant.

(ix)

Earths	43	Salts	04
Sands	10	Alum	03
Gravel	01	Vitriol	04
Stone	17	Nitre	02
Alabaſter	01	Sulphur	00
Marble	41	Arſenic	01
Pebles, Flints, Agats,	253	Pyritæ	46
		Marcaſitæ	55
Foliaceous Talcs	52	Antimony	06
Selenites	59	Calamin	06
Fibroſe Talcs	20	Black-Lead	07
Ludus Helmontij	52	Copper-Ores	77
Lapis Syringoides	24	Tin-Ores	30
Belemnites	66	Lead-Ores	138
Corals, and coralloid Bodyes	153	Iron-Ores	107
		Load-Stone	02
Cryſtals, Spars, and cryſtalliz'd Gemms	221	Mangeneſe	02
		Bezoar Min. Geodes, Enhydr.	24
Vein-Stones	11	Mineral Delineations	14
Bitumens, Coal, Jet, Amber	22		
	1046		528
	528		
	1574		

So great a Variety as fifteen hundred Bodyes, and upwards, and each ſo much differing from other, that in the whole there are ſcarcely any two alike, in every reſpect, to be produced within the Bounds of one Country, muſt needs be allow'd to be very conſiderable.

John Woodward *List ofminerals* 1728-9

Left top: Digitally routed drops of water on the surface of the cave. The thin columns of polystyrene are noise caused by the droplets of water falling from the ceiling of the cave recorded as positive forms during the process of laser scanning.

Left bottom: After the routed polystyrene has been cleaned and all noisy artifact removed it is covered with wax, moulded from the surface of the cave. This increases the apparent resolution. Various colour-coded textures were cast in pigmented beeswax to produce this beautiful smelling surface. The cracks and pock-marks in the rock were then routed through the surface from additional photographic data..

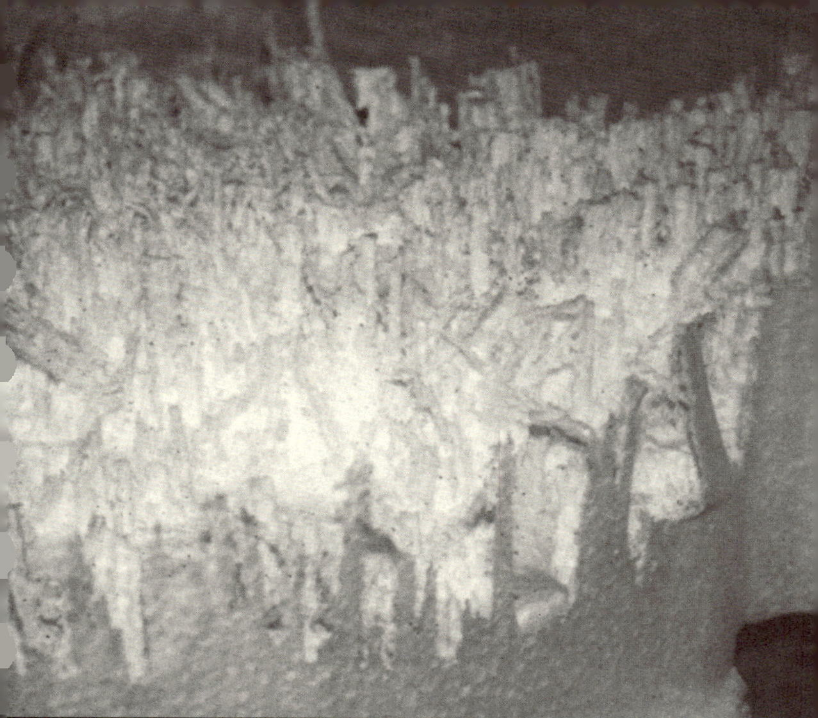
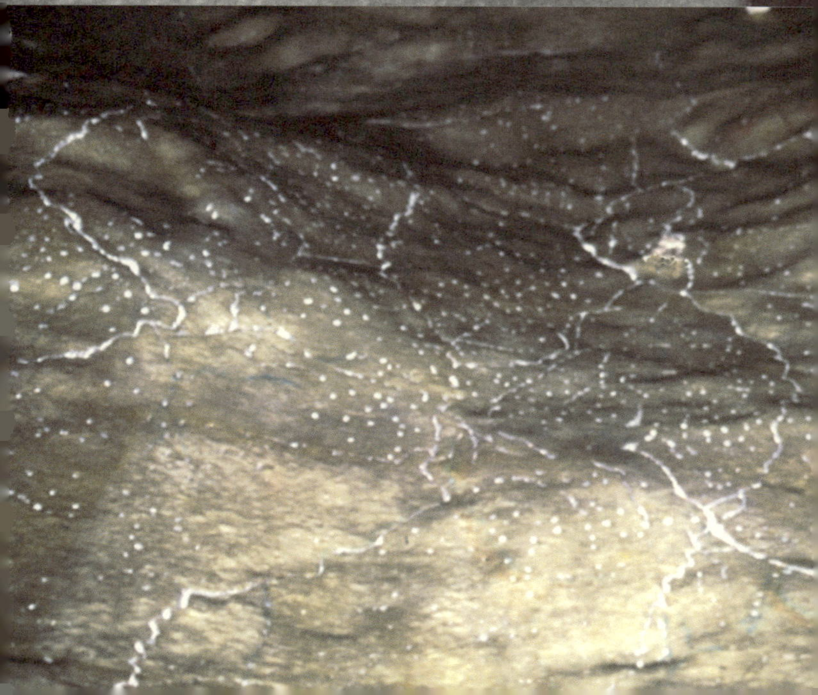

Robin Boast Curator at the Cambridge University Museum of Archaeology and Anthropology.

Sven Nebel Artist, technical engineer and director of Tragacanto. With Manuel Franquelo he is responsible for the facsimile of the cave at Altamira.

Manuel Franquelo One of Spain's most important hyper-realist painters. His works, in a variety of media, are painstaking representations of visual and non-visual information

John Woodward (1665-1728) A draper's apprentice and eccentric London physician who in 1695 announced that fossils were the remains of animals and plants destroyed, dissolved and deposited during Noah's Flood. The proud owner of a notoriously faked antique shield and the fierce proponent of his own medical therapies, in 1719 he fought a duel with one of his critics, the eminent physician and antiquarian Richard Mead, and lost. He sued the Royal Society, of which he was a fellow, when expelled from its council for insulting the president Hans Sloane. At the end of his life he published remarkable catalogues of his vast fossil collections, many gathered in Gloucestershire, and left them to Cambridge University in his will, together with cash to establish a post for an unmarried layman to lecture on the subjects of Woodward's publications.

Maria Sanz de Sautuola The grandmother of Emelio Botin, the owner of Banco de Santander. The Botin Foundation part-funded the production of the replica. Maria was the first person to notice the painted animals on a visit to the cave with her father in 1879.

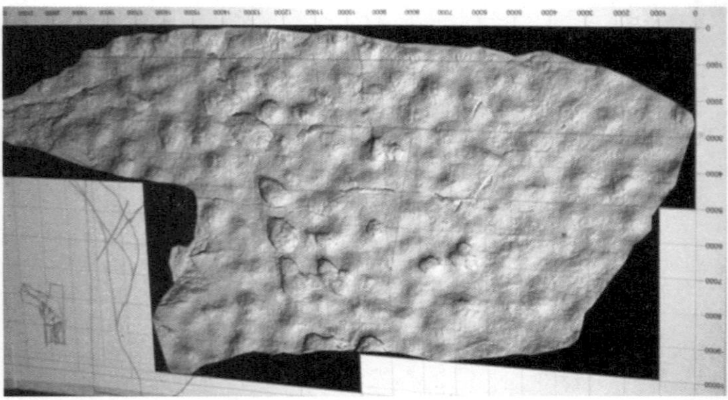

An image of the painted area of the ceiling of the cave at Altamira in Northern Spain produced from laser scanned information. The raw data was put through various filters by Manuel Franquelo to produce this image which appears to have a light source and texture. This data was in turn converted and sent to the specially constructed digital router which outputs physical form.

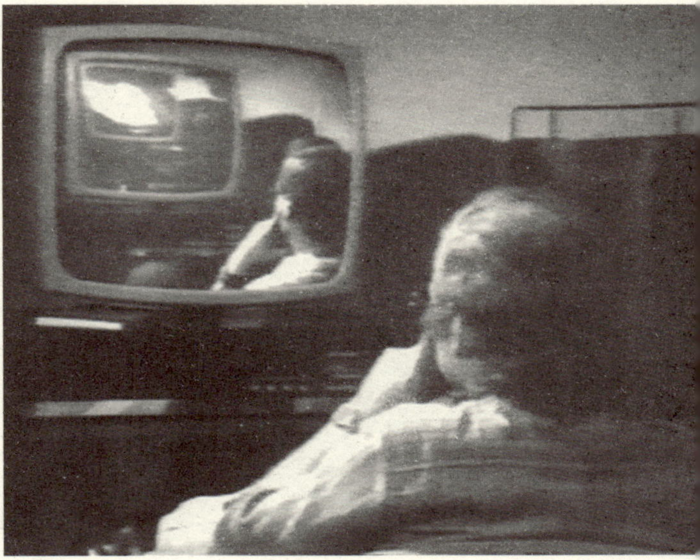

Peter Weibel
Video Stills from *The Endless Sandwich* and *Time as Code*
Peter Weibel's writing on Noise and Information in physical and social systems have influenced generation of Media Artists.

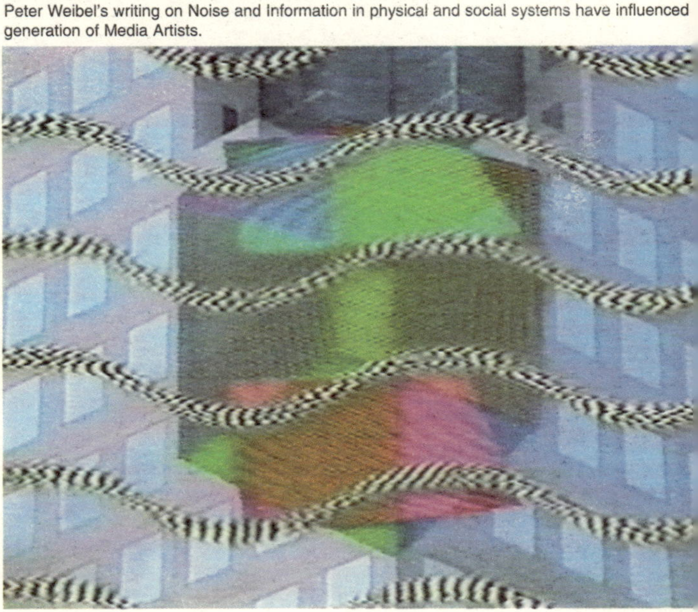

Paul D Miller *Synchronia* 2000

Simulating Sound

Working at the House Ear Institute, Los Angeles **Robert Shannon** has produced a series of computer programmes to simulate the sound heard through a Cochlear implant under a variety of conditions.
These recordings demonstrate that words can be identified in speech even at a relatively low resolution and as a result the cochlear implant can return a remarkable level of hearing to patients who have become completely deaf. (recently there have been attempts to implant the device into children born deaf and if the operation is done early enough the child will develop a reasonable level of hearing).
The Cochlear implant is less successful when dealing with more subtle qualities of sound, such as listening to a singing voice or a piece of music. For **n01se** the composer **Georgina Brett** has produced a series of short musical compositions which have been fed into the computer programmes. The results demonstrate that complex sensory information, the fabric of music, present a different challenge to that of speech identification and are not easily distinguished from noise.

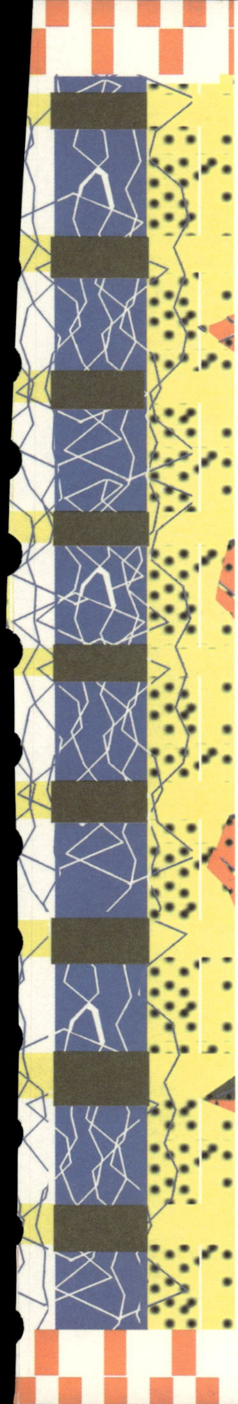

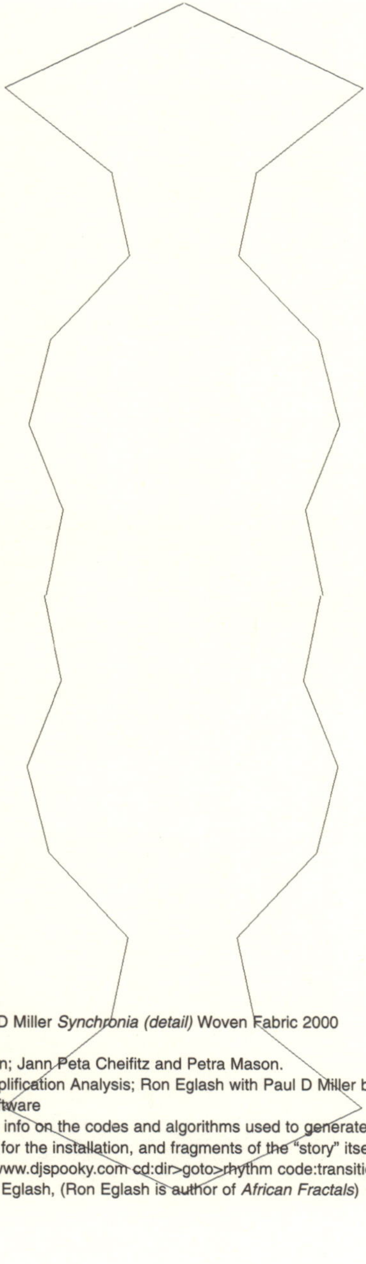

Left:Paul D Miller *Synchronia (detail)* Woven Fabric 2000

Fabrication; Jann Peta Cheifitz and Petra Mason.
Wave Amplification Analysis; Ron Eglash with Paul D Miller based on Maple Software
Additional info on the codes and algorithms used to generate the "material" for the installation, and fragments of the "story" itself can be found at:www.djspooky.com cd:dir>goto>rhythm code:transition analysis:> Ron Eglash, (Ron Eglash is author of *African Fractals*)

Paul D Miller aka DJ Spooky that Subliminal Kid An artist, writer and DJ based in New York

The Hieroglyphics of Horapollo A text apparently composed in Alexandria in about 500 AD, purporting to be an Egyptian account of the true meaning, of hieroglyphics, though it obviously includes much material unrelated to ancient Egypt. The manuscript was found on an Aegean island in 1419 and printed with Aesop's fables in 1505. It soon became the indispensable guide to Egyptian learning in the Renaissance, and was included in a vast commentary by the Roman scholar Pierio Valeriano in 1556, in which version Isaac Newton and many others consulted it as guidebook.

Robert Shannon Researcher at the House Ear Institute in Los Angeles working with Cochlear implants

Peter Weibel Director of ZKM (Centre for Art and Media) Karlsruhe and founder of Ars Electronica Linz.

Georgina Brett Composer and DJ working in London

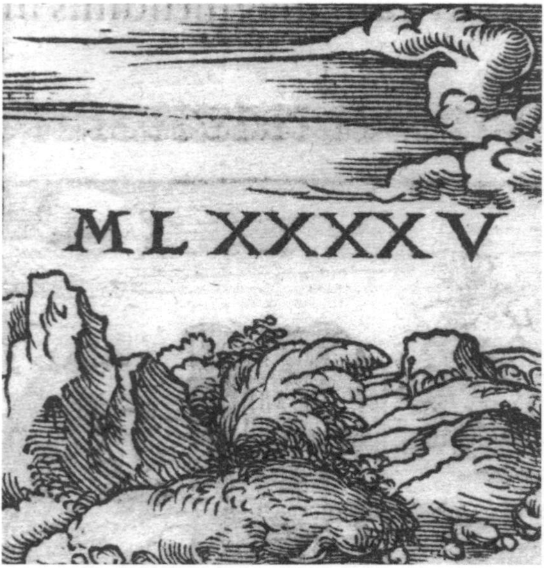

Horapollo, *Hieroglyphica* Lyons 1626
Reproduced by permission of the Master and Fellows of Trinity College Cambridge.

Book 1; Number 27; 'Silence'
When they wish to denote silence, they dfraw the number 1095, which is the extent of three years, since the year is composed of 365 days. For if during this time a child does not speak, it is indicated that the tongue has failed.

African American theorist Henry Louis Gates refers to as "tropological revision" - how we change ideas and the contexts that surround them - is an informing motif of the project, but it's also about how we translate ideas into code into art and back again Synchronia - body mnemonics.... textured textuality the medium beyond the message.... ambiguities, puzzles, and paradoxes of human experience. Mapping a cartographic space that is physical without a fixed position, a kind of social identity and memory encoded, revised palimpsest like into a milieu where the only constant is the codes informing how we relate to the world around us....Here in Synchronia, history becomes a legend, an invention of the present, a kind of cognitive cuing structure, or maybe a modern update/upload of the concept of what was called in Europe an "ars memoria." Memory embodied, clothed in code... a mnemonic melody wafting through the fiber optic cables, cellular land networks, and satellite transmissions holding it all together - multi-referential, performative, hyper-textual... it goes on and on with the kick drum, yes folks, this ain't no re-run. I write to you from a world culture that meshes digital technology, theater, performance art, and a wholesale use of information in all its sundry forms for entertainment. DJ culture is a world subculture and one of its main tenets is "the mix," but again, in our contemporary post-industrial world, culture and technology have blurred together to a point where it's difficult to determine where one ends and the other begins. The cultural origins of this world of revisions and recitations. The reconstruction of experience through many voices, like Russian "matrioska" dolls - layers within layers, or something like that... form and function, fact and fiction, translation and transposition think and link... it's been said that the act of exploration is not one so much of seeking new landscapes but of fashioning new eyes... a strange evolving drama, a nebulous engagement with the world condition as we've fabricated it... thinking out loud about a world like something straight out of Edwin A. Abbott's *Flatlands*: a world condition where we've created, a fabric that we have woven, a text we have written (biomechanical/immersion, fabric/memory/ luba - (cybernetic/anansi)... aggregates of spatial and temporal values: equate communication and community...complex social construction/technologically mediated met morphosis - a play on biomass and infomass, or what the French call "paysage insolite" the "unfamiliar landscape" economy of presence and absence, or as Richard P. Feynman wrote so long ago in his essay: *The Uncertainty of Values*, "The dream is to find the open channel. What, then, is the meaning of it all? What can we say today to dispel the mystery of existence? ...Admitting that we do not know and maintaining the attitude that we do not know the direction necessarily to go permit a possibility of alteration, of thinking, of new contributions and new discoveries for the problem of developing a way to do what we want ultimately, even when we do not know what we want....

Feel the fabric, check the cross-fade in the mix... like Willie Wonka said in the "Chocalate Factory": "we are the music makers, we are the dreamers of dreams"

Synchronia - a hypnogogic state, a condition of debate: a signal with no fixed rate.... a website in a state of perpetual update....

cd:dir>goto>fadeout

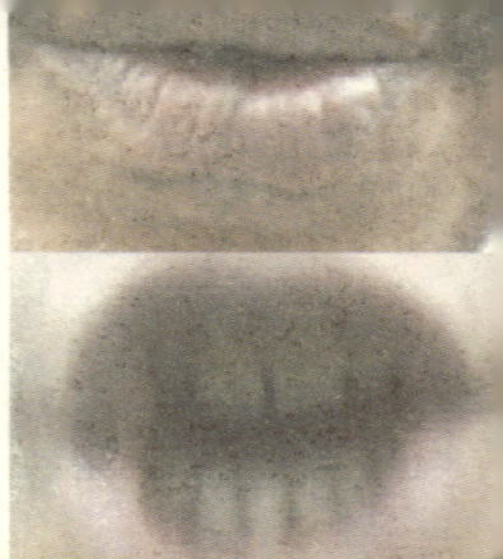

What's the story here?

Synchronia: Myth, Fabric, Thought: Uncanny/Unwoven, re-woven....

PAUL D MILLER aka D.J Spooky

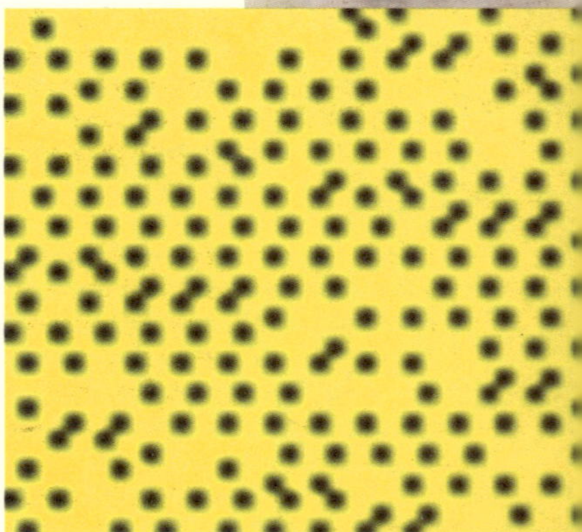

Invisibility
Rise lightly from earth
And try your wings
While I make the darkness invisible
The visibility of the day
Is the invisbility of the night
The invisbility of the day
Is the visibility of the night
So rise lightly from the earth
And try your wings
Try them now
While the darkness is invisible

Sun Ra

[tropes...What's the story here? What's the 411? Fixed floating, signifiers and signs adrift on an ocean of information. An invocation. An investigation. A "roman malla-parte" with no beginning and no ending, only an incidental drift across the vast amount of codes and ciphers that inform everyday life. Thoughts like rain, down-load, upload, test the signal again... lost in translation, feel the permutation of the nation. Upload, upload, upload   Think and link. Synchronia and its cognates: syn, synthesis, synchronic, synopsis... the list goes on but the point is clear - it's a word that conveys a sense of recombination and condensation, convergence and collateralism... The installation that I've created is a reference point for a kind of dematerialisation of culture that I reference partially through music, partially through video, and partially through the internet. Basically "Synchronia" is a play on Bakhtin's notion of "diachronic/synchronic" narrative play, and its place in a world become total theater. But there are other resonances. It's been a long while since Freud wrote in his 1930 classic *Civilization and its Discontents* that "with every tool man is perfecting his own organs, whether motor or sensory, or is removing limits to their functioning... writing was in its origin the voice of the absent person..." The phrase has hung over digital culture like some sort of shroud ever since it was written or pronounced, and in one way or another its a kind of psychological exploration (if only in a form of outdated narrative description) of the way we relate to technology.

I like to think of the material I've created for the installation as a convergence of code and cathexis - emotive, yet "functional" as an element of a larger backdrop of society's immersion in technology accelerates and becomes even more profoundly problematic. *Techne* and *Logos* - two terms that relate to how we resolve the issue of skill and craft as linguistic code, and that's what Synchronia is about. What